The Accurate Rifle

The Accurate Rifle

by Warren Page

Winchester Press

Dedication

This book is dedicated to all the thousands of riflemen and hunters in this country who have been my friends and correspondents for many years, in the hope that it will somehow aid in their efforts to make of the modern cartridge rifle a more efficient instrument.

Copyright © 1973 by Warren Page
All Rights reserved

Library of Congress Catalog Card Number: 73–757665
ISBN 0–87691–102–5

Fourth printing 1975

WINCHESTER PRESS
205 East 42nd Street
New York, N.Y. 10017
Printed in the United States of America

Foreword

It was hotter than Hell-in-August that Texas summer of '64, but the special undercurrent of excitement which earmarks any national-level competition was much in evidence. Exotic-looking rifles, super-tuned to near perfection, adorned benches along the firing line. In the shade of the covered reloading area, competitors clustered in random groups to discuss the mysteries of wind and mirage, to debate the merits of bullets and case design, perhaps even to speculate on the outcome.

The scene of this organized chaos was a gun club on the outskirts of Abilene where the most highly specialized group of precision riflemen in the world had come to decide the National Varmint and Sporter Rifle Championships. Contenders included such demigods of the accuracy game as the late Paul Gottschall, L. E. Wilson, the late Dr. Sam Nadler, Bob Hart, L. E. Cornelison, Tom Gillman, and others. Many others.

To an impressionable country boy, the spectacle was absolutely awe-inspiring. I spent the next four days there, watching. *Just* watching, because I was far too timid to talk to anybody, yet much too interested to leave. And long before the final match was fired I had decided that this was the game for me.

Why? Darned if I know. But whatever it was that ignited my interest has touched a similar chord in hundreds—no, *thousands*—of riflemen through the country, and it's been that way, more or less, for two coon's ages. And today's hunters and shooters owe a great debt to those bench deities. After all, for every group shooter there are a hundred varmint hunters, for every match competitor a thousand deer hunters; yet all are concerned with the accuracy of rifles.

Of course the evolution of modern rifle accuracy competition had a much more recent genesis. While some early and informal bench rest matches may date back to the '30s, the sport didn't achieve organized status until after World War II, and it wasn't until 1960 that competitive bench rest shooting with more or less practical rifles became a national sport under roughly the same rules and guidelines used today. National competition for all three classes of varmint rifles—heavy varmint, light varmint, and sporter—premiered in San Angelo, Texas, that year, and John I. Moore, Paul Gottschall (both deceased), and R. L. McLaren became the NBRSA's first national champions under the then-current program. The No. 2 man for the whole shoot, when all the results for all three rifles were totted up, was a Yankee type. Of him we'll have more to say later.

Moore won the heavy-varmint championship, using a then-new 40X Remington rifle—one of only two at the matches. His grand aggregate measured .507 M.O.A. (That same aggregate would have been good for thirty-third place at the 1972 NBRSA National Varmint and Sporter Rifle Championships as fired at Tulsa.)

Although the earlier-mentioned Yankee won the 100-yard stage, the light-varmint crown for both yardages went to Gottschall, with a .636 total. His score would have been worth seventy-eighth place at the '72 nationals. Even more graphically illustrating the effects of recent technological advances was McLaren's standing in the sporter contest. Shooting a standard Model 70 Winchester .243 with a 6X Weaver scope, he put together a .944 M.O.A. in a photo-finish with Gottschall and the late L. S. "Cowboy" Rucker. In 1972, that same aggregate would have taken a back seat to no less than 103 shooters!

Smallest group fired at that 1960 riflefest was a .195 by Ed Shilen, creditable even today. Ed won the 100-yard heavy-varmint title with a .343 aggregate, shooting the prototype of his own custom action built earlier that year. His success with the action (he won the light-varmint nationals the following year) paved the way for production of 250 Shilen actions, now collector's items more valuable than when they were in production.

Probably the earliest major technological contribution to competitive precision shooting came from Clyde Hart, who was building match-grade barrels as early as the 1950s. The Hart name has been synonymous with rifle accuracy for at least fifteen years, since more contribution came from R. W. Hart, who perfected techniques and equipment for bullet-spinning. Although experiments with bullet-spinning were nothing new, Hart was probably the first to isolate the important factors in measuring bullet eccentricity.

In 1963, Shilen joined Shooters Service & Dewey (SS&D) in New York and the firm began building button-rifled, match-grade barrels along with the Shilen custom action. It was here, also, that Shilen began experimenting with an aluminum action sleeve, which he later produced through his own company in Texas.

Equally important to the advance of the precision-shooting game has been the evolution of custom bullet-making dies. Probably the first really *good* handmade bullets were produced in RCBS dies back in the early 1950s. When RCBS got out of the market, dies built by Biehler and Astles became the benchmark for the industry and remained so for many years. The next plateau of precision-die development was reached by Ross Sherman, who produced the first carbide dies, along with custom actions bearing his name.

The decade of the '60s saw a great number of "revolutionary" developments for the ultra-precisionists, including the Redfield 3200 target scope, custom actions by Charles A. Williams, Pat McMillan, and others, bullet-making dies by McMillan, Don Rorschach, Bob Simonson, Ferris Pendell and Clarence Detsch, RelodeR 7 powder by Hercules, and obviously, the 40XB-BR rifle by Remington.

Still, the ten-year era beginning with 1970 is an odds-on favorite to yield the biggest volume of new goodies for the rifle accuracy specialist. Already there are new rifles and actions, fiberglass stocks by Brown Precision Co., 20X and 24X lightweight scopes by Lyman, Remington, Unertl, with more coming, new match-grade barrels by Pat McMillan, commercial bench rest bullets by Remington. Heaven knows what else lies around the corner.

But technical developments tell only part of the competitive rifle accuracy story. Equal credit is due the folks who have nurtured the fledgling bench rest game from a shaky adolescence into what might now be described as a "nervous maturity" plagued by growing pains.

Perhaps the only black mark on the bench rest sport's development was the lamentable 1970 "split" in the NBRSA, which resulted in the creation of another organization, IBS or International Benchrest Shooters, international because of current matches with Canada and Australia. Despite this schism, the game itself continued to prosper, now counting more active participants than at any time in history. Still, a solution of differences between the two groups, before any divergence in rules occurs, would no doubt enhance the sport's success.

Any attempt to capsule a quarter century of shooting history in a thousand words would be futile, especially when in addition to match shooting the accurate hunting rifle must be considered. That calls for at least a whole book, and an unusually well-qualified guy to write it—somebody like Warren Page.

To my knowledge, Page and Mike Walker are the only living shooters who have actively participated in the bench rest game for a full twenty-five years.

Page ventured into the arena at the second meet ever held in the East, at Princeton, New Jersey, "and I've been messing with it ever since," he says. Messing, indeed!

After piling up a string of top listings with the early bench rest rifles, in 1960 he won the 100-yard light-varmint national championship. In 1961 he annexed the 100-yard heavy-varmint national crown, the grand aggregate heavy-varmint championship, and became the NBRSA's first three-gun aggregate national champion.

The following year he became the only man ever to win back-to-back three-gun aggregate championships with another overall victory, along with the 200-yard sporter title. And in 1963, he added the 100-yard sporter championship.

By virtue of these victories, Warren Page is one of only six men in history to qualify for membership in *Rifle Magazine's* Bench Rest Hall of Fame, sharing the limelight with Gottschall, Gillman, Cornelison, Shilen, and Dave Hall. His most recent triumph came in 1971, when he won his second IBS national crown, that for the three-gun aggregate title.

In addition, Page's credentials include an equally impressive history of successes afield with hunting rifles. Shooting editor for *Field & Stream* for the twenty-four years between 1947 and 1971, Page has hunted all the world's continents offering sporting game. More than thirty of his trophies have rated mention in listings by Boone & Crockett and Rowland Ward. He earned the Weatherby Trophy, top accolade in big-game hunting circles, as early as 1958, and hasn't slowed up since. His western bongo was the first taken by an American in twenty years, his Yakutat Bay glacier bear the first shot by any sportsman in nearly half a century. And so on and on.

From a technical standpoint, Warren has been directly involved in the development of such commercial cartridges as the .222 Remington, 7 mm. Remington Magnum, 6 mm. (.244) Remington, and .243 Winchester, that being a latter-day offshoot of his wildcat .240 Page Pooper.

Today, as president of the National Shooting Sports Foundation, he's one of the nation's strongest voices for practical conservation, and a prolific ambassador for all aspects of the shooting sports.

In these respects, it would be difficult to find one better qualified to comment on rifle accuracy, both sporting and competition rifles, than Warren Page—a man who has heaped victory upon success in a lifetime of precision shooting. I count it an honor to introduce him.

HOUSTON, TEXAS
NOVEMBER 1972   —JAMES GILMORE

Acknowledgments

Anyone who has ever been involved in precision riflery owes a vast debt to his fellow accuracy nuts, since there is no style of shooting, no concern of riflemen, in which bits of knowledge or items of progress are so freely shared. A nickel's worth of new fact—or even of unproved supposition—is so instantly circulated among novice and old-timer alike that it becomes a treasure of novelty; and I have never yet attended a shoot when I didn't pick up one tid-bit or another.

The primary responsibility for my long-time interest in accuracy matters, whether with hunting rifles or specialized competition jobs, probably belongs to the late Al Marciante of Trenton, New Jersey, a precisionist considered by his friends and peers to be the gunsmith's gunsmith. Wildcatters may remember his name because of the .22 Marciante Bluestreak—so called because it was so hot all but the strongest jacketed bullets zipped down the range with a trail of lead smoke behind them. I shall never forget Al, not because he made a few rifles for me, or introduced me to the esoterics of precision reloading, but rather because of the simple pleasure and the multiplication of my fund of gun savvy gained during late evenings in the Marciante household. There gun talk ruled until after midnight, interrupted only by the wanderings of Al's pet budgerigar, and at the witching hour his Laura called us to an Italianate snack of muscular coffee and manly cheese.

After Al came the deluge, because by 1948 I had become involved in bench rest shooting while it was becoming a competitive sport, as distinct from a system of rifle testing—and from there on out there was no lack but a plethora of helpful information. Riflemen do not keep secrets. They broadcast them.

Over the years, of course, certain individuals have given me particularly helpful nudges along the primrose path. Colonel Whelen, for one, I suspect primarily because he was both a sterling example of what riflery is all about and also a friend and confidant to an upstart gun writer. Bob Wallack, for another, not because he also made a rifle or two for me but because he was a person of sufficiently individual opinions to start other people thinking. Bob has also been helpful in this book as a source of photographs of early shooters. Harvey Donaldson, who puffed lousy cigars but through the smokescreen occasionally popped out with historic wisdom. Sam Clark, who like so many of us occasionally got off on a fruitless bypath but without realizing it taught me hugely about bench competition. John Collins, the Kodak employee who periodically astonished the bench rest world and lightened its seriousness with items like the first scrubbing-brush forward rest or the first golf-cart carrier for unrestricted rifles. Bill Cutter, who chambered up the first .240 Page and then went into banking. Larry Rucker, who conned me into shooting at the wrong instant during the first national varmint-sporter matches at San Angelo and thereby taught me never to pay attention to another soul during the seven-minute firing time, unless it be the range officer. Bernice McMullen, who has taken my NBRSA dues for many long years and never failed to answer a foolish question, and Emory Tooly, who has taken the IBS money for a shorter time but lets me reload under his tarp and listens to my mutterings about the cussed mirage without any sympathy whatever. The list could get pretty long. I don't know anybody I've ever met in the bench rest game I didn't like. Some more than others, of course, but there's really nothing so congenial as a group of self-confessed fanatics.

And needless to say, I owe a considerable debt more directly to those people who have contributed in words or wisdom to the writing of this book. People like Mike Walker, whom of course I can beat anytime I've a mind to, but who knows infinitely more than a man should as to what makes guns shoot. Or Ed Shilen, who is considerably less muscular than his partner Allen Hall and can't get off five shots quite as fast but has managed to spread a reputation for making fine barrels and fine rifles from mid-New York State clear out to western Texas without snapping the string. Or Clyde Hart, who made the leap from making tallow to making fine barrels and acquired a first-rate reputation and an ulcer at the same time, and I suspect for the same reasons. Or the late Doc Nadler, who by the depth and catholicity of his interests reminded me that Renaissance man was not dead. Or Bob Hart, who runs the smoothest range operation in either East or West. Or Ted Boughton, a canny gunsmith who has had much to say about the actions commented on in this book. And Ferris Pindell, long associated with the precision game, who was generous with his expertise in the "big rifle" chapter, a part of accuracy shooting I have stayed out of since the "practical rifles" got their start. There's a little piece, or perhaps a big piece, of all these people and of hundreds more, somewhere in this book.

And I am grateful to them, as shooters should be to the whole accuracy clan, for passing over so freely the bits of procedure and information that make the difference between scattergunnery and precision riflery. It is people like these who make the accuracy world go round.

WARREN PAGE
RIVERSIDE, CONNECTICUT
JANUARY 1973

Contents

The Accurate Rifle

How Accurate
Is Accurate?

Two days before typing these comments I returned from an NBRSA National Championship in Tulsa, at the John Zink Range, where to win an individual match in any of the three competition rifle classes required a group well under $\frac{1}{4}$ minute of angle, in virtually every case under $\frac{1}{5}$ minute, which is to say under $\frac{1}{5}$ inch at 100 yards. The next day, just one day before setting to work on the chapter, I check-fired a hunting rifle, a 7 mm. magnum, as a sort of advance preliminary before taking it to Montana for elk in the fall, and was more than pleased when it delivered a couple of groups reliably close to its pre-established impact point, spreads of $1\frac{1}{8} - 1\frac{1}{4}$ inches.

For their specific jobs and expectations, both the bench shooter's rifle and my elk rifle are accurate, albeit at vastly different levels. They do not look alike; their scopes are different; their loads are markedly different. But they operate under the same physical laws, and the principles involved in achieving accuracy, as I will say throughout this book, are much the same for the one as for the other.

Any rifle, as the term is presently used, comes in four sections: action, barrel, stock, and sights. Similarly, any rifle cartridge is a four-part unit: case, primer, powder, and bullet. The problem in achieving accuracy, which may be defined as the ability to put shot after shot into as precisely the same selected area as is possible, is then to maintain each and all of these elements at optimum level and in perfect relationship, or as near to that as is possible, for shot after shot. Considering that we have in our equipment itself at least eight elements, each with its own sub-elements that can vary, plus an unknown number of factors both physical and psychological in the human term of the shooting equation, it often strikes me as a near miracle that we are ever able to hit a barn. The plain fact is that we frail humans do far better with those eight basic bits of shooting equipment than we have any right to expect or even to hope.

The essence of accuracy, then, is duplication. It is, for example, self-evident that if a projectile is to fly accurately and to the same impact area as its brothers it must not only be correctly balanced in mass and perfectly round or true in dimension, but it must also be exactly like its brothers in all respects, and it must, while in the gun, be subjected to forces and effect identical to those that work on its brethren. Since human effort always presupposes tolerances, such duplication is decidedly not easy. With the hunting rifle, of course, a further dimension of difficulty is added in that we expect the rifle to maintain its point of impact month after month.

We do not, seemingly cannot, presently load ammunition which is identical shot for shot. A chronograph indication of plus and minus 10 foot-seconds variation, even from the same barrel, is downright phenomenal, and it appears that no amount of careful titivation of powder-charging methods, no amount of spinning and mixing and weighing and examination of bullets, no hours of checking of flashholes or measurement of case brass, will bring the delivered speed to truly identical levels, round for round.

We then know that pressures and velocities, even in a rifle where the stability of the metal parts is 100-percent assured in relation to the wood or plastic elements which serve as their handle, simply cannot be held to such precision that the time-up-the-barrel factor—that tiny continuum registrable in milliseconds that it takes our projectile, once the striker has fallen to crush the primer pellet to set off its flash to ignite the powder to establish the pressure to push the bullet up the barrel tube from case mouth to muzzle exit hole—is absolutely identical for each shot. If the shooting millennium were to be reached—if the perfectly balanced projectile was driven out of the barrel in identically the same time so that it exited the muzzle at the identical positioning of that hole during its violent vibration and flexing under the stresses of firing and recoil, and if the gun itself was for each shot supported by the same cushioning and recoil absorption forces, and if the action of such outside forces as wind on the bullet and light on the target was also to remain identical—presumably each bullet would indeed go precisely through the hole made by its predecessor.

But somehow or other all this doesn't quite happen. It comes agonizingly close. We can only keep trying to make it happen, time and again.

We do keep trying. It is inherent among serious riflemen to keep trying. Otherwise they might as well be shotgunners, where approximations rule and skilled shooting is an art rather than a science.

How successfully we try is itself measurable only in fractions. To the deer hunter, or even the military ordnanceman in whose lexicon 3 inches of spread at 100 paces is good shooting indeed, those fractions are pretty large, since it's a sorry hunting rifle today that won't beat 2 inches and 1 inch is quite within reason. But among the true accuracy devotees progress comes slower and smaller, also harder.

It may not seem any great shakes that the 1950 any-rifle record of .1057 for 100 yards has been shrunk only to the .063 fired in 1958 or to the .090 shot with a fairly comparable weight of rifle in 1968; but over *aggregate* courses, where the freaks of luck so common in single-group firing are ruled out, the real truths about modern accuracy appear. For one single five-shot group at 200 yards back in 1950, Bill Guse achieved a phenomenal .3896. By 1967, Engelbrecht had managed not one but *five* consecutive groups only very slightly larger.

Or, to put matters another way, in 1961 I won the three-rifle aggregate and the *Field & Stream* trophy with .56916 m.o.a. In 1972, such an average for the thirty-group course of fire, shot with three distinct rifles, would have placed worse than halfway down the ranking of all 120 or so shooters! Only two of the top twenty aggregated as badly as a half inch. Five years before, a half-minute in the three-rifle would have won all the potatoes.

Improvements, then, come small in dimension, perhaps, but vast in meaning. Among the true accuracy bugs the talk is not of inches but of tenths, hundredths, even thousandths. We're talking about a science, not an art.

Man's Search
for Accuracy

Since the discovery of rifling, nay, since the discovery that gunpowder could be used to drive a projectile out a tube to give forceful impact on distant objects, accuracy has been a Holy Grail to the firearms fraternity. It has never been enough just to drive the projectile with useful force; always the demand has existed that it be driven precisely to a desired spot. The only difference, really, has been in the level of precision required.

The ancient Chinese defender of a walled town or the medieval European hammering a castle with rounded stones lobbed from a bombard were probably—and necessarily—satisfied if their balls went in the general direction of the enemy. The footsoldier operating a sixteenth-century wheellock asked little more. Armies using flintlocks and smoothbored muskets were pleased that the solid mass of opposing infantrymen, rather than a single man or a spot on his body, offered a practical target at 100 yards. Yet very specifically aimed fire was not only possible but began to be employed by the later eighteenth century. Ferguson's Rangers of our Revolution used rifled muskets patterned after the jaeger carbines developed for Middle European hunters; and the small-caliber "Kentucky" rifles made by Palatine Swiss in the Lancaster, Pennsylvania, region have become a symbol of fierce colonial independence. With a patched round ball they were capable of hitting a redcoat in the chest at 100 paces, or in the hands of a squirrel hunter, in the head.

The percussion period beginning in the early 1840s inevitably saw accuracy improvements with faster and more reliable ignition, but despite the stimulus of the Civil War there is little evidence of vast general changes in the shooting ability of guns in ordinary use. The Hawken rifles of the later mountain men were not all that much better than converted Kentuckies. Actually, the arrival on the battle scene of Colonel Minié's hollow-based skirted projectile, because it permitted multiple firings without laborious swabbing away of black-powder residues between shots, was an aid to practical military accuracy but not necessarily to the theoretical ideal. The sniper tack-drivers of the War Between the States showed progress toward one-hole perfection primarily because they used optical sights as an aid to holding, so that with rather heavy-barreled muskets a sniper could roll a general's horse at several hundred yards, rather than because the rifle itself had improved.

Both before and after Appomattox, however, the pot was steadily boiling among devout riflemen. Earlier "hog rifles" or rest rifles of the percussion sort had been in vogue among accuracy seekers, often massive affairs in the 20-pound class with hexagonal or octagonal barrels of three-inch diameter and cap ignition, frequently by underhammer powered by the trigger guard acting as a spring. But the breechloading developments which had begun during the war eventually seized the fancy of riflemen. In the last quarter of the nineteenth century and well into the first quarter of the twentieth there was constant experimentation with breech-loading single-shots, and levels of accuracy were achieved that are highly respectable even today.

Serious students of this nineteenth-century transition period revere such gun-building names as Vermonter Norman Brockway, New Yorkers Lewis and Billingshurst, the great Morgan James, George Schalk, N. G. Whitmore, and Horace Warner, all Olympians of muzzle-loading mythology. Whereas the hunting-weight rifles of their day (9 to 15 pounds) were usually fired in local offhand competitions at 20 and 40 rods—40 rods being 220 yards—at targets like an actual turkey or a charcoal-marked shake or oversized shingle, the experimental rifles of the time were shot from either prone or table rest, a muzzle brace or clamp then being preferred over the sandbag arrangement of later days.

Following the percussion cap's arrival, amazing advances had been made with muzzle-loaders. A primary step was the false muzzle, essentially a bored and rifled barrel extension which mated perfectly to the rifle muzzle with pins. It had a slight flare at its own muzzle, so that a soft-lead bullet, usually patched with paper or cloth, could be hand-started dead straight and without deformation into its bore and so into the barrel, the slug imprinting itself into the rifling as it was forced smoothly home over the powder. With picket or conical bullets and their short bearing surface the false muzzle was virtually a necessity; and it also helped guarantee the true flight of the far heavier and long paper-patched cylindrical or cylindro-conoidal bullets developed for the rest rifles. By midcentury, any respectable muzzle-loading equipment could be expected, some say, to strike into 4 inches at 40 rods, although I find this hard to believe as a reasonable general expectancy.

Ned Roberts' immortal book *The Muzzle-Loading Cap Lock Rifle* tells a story of Colonel Berdan, the Civil War sharpshooter leader, which illustrates the true efficiency, at least in the hands of an expert, of the best rifles of the 1860s. At a Weehawken exhibition, I assume to recruit men, Berdan appeared with a 32-pound .48-caliber percussion rifle, its 31-inch octagonal barrel fitting a false muzzle. The piece was topped by one of the full-length telescopes of the period, low in magnification, field, and brilliance but still superior to iron sights for precision work. Shooting at a "Jeff Davis" figure from something over 200 yards, once Berdan had checked his sights against the day's conditions, he proceeded to shoot out the figure's eyes, nostrils, and vest buttons, more or less at will. Since recruits to Berdan's famous regiment were required to put ten consecutive shots an average of 5 inches from the bull's-eye at 600 feet, there is no saying how many new men lined up that day in Weehawken.

When the National Rifle Club was formed in Framingham, Massachusetts, in June of 1858, however, with the immortal Brockway as one leader, and arranged a shoot at Waltham for the following October, it must be noted that one T. Spencer took home the silverware for a 50-shot day at 40 rods or 220 yards totaling 54 inches string measure. In today's terms, that would mean the 50 shots averaged only 1.08 inches from target center. That would be a most creditable performance with most modern equipment other than outright bench rest rifles, believe me.

In some ways, incidentally, the string-measure system of grading targets is superior to our "greatest spread between centers" approach. The method varied regionally, but essentially string measure involved spotting one end of a string at the target's center, then carrying the cord in loops out around each of a number of plugs, usually ten, inserted into each bullet hole, and so back to center each time. The string was cut after reaching center the last time, then measured for length. A more modern approach might be to measure, with a caliper, from target center to shot center for each hole, then total the measurements thus obtained. In short, the string system, however cumbersome and slow, gives us an index of the rate of shot dispersion, whereas our present spread measure may well indicate only the semi-accidental effect of a single shot. String measure is still being used by some contemporary purists among the muzzle-loading clan.

The postwar switch from muzzle-loading to breech-loading rifles probably peaked in the activities of the Massachusetts Rifle Association at their Walnut Hill Range, which eventually succeeded the Vernon, Vermont, range of the National Rifle Association as the Mecca of accuracy fans. By 1883, Walnut Hill shooters had gone entirely over to breech-loaders, although in the great Creedmoor matches at 800, 900, and 1000 yards (which were fired in September of 1874 on a Long Island range built, interestingly enough, with an appropriation of land and money from the state of New York and the cities of New York and Brooklyn) the battle between the Irish muzzle-loaders and the American Remington and Sharps breech-loaders was inconclusive. The Americans won the match, true, but one Irish gentleman shot on the wrong target and some of the breech-loader shooters were loaded from the muzzle! But certainly by the 1880s the muzzle-loading rifle, as far as accuracy events were concerned, was passing into disuse.

Not easily abandoned, however, were the false muzzles which ensured undeformed bullets. The system of using a breech-loaded cartridge, the powder sealed in under a card wad, with the soft-lead bullet first carefully started and then as carefully rammed down into the chamber throat, held its adherents for years. With the breech-loader, however, began the day of Pope, Schoyen, Rowland, of the Schuetzen rifle as made in this country by Stevens and Ballard and perhaps Sharps and Remington, overseas by Aydt and Martini and Farquharson and the rest. These were one-shot rifles of falling- or dropping-block type, with or without outside hammers, often remarkably decorated and equipped with stocks of one-purpose design, heavy barreled and in a multitude of calibers—new ones appeared constantly—all remarkably like the .32–40. I firmly believe that only four factors prevented the appearance between 1880 and 1920 of rifles capable of grouping alongside our modern practical-weight pieces: first, the necessary usage of black and very early smokeless propellants, which caused fouling problems beyond solution even by the mysterious Leopold Bullet Lubricant (a mix of beeswax, tallow and plumbago); second, the unjacketed lead bullets of the day, vastly difficult to deliver into flight without some deformity; third, the two-piece stock construction which has ever since given fits to makers of one-shot rifles by its tendency toward vertical impact shift; and finally, the lack of highly developed optical sights.

Probably the most famous group ever fired by one of these Schuetzen-style rifles was that ten-shot Rowland one-holer fired at 200 yards in Boulder, Colorado, on May 16, 1901, and measuring .725 by modern methods. It was generally accepted as a world record, exemplary of the finest attainable with turn-of-the-century equipment. Using Hazard's FG black powder, Rowland fired a .32–40 breech-loader, with each lead-alloy bullet inserted from the muzzle, the rifle being a Pope-barreled Ballard, and a Pope machine rest was employed. That in 1948 Bob Wallack, at the time a gunsmith, at one of the very first modern-day bench rest matches outside Princeton, New Jersey, fired a .531-inch five-shot 200-yarder, or that the present (1968) record for ten rounds at 200 yards is a tiny little .298-inch hole, cannot really detract from the Rowland performance. No one since has made black powder and lead bullets shoot that way!

In May of 1931, of course, Rowland fired another group to prove that his earlier feat was no freak, using a Schoyen-built rifle which last I knew was owned by Sam Clark of Oakland, Maine, once a bench rest great but now, alas, committed to a rather more childish sport called golf. Spreading the firing over several days to be sure of correct conditions, Rowland and his

Pope-style machine rest fired forty bullets of 200 grains weight and .32–40 caliber, each load using over 12 grains of Dupont shotgun powder, which make a cluster $\frac{1}{2}$ inch high on centers, $\frac{1}{2}$ inch wide.

Twentieth-century bench rest shooters, then, had something to shoot at.

Very possibly because of the wars of the period—though these seem to have had no effect on the proliferation of modern hunting and varminting cartridges and rifles—the second quarter of this century showed less accuracy activity than had been the case during the fifty years preceding. Experimentation seems to have been confined to individuals, or to very small cliques, often followers of one gunsmith like Gebby Whelen or a writer like Fred Ness, who cooperated to contrive varminting combinations like the .22–250, the .220 Swift, and the .257 Roberts, for example, but there was little attempt to spread rifle knowledge through accuracy competition.

In 1944, however, a group of woodchuck shooters and gun nuts in the Northwest decided matches would be both fun and productive, so they organized as the Puget Sound Snipers Congress and held 100-yard and 200-yard competitions for the Seattle area.

Men like Dr. Rod Jansen, an obstetrician of local note, and Roy Meister headed a casual operation, with a multiplicity of rifle classes, which permitted "any dead rest, including machine rest, sandbag rest, rest over a sack of sawdust or horse feathers," and the first (1944) matches were won by Meister with four 200-yard groups averaging 2.235 inches, hardly phenomenal. Four years later the same Meister had shrunk his 200-yard average to 1.39 inches, however, and the direction of development was clear.

Eastern shooters had been thinking along similar lines, in good part under the spur of Harvey Donaldson of Fultonville, New York, a man unique in that the span of his shooting lifetime—and at this writing he is still very much alive, smoking abominable cigars and telling thirty-minute anecdotes at the drop of a hat—began back in the Schuetzen period, so his viewpoint is of great worth. The first Eastern matches were in Machias, Maine, an informal affair quickly followed by a famous inaugural event at the Pine Tree Rifle Club of Johnstown, New York, held over the 1947 Labor Day weekend.

Possibly the only extant photograph from the first formal bench rest matches, held at Johnstown, New York, in 1947. Reading from left to right: Jennings Prescott, who used his own folding bench, and reloaded the same cartridge case over and over for each shot; then three old-timers whose names I do not recall; next the tall Ray Biehler, precision bullet diemaker; turned away, Sam Clark, referred to by his friends as "Slippery Sam"; Harvey Donaldson, who smoked evil cigars even then, drove a hot Corvette, and designed cartridges up to his death in 1972; Virginia Bill Curtis; and Al Marciante.

That Johnstown affair—and there have been matches at Johnstown ever since of either a regional or national sort—sparked rapid development. An association was set up, with Donaldson as president and the late Colonel Townsend Whelen as vice president, Sam Clark as executive officer, and Frank Hubbard as secretary-treasurer. I was appointed one of a twenty-man planning committee which included such early names in bench rest shooting as Al Marciante, J. E. Smith, Al Barr, Lucian Cary, M. S. Risley, Hal Mallet, R. K. Nelson, Clair Taylor, and Don Robbins.

The first event I attended was in 1948, at the ranges of the Princeton Rifle and Revolver Club and referred to as the Trenton Shoot. Others, at Oil City and Dubois, Pennsylvania, at Johnstown, as well as in Seattle, were huge successes, and by 1950 and 1951 it was not exceptional to find 150 men out at Dubois—which was even then a hard place to reach from almost anywhere—or at Johnstown. Four years after the Seattle matches the idea of bench rest shooting not for singlehanded testing but in competition had spread over virtually all the United States, with the possible exception of the extreme southeastern area, which has never really been rifle country, and matches numbered as many entrants, in some instances, as they do today.

Modern bench rest shooting, then, was under way.

It has gone through all manner of vicissitudes since. Early reorganizations or regional groups early in the game linked

The inaugural shoot at Princeton, New Jersey, often miscalled the Trenton Shoot, at which Wallack (extreme left bench) shot a 200-yard .53125. The author, then a natty dresser, stands behind Marciante at far right. Note the 1948 idea of a "sandbag rest."

The great Colonel Townsend Whelen, true dean of American writers on riflery, was an ardent bench rest competitor until failing eyesight forced retirement. In the early 1950s, he is here shooting the top equipment of that day: an adjustable tripod carrying a Taylor & Robbins-made rifle chambered .219 Donaldson Wasp, its barrel probably of Gregoire origins, and using the big Unertl scope. Note even then the canny Colonel had loosened the scope return spring so it could be returned to battery or firing position by hand, positively.

them all into the National Bench Rest Shooters Association. This lasted as the sole governing body until 1969. Then, in a hassle over the questions of a "national home range" and that of the official publication, plus assorted other factors of disagreement that have no place in this book, a schism occurred.

The International Bench Shooters, primarily Eastern-oriented though both IBS and the NBRSA have members from all over the nation, was organized as of January 1, 1970. As this is written, that schism, on which I flatly refuse to have a publishable opinion, still continues. I definitely plan to continue attending national matches in both camps whenever I am able. I trust the schism can someday be healed by compromise, since as of now the rules, regulations, and basic procedures of each group are either identical or closely parallel and the basic interest of each, the absolute ultimate in rifle performance in terms of accuracy, is still the same.

Not that bench rest people agree, really, on much of anything. I'll bet that old-timers of the black-powder period like Herrick and Leopold argued over the time of day. The evolution of competitive rifle classes has not been easy, from the earliest "any centerfire" rifles—which were in many ways the same as what are now termed heavy varmint rifles—to our present listings of bench rifles under no weight limit but a division for scoring purposes into restricted (sandbag rests only) or unlimited categories; to our heavy and light varmint classes and sporter groups of $13\frac{1}{2}$-, $10\frac{1}{2}$-, and $10\frac{1}{2}$-pound weight limits, and the developing hunter class which is limited in caliber (above .23), in case size (.30–30 capacity or larger), in scope power (6X) and in weight ($10\frac{1}{2}$ pounds). Definitions and redefinitions have been battled out along the way, usually because some venturesome soul followed the letter and forgot the spirit of the basic rules. Despite amazing progress since the heyday of Morgan James, there is certainly no agreement whatever, as you will note in ensuing chapters, as to what constitutes the best caliber choice or the best rifle design or the best formula for group-tightener or anything else, much.

But one point is sure. The bench rest shooter, descendant of Brockway and Rowland and Roberts and Pope, is the greatest sharer of knowledge the sporting world has ever known. No secrets exist. What Tom knows about bedding he will freely impart to Dick; what Waldo has discovered about bullet-making he will tell the very guy who beat him at last week's matches; the powder charge Harry has developed for his .308 sporter shoulder-buster he'll announce to all who listen and some who do not want to hear. Ed Shilen will tune the bedding of my light varminter so I can trim him in the 200-yard event; and I'll tell Mike Walker which flag I think is the one to watch

Very probably the first feminine accuracy competitor was Betty Wallack, who entered the 1949 Johnstown matches and shot a set-trigger Mauser with Fecker scope put together by Bob Wallack, in those days a gunsmith. Betty paved the way for dozens of lady shooters who have set records, and often clobbered the menfolk. The accuracy game requires little muscle but lots of mental control.

off Bench 24 so he can beat me next match. Hard-fought competition, but no secrets.

And that is why, in the history of the search for ultimate rifle accuracy, every bullet through the hole made by the first, bench rest shooting is fast approaching the millennium. Today's world record of .070 inches for five rounds at 100 yards from a perfectly practical woodchuck rifle was *not* achieved by keeping secrets.

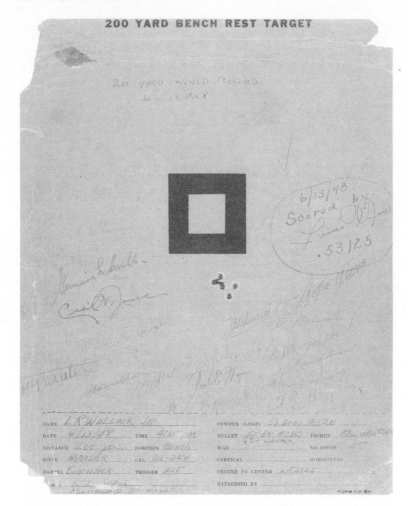

What a "world record" looked like in the early days. This target was fired by Bob Wallack at the Princeton, New Jersey, shoot of June 13, 1948, and was signed by 21 shooters to prove it measured .53125, although how measurement to five places was then possible is a mystery. Shot with a Mauser-actioned .22-250, it was phenomenal in a day when the match aggregate for 20 competitors at 200 yards was 2.05 inches; today it would be good but unremarkable, one of many half-inchers.

3

The Quarter-Minute Rifle

Ten years ago or a bit more I wrote a piece for the Shooting Department of *Field & Stream* under the title "The Half-Minute Rifle." It hailed, with all the fervor of a messianic pronouncement and with a bundle of appropriate statistics, the development among the accuracy clan of rifles, bullets, and loads which were capable of averaging $\frac{1}{2}$ inch at 100 yards, or an inch or so at 200. Not for one wallet group, but for *averages*. Not for every rifle every day all day, but most of the time and under good conditions. That article, I have been told, had greater effect than any other single piece of gun writing in inspiring varmint shooters and those hunters more than usually concerned with field-practical accuracy into leaning toward bench rest competition, or at least toward its methodology. Could be. But the proclamations made in that article a decade back are now strictly to laugh!

At this stage of the game, the plain fact is that a $\frac{1}{2}$ minute rifle, however deadly on woodchucks, is in bench rest competition about like a nickel before a Coke machine—sadly inadequate. It will win you nothing but sympathy and not very much of that. In the year of our Lord 1972—and we hope it may con-

By Labor Day of 1948, the basics of a formal bench rest layout, and an acceptable plan for the benches themselves, had been formalized at the Johnstown, N.Y., range.

tinue since there are no exhaust-emission standards to emasculate the rifle as there are for the automobile, though there are a few gun-haters in the political arena whose aim, avowed or otherwise, is to eliminate all firearms—it is perfectly possible to buy a varmint rifle of totally conventional design and appearance and tune it to shoot good handloads to the $\frac{1}{2}$-minute mark. The competition rifle has to be good for a $\frac{1}{4}$ minute.

Before me as this is typed is the voluminous shoot report compiled by the Tulsa Club of NBRSA on their 1972 National Championship shoot, the largest multiple-rifle bench doings ever held, with 115 entries in the sporter class, 127 in the light-varmint group, 151 in the heavy-varminter category. The statistics on this shoot—and it was fired during four days of conditions which as I know from being there were perhaps mild for Tulsa, but were both exacting and exasperating—are absolutely amazing. To any but a devout accuracy bug they might seem incredible.

For example, of all matches fired over the National match course, thirty matches with three rifles, only one was taken with a group larger than $\frac{1}{4}$ minute. That was the first 200-yarder with the sporter, which I won with a measurement of .581, probably only because everyone else had suddenly been struck with some strange Asiatic fever. The match-winning 100-yard groups for three classes of rifle were in all save one instance (a .225 with a sporter) under $\frac{2}{10}$! The average winning measurements at 100 yards were for the sporter class .187, for the light varminter .162, for the heavy varminter .145. At 200 yards, in the same minute-of-angle terms, the corresponding figures were .2144, .2189, and .2065.

Figures like that mean little to the average layman, but consider these. The diameter of the average lead pencil is .305 inches. A dime from my pocket mikes .703. The 100-yard winning groups, then, were much smaller, almost half the size of the lead pencil, and all but one of the 200-yarders could be hidden under the dime!

All of which means that individual match wins demanded much less than $\frac{1}{4}$ minute, ordinarily less than $\frac{2}{10}$ minute. This same Tulsa match series saw possible records—they may even have been officially remeasured by the time this material is in print—with Jim Stekl's range-measured 100-yard sporter aggregate of .2482, or this possible new sporter figure for both yardages of .3441, or the 100-yard heavy-varmint aggregate of .2172 which was fired by Don Geraci of New Orleans with a rifle he borrowed from Jim Ridings. Other potential records for individual groups like Hulet's H. V. 100-yard .057 or Prachyl's 200-yard .194 are I think less notable than the aggregates, phenomenal though they may be.

The results of the IBS Nationals at Fassett, Pennsylvania, have not been sent on as this is written, but I do have in front of me data on a recent IBS event I also attended at Wapwallopen. The 100-yard winning performances there (.197, .206, .191, .200, and .209 in the heavy-varmint class, for example, and so still at the $\frac{2}{10}$ level) undoubtedly reflect more the vagaries of the day's conditions than anything else, although it's perfectly evident that when you get twice as many top shooters assembled in one place you're that much more likely to get some fancy results, and the Wapwallopen shoot mentioned was a local affair, with less than seventy-five shooters.

Nobody but nobody yet registered seems able to maintain such a pace through all the vicissitudes of breeze and boil, and the idea of a $\frac{1}{4}$-minute aggregate for both 100-yard and 200-yard events may probably be impractical for a time, yet even the gross figures show what has happened since I wrote that "Half-Minute Rifle" piece a decade back, when all-gun winning aggregates for all three rifles of .56916 and .53012 were solid indications of $\frac{1}{2}$-minute support. In those days, individual matches could sometimes be won with .3 or even worse! At Tulsa in '72, with a surely record number of three-gun aggregate competitors with 92, we had to go down the list to Number 19 to

By Labor Day of 1949 the Pine Tree Rifle Club of Johnstown at least had covered benches and target butts at 100 and 200 yards, and showed 86 competitors, including the author at extreme right, judging from the upper group picture. By 1951 the lower group photograph showed 117 entries. The custom of taking all-competitor group photographs petered out during the 1960s, unfortunately for historians of shooting.

find a $\frac{1}{2}$-minute average for four days, three rifles, thirty matches, and 150 measured shots. The first figure for every man above that was a .4, and the top dog for the four days, Jim Stekl, had posted a .4076. That may not be $\frac{1}{4}$ minute, to be sure, but consider the type of yardstick we're using here. The three-gun champions during the history of varmint-rifle competition have never come close. As far as I can recall, the best ranking earlier made, a .4554 by Tom Gillman back in 1966 (Tom won in 1970 with a .5130), would have been good for only about eighth place in the top twenty rankings at Tulsa.

Quibble if you must about the $\frac{1}{4}$-minute business—though I tell you now that if you and the musket you brag on will not, under optimum conditions, shoot .250 groups you're not likely to come home from matches laden with either silver or gold— but it is evident that something has happened over the past decade or so.

Essentially, of course, it's the same thing that happened over the decade before that, just more so: consistent betterment of the accuracy quotient in gun-building. It is obvious that im- provement in accuracy comes in slow degrees, rating in diffi- culty according to where you start from. If you begin with 3 minutes of angle, bettering things by an inch is a cinch. If you begin with .3 minutes of angle, squeezing $\frac{1}{10}$ inch is creating miracles. Yet something like that has happened.

Today's 13$\frac{1}{2}$-pound rifles which are characterized as heavy varminters are ahead of the bench rest rifles with which we shot during the early '50s by four miles and six of Gulliver's leagues. Yet they're not all that much ahead of what heavy varminters were half a dozen years ago, if you study the shoot reports. There is sharp betterment, however, particularly in the area of bullet availability, there now being purchasable for either cash or sweat bullets to better the $\frac{1}{4}$-minute mark. That I characterize as one of the great advances of the past decade. If you don't want to make match-winning bullets you can buy them.

Where the vast jump has been made is in the small-rifle classes, in the so-called practical-weight types referred to as the light varminter and the sporter of .243 caliber or greater. As I see it, that progress is due to several quite obvious factors.

First, of course, has to be the bullet availability factor already mentioned. That goes for all rifles, but perhaps especially for the sporters since we have not only the excellent match-quality

The earliest 50-bench range was laid out at Johnstown and remains the longest firing line available in the East. Tulsa boasts 50 benches, but this range, once considered as a "national home" for rest shooting, may eventually be lost by flooding. As the game has grown and entries in a single rifle class reach and surpass 150, the 25- and 35-bench ranges face great problems in running off a national-level match in reasonable time. Further growth of the sport waits on the building of more 50-bench facilities.

168-grain .30s from Sierra and Hornady, and the 60-grain Sierra 6 mm.'s which are competitive in many rifles, but also the .243-diameter projectiles of the 70-grain class which are handmade and sold to known bench rest bugs—not to the general public because he could never fill the demand—by Clarence Detsch. Detsch may change his dies now and then, altering dimensional factors so that the riflemen must make load adjustments, but he has not turned out any bad bullets for years.

Perhaps even more important, since .224 bullet availability has always been less a problem for the 10½-pound light varmint class, has been the appearance of the short, light, and now in some versions internally adjustable scope of target optics but a half-pound less weight which has made possible the ultra-stiff barrels now feasible on the lighter classes of rifle. Look back at those Tulsa figures—when can you last recall firing in a match when the spread between top-performing heavy rifles and the light varminters and sporters was so small, the distinction so consistent? It is not that the heavy rifles have gone back but rather that the light ones are so much better.

By 1960 bench rest rifles had grown in massiveness to the point where Gene Beecher, designer of the Beecher front tripod and always a practical man, moved his around on a modified golf cart.

The use of a cart was all but necessity with this 1960 rifle, which nowadays would be classed as an unlimited type. It featured a log-of-wood stock, steel-block attachment of the barreled action to the stock, and some 40 pounds of weight.

Another reason, perhaps connected with the lighter scopes, is the greater use in 10½-pound equipment of either the heavy cylindrical actions or of sleeved actions, which in either case increase the basic stiffness of the piece, simplify bedding problems by making them less sensitive, and provide not only surer and quicker firing-pin fall but essentially a more solid base for the piece. In short, the 10½-pounders have trended toward becoming shorter-barreled versions of their heavier brethren. They *can* shoot virtually as well, but are a bit harder to hold, I think.

Remember that it was not too long ago when the normal light varminter and sporter—very often the same rifle is still made to do duty in both categories, a plan particularly feasible now that we have good 6-mm. bullets—featured long and relatively slender barrels, actions which were of bench rest design only by courtesy, sometimes being unaltered magazine actions, and weight-wasting full-sized target scopes.

In competition terms, then, the sporter and light varminter of 1972–73 shoot as well as did the so-called heavy varmint rifles of a half-dozen years back, and they in turn beat the full-weight bench rifles of a dozen years ago. The question as to whether or not we have actually achieved the $\frac{1}{4}$-minute rifle is a matter of academics, of quibbling if you will. We've made a carload of 'em, but only a few $\frac{1}{4}$-minute men, it seems to me.

4

The Bench Rest

M aking flat statements is, they say, one style of forceful writing, though making flat statements that can be contradicted is a fine way to make a fool of yourself. But in this instance I feel that there can be no real argument. In all the years I have been in any way involved with bench rest shooting I have never yet encountered—and there have been literally dozens of designs offered to the public with high hopes—a takedown or transportable bench rest that for serious work was worth a tinker's damn.

The value of a bench, in terms of pinhole accuracy, depends almost entirely on its steadiness. Of the portable types, a good many are quite adequate for sighting in hunting rifles—after all, you can do that quite efficiently leaning across the hood of a car or lying down behind a jacket-padded log. Certain of these, the commercial best probably being Basil Tuller's fold-up type which swiped its legs from Sears Roebuck, can be steady enough for meaningful testing of a sporting rifle, one that shoots anywhere from 1 to 3 minutes of angle. All of which has little to do with the requirements for a true bench rest. If you expect consistent groups, the rest simply cannot quiver like a virgin

Early bench matches used crude equipment and crude ranges, but the principles were the same as in the 1970s. Competing at Bradford, Pennsylvania, in October of 1948, on a six-bench layout, were from front to rear Al Marciante, Alex Hoyer, Glen (last name unknown), Joe Rich, D. E. Barr, and Rex White. At least five of these riflemen have left for quieter ranges.

bride outside the motel office. On the contrary, it must out-steady the Rock of Gibraltar.

It must also be large enough on top to permit strewing around the paraphernalia common to accuracy work—the block or blocks of ammunition, a handy screwdriver, a propped-up stopwatch if you're one of the nervous types of competitor, perhaps a spotting scope set where it can be used with minimal position shift, plus any rabbit's feet, spare ear plugs, extra sandbags, or elbow pads that you feel are necessary to your style of shooting. The bench top must be long enough so that your front rest does not tip off the forward end or the back rest crowd your elbow off the rear. It must be reasonably smooth so that the mild recoil of a rest rifle does not chew up elbows—either your own or the jacket's—yet either rough enough or soft enough to hold the peg-shaped points of your front tripod—we shall assume that you are not back in the dark ages of piled-up 2 × 4's or oversized sacks of wheat such as Roy Meister, I think it was, used to prefer, and are using one of the adjustable sandbag-holding tripods as made by Beecher, Wichita Tool, Bob Hart, and half a dozen others. And if humanly possible the bench top should be both level and flat, neither humpy nor tipped to suit the angle of the range, as is lamentably the case clear across the firing line on a famous range otherwise almost perfect.

In the fair state of Texas, where concrete and cinderblock are used for everything from chicken coops to highways, the normal bench uses a 4-inch cast-concrete slab, polished topside and set on three massive legs of cinderblock, the whole sitting on one concrete flooring slab running across the firing line. So long as the mortar holds these are steady; if it lets go the assembly doesn't shake but teeters. And in the Southwest, where the problem of heavy winter frost doesn't exist, such a slab footing can be laid pretty much on the local earth. In upper New York or Maine, chances are the concrete benches would come apart under frost action in the mortar. In northern climes the firing-line slab will stay unrumpled, without frost heaves, only if it has been laid on a carefully drained base. Several cold-country ranges use the more malleable blacktop footing.

Away from termite country, wood is still widely used for the bench. Common are benches topped with painted 2-inch planks, with three posts, either 6- or 8-inch logs or 6 × 6 timbers, acting as legs, two in front and one at the rear. The leg assembly is stiffened by 2 × 6 planks spiked vertically around their upper ends so that the crosswise 2 × 6's or 2 × 8's of the top can be nailed to the planks as well as to the posts. The flat top should be very close to 34 inches above ground level.

The usual dimension for the bench top is 4 feet across the front; the overall length is usually 5 feet. The sides of the upper planking are sawed straight back for about 2 feet, then meld into a gentle curve, ending in a corner at least 8 inches either side of the central back post, so that the rear edge is actually a full 16 inches across. Any less leaves your right elbow without proper support. If the curve is repeated on both left-hand and right-hand sides, the bench obviously can handle either right-handed or left-handed shooters.

The bench which for over twenty years I used for all experimental rifle work on the range of the Camp Fire Club of America, some forty miles north of New York City, was built to this design. There were, however, three personal additions, all of which I recommend. First, the posts, actually what the lumber trade calls 8×8's but more like 7½×7½'s, were cut for more than the 2 feet of penetration below ground level usually recommended. On that bench they go down at least 4 feet, and their bottom ends are anchored in a colossal chunk of rough concrete, coming up to within about a foot of ground level, at least as big as a glacial boulder. Winter frosts have so far had absolutely no effect.

DuBois, Pennsylvania, was a bastion of early accuracy competition, eventually achieving over a hundred entries. This faded photo is of the first matches held there, in 1949, when benches were benches and casualness was the order of the day.

I am at the left, and facing the camera is the man who started me on the accuracy search, the late Al Marciante, who was known as "the gunsmith's gunsmith." Taken at Altoona in 1952, on a day when the wind blew virtually everybody off target at 200 yards.

Second, to the vertical 2 × 6 planks running between forward and after posts, I added a third across the front.

Finally, to assure a flat surface with minimal warpage I had a piece of marine plywood laid over the 2-inch topping and that well painted, with new paint annually. This bench is fully exposed to the weather but after two decades the only real wear is where my tripod's pointed feet have gnawed a bit at the easily replaceable plywood topping, and I'm sure it will be good for another twenty-odd years.

On ranges where competition is expected, or even much serious test work, overhead roofing is common, with sheet metal or fiberglass sheets and drill-pipe posts in the Southwest, a wooden roof in other sections of the country. Keeping off the blazing sun or the incipient rain or even the full thundershower is all very well, but bitter experience indicates that this roofing must be contoured without any overhang in front of the rifle muzzles, or certainly with any overhang still slanting upward. Otherwise the rumpus of anywhere from fifteen to fifty rifles whanging away in concert, or more particularly the horrible jarring rap of the .30-caliber the joker next to you is squeezing off, a jar stout enough to move your entire rifle off the aiming

At the Citizens Rifle and Revolver Club of Princeton, New Jersey, in June of 1948, the late Bill Curtis of Virginia shot a rifle typical of the day. Note the scope mounted entirely on the barrel, the Mauser action, and the sling, still in place as conclusive evidence that this was a practical varmint rifle. During the earliest beginnings, a sandbag was a true sandbag and tripods were unheard of.

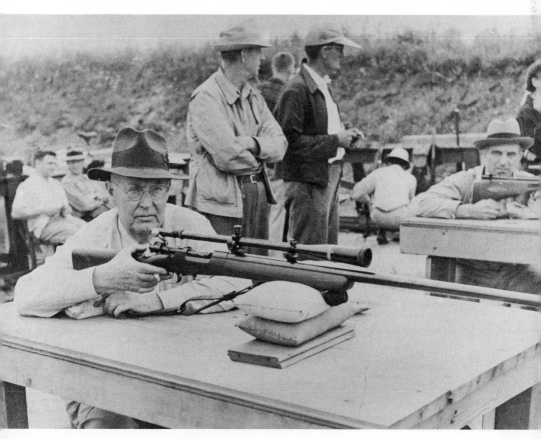

point, is not directed outward, uprange, but back into the ears of the shooters. In Millerton, New York, there is a range where the winter months are marked by great activity on Sundays with Snowball Matches. These cold-weather shooters long ago went beyond ordinary ear plugs to the custom-fitted variety or to the ear muffs developed for industrial uses, because the Millerton roof, handsome enough, comes down on the outside at a perfect angle to trap and bounce back all possible muzzle racket. Bob Hart's range at Wapwallopen, Pennsylvania, started its life with a similar but not so serious roof problem, but Hart has helped it greatly by laying house insulation up under the planking.

A bench rest match range for regional or national championships must have complex target frames, properly and visibly numbered, with empty air behind the bullet's passage through the target paper, behind that a moving backer to ensure that the correct number of shots is fired for each group, and behind that a stationary backer far enough away to permit accurate determination of the source of any crossfire.

On the Council Cup Range at Wapwallopen, Pennsylvania, owned and operated by Bob Hart, each target paper is stapled to its own board and slipped down into the holder left of its proper number. In a full relay, all target positions are fired, the target numbers corresponding to bench numbers back at the firing line, and in national competition the shooters shift benches to equalize firing line conditions. Note clean stationary backers ready to catch crossfires a few yards behind the target position.

On a competitive firing line—and existing ranges have anywhere from fifteen to fifty bench firing points—the benches are located up to 6 feet from one another on centers. Closer means some degree of interference and a considerable degree of annoying neighbor noise; further apart means a very long firing line and, worse, problems down at the target end. During registered matches there must be, behind the target-holding boards, both fixed and moving backer strips. These fulfill two purposes, one of indicating and identifying either deliberate or accidental crossfires, and the second of making sure that the requisite number of shots pass through the scoring target. They are hardly necessary for hunting rifle tests, sighting in. I am not going to try to describe the mechanics of the boards and

At Council Cup Range the moving backer paper is on a short roll behind each target, in order to avoid the problems of wind on a single sheet of paper stretching across the range. Then the whole backer frame is motor-driven slowly sideways as "Commence Fire" is called. In this instance, alas, it shows only four holes, cause for disqualification. The moving backer system is almost infallible and only the fastest shooter, or a breakdown of the machine, can bamboozle it into making four out of five.

backers. Both NBRSA and IBS can make available drawings of the systems now in operation, and any club planning to set up a match range should first send its best mechanical or engineering mind on a tour of well-established layouts to see firsthand how they work. None is perfect, that's sure, and it is equally sure that the functioning of a shoot is no better than the crews operating the boards and the backers.

A full match accuracy range, then, is not cheap. Your own testing setup can be, since you're the only one who gives a hoot whether you fired four or five shots into a group, and whether you get off all your shots inside a 7-minute time limit, as is today expected in varmint and sporter matches, for example, is your own business. The shooter who has easy access to his own private bench is a lucky feller, believe me.

Running a range for serious matches requires a considerable crew, usually six to eight on the targets, four in measuring and statistics, a range officer and his back-up, plus a kitchen staff and one chief to watch all the Indians. Here two of the Wap-wallopen target crew change the high-number end of the butts during a 200-yard event at the Pennsylvania shooting layout. Note the separation between holder for the scoring targets and the stationary backer setup.

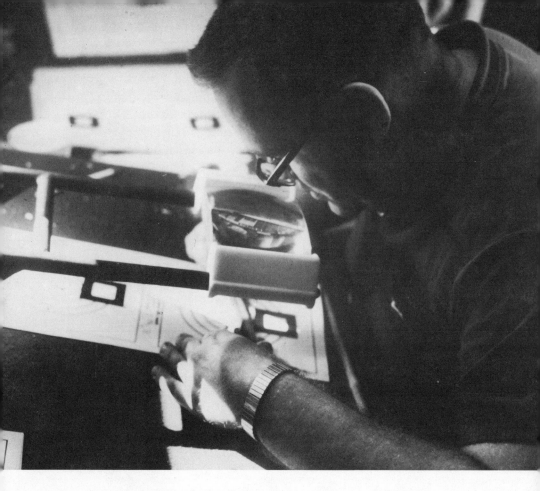

The unsung and thankless job of target measuring is done with magnifiers and devices capable of three decimal places, matches and aggregates alike depending on a few thousandths one way or another, although under some conditions 200-yard targets could probably be measured with a common yardstick.

Opinion is split on the matter of seats. Originally, for wooden benches a pair of seats 18 inches off ground level, set either side of the bench but carefully not connected to it, seemed to suffice. Then rebellion stepped in from Long Johns and Five by Fives alike, and most ranges today offer some sort of stool. Since most of these are as jiggly as Raquel Welch coming down a stairway the perfectionists bring their own—piano stools, homemade adjustable jobs, kitchen stools, and you name it.

At this point we can explain the business of using a bench rest. First, you sit at it. And your stool, no matter whether it be a rickety affair of aluminum tubing and canvas, a couple of stacked cinder blocks, or an adjustable swiped from the family Steinway, should ideally be of such a height, and so placed in relation to the bench, that when you sit squarely and straight-spined on it, with the right-front corner of your ribs in contact with the bench top at just about the vestigial mammary or nipple, if you'll pardon the expression, and with your shoulders and head comfortable in relation to the rifle, the angle of your thigh and shin bones will be just about 90 degrees. Your Number 11's will be set flat on the ground or concrete under the bench. Firm, square, solid, but relaxed. And in shooting, let yourself sog—not sag, sog—down onto the stool so that it seems to support most of your weight.

I am no churchgoer, though many bench rest fans are—in a few cases, I suspect, because they are hoping to get the good Lord on their side. But even the atheists among experienced accuracy experimenters agree that the proper hymn for sitting at a bench is "How Firm a Foundation."

5

Table Techniques

The average nonshooter, watching a man firing from a bench, figures something like this: "Heck, any jerk can hit the target every time that way. He isn't even holding the gun." Be it understood that such an average nonshooter, or anyone else who believes that the use of a bench totally and completely removes human frailty from the shooting problem, is off his wheezer. Proper shooting off a bench is both a technique and something of an art; and, alas, the human element is always there to some degree. Especially the human element that dwells between your ears.

But there are basic principles on which we can operate to minimize human wiggles and waggles, even to minimize the frailties which are, believe it or not, intrinsic in the firearms themselves. If I had to summarize these in single words, I'd say the two secrets were solidity and uniformity. And without touching the mysteries of mirage and wind—which are also part of that element in fine shooting which dwells between your ears—it is for certain that observance of those two principles is a matter of technique. Not automatic technique. Technique to be learned, and once learned, to be practiced over and again.

The concern with solidity was evident in the preceding chapter, in the matter of the bench's inherent or basic stability, and the stability of your own base or butt. The importance of these points is fairly obvious.

Going up a step, the question of contact or no contact between rib cage and bench top is hotly debated. Unless the bench itself is as shaky as Jello, I favor a slight but not driving or thrusting pressure between thorax and bench, and I shoot with a low rifle position. Others carefully avoid touching the bench, especially those who set up their rifles relatively high on forward and back sandbags and who touch off the rifle with either no contact or with minimal contact at any point other than the trigger finger, letting the rifle recoil absolutely free for a discernible distance.

It becomes evident, then, that there will be personal differences in rifle holding and let-off. I think that these differences, assuming we are shooting off sandbags and not with a return-to-battery rest, essentially depend on the rifle height off the bench. That in turn depends on the bags and tripods you use.

These come in a considerable assortment of types. As was earlier mentioned, tripods which can be adjusted in height, are to a degree locked to the bench by pointed feet that are themselves adjustable so as to keep all level, and will carry a fitted fore-end bag on a proper tray are made by several outfits. Lightest of these is the tripod made by Gene Beecher of Galeton, Pennsylvania, and designed to accept Tuller's sandbag models properly. The heavier rest made by Bob Hart of Nescopeck, Pennsylvania, also takes such standard bags. So will the massive rig made by Ed Bagrosky of Philadelphia. Wichita Tool is in the tripod business with a good one; Midwestern and Southwestern shooters also like outfits by Womack of Shreveport, Louisiana. New ones appear at every major shoot, and a minor sport for gunsmiths and machinists interested in accuracy work is milling out their own. All save the minutely adjustable jobs intended for the Teflon or metal bearing surfaces of the return-to-battery rests used with unlimited-class rifles, are simple and involve the same principles, so that picking one is a matter of choice. Just insist on solidity and adequate adjustment.

Since accuracy rifles are designed with flat fore-ends, which in the varmint and sporter matches are under 3 inches in width,

A multiplicity of front rests or tripods exists, all of which involve pointed feet, adjustable to square the rest on a canted bench; a wide range of vertical adjustment of the bag-holding tray; and usually a fore-end stop, which some shooters use, some don't. Some run heavy, and some, like the Beechers at left, are on the light side. Most vital need is that the supporting sandbag be contoured to fit the fore-end of the rifle in use. For that purpose Tuller and others make a variety of bags.

and since the rifles we ordinarily use in hunting are fitted with much slimmer and more rounded forestocks, the bag tied to your tripod should be contoured according to intended use. The flat-topped bag, presumably adaptable to anything, lets a rifle slide around sideways, so I long ago abandoned it and use for bench competition a narrow type, about 1 inch thick, with a U-shaped notch of a width fitting the fore-ends of my competition muskets. For test work with sporters, I switch to a similarly narrow type which is sausage-shaped and long enough so that on the tripod tray it forms a V to accept firmly almost any hunting-rifle fore-end. Bags are inexpensive and are made in a variety of shapes. Both fit and sand consistency are important.

Just bear in mind that in the varmint/sporter classes, indeed all sandbag matches, the bag or bags on which your rifle rests must be malleable, and must not mate with any tracks or edgings or special grooves so that the rifle is so tightly stabilized that it can be returned to firing position after a shot without resighting.

For the first fifteen years or so of my own bench competition I used for a rear bag a simple suede sack of beach sand, about the size of a large grapefruit, and finger-molded it into shapes more or less suitable to the undersection or toe of the rifle stock. It would fit any stock, but none well, and required that I use a firm hold even with the light-recoiling match rifles. I even won matches that way. There can be no doubt, however, that the present generally accepted style of rear bag is more efficient: rectangular in body shape, about 4×6 inches square and $2\frac{1}{2}$ inches deep, with the top surface tapering down aft and fitted with either pronounced rabbit ears or the less obvious bunny ears on top to form a V-section into which the stock toe slides. This bag design, when filled moderately stiff, can be manipulated with the fingers for elevation and windage corrections, and the ears definitely do help control recoil reaction and realignment of the rifle. Under no circumstances use a rear bag so shallow that the toe of your stock can touch the bench top, or so mushy that the corner of the stock toe drives into the bag, not over its top.

But we have left our shooter sitting at the bench, learning how to keep his back reasonably straight yet at the same time "sog" his weight onto his stool.

Presumably, of course, he has already had sense enough to set his tripod and rear bag on the bench and has adjusted the tripod height so that when the rifle is placed on them its sight aligns on or a mite above the aiming point. Presumably, also he has positioned the equipment in a way comfortable for him. I for one like the rear bag *center* about 5 inches in from the bench edge.

Very evidently, any strained position will be expensive either in terms of muscle tremor from fatigue or, more likely, from an attempt to "steer" a misaligned rifle back into proper target line. That really is the kiss of death, because steering with the cheek or with the right or trigger hand, or hitching the rifle back and forth on the bags with the shoulder, inevitably means a variation of the pressures on the rifle at the instant of firing. That will as inevitably mean a displacement of the shot. Proper alignment of the rest and rifle, then, is the primary step in observing the principle of uniformity.

Your left hand becomes the master of the operation thereafter. By squeezing or very slightly urging the rear bag, it controls both horizontal and vertical alignment of your sight. Recall that

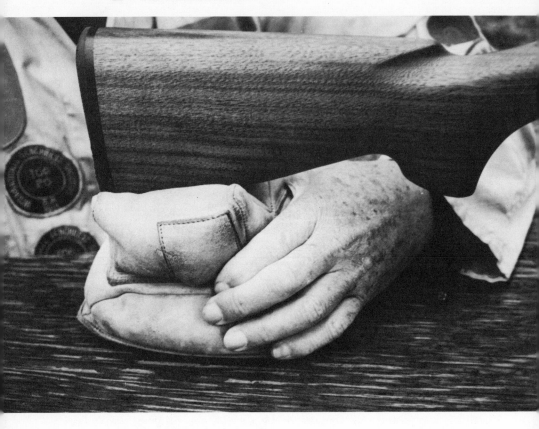

Key to sandbag shooting is the left-hand control of the rear sandbag, through which all aiming is done. Squeeze to change elevation, etc. The rifle must not be aimed with the shoulder or by hand or cheek pressure. This bag is a Tuller rabbit-ear type, filled only moderately hard. Note that the stock toe is positioned to slide back off the bag in recoil, not catch on it, and the left hand does not contact the rifle.

I suggested the primary lineup should have the sight on a point slightly above, say 6 inches or so, the ultimate aiming marker, be it square, bull's-eye, or X-ring. Merely gripping the bag then lifts the butt to drop the crosshair to the dead-on level. I repeat, the aiming of the rifle is done with the *left hand,* and the left hand alone, not by force from any other part of your body.

There exists disagreement as to how much contact there should be between shoulder and buttstock of match rifles. With any hard-recoiling rifle, lightweight hunting equipment, or Remingchester's new magnum, the contact must be absolute, truly firm, if you value your new bridgework. But for peak accuracy with either, there is total agreement on one point. If impact is to be the same, the stock-shoulder relationship must be the same for each shot. As a general rule, with the assorted bench rest equipment I have owned, an ultra-loose hold or no contact will give a shot hole higher on the target than will a more solid thrust of shoulder against butt. I suspect some rifles work out the other way. This is not so much the effect of shoulder pressure on any back-driving recoil that might occur while the bullet is still in the barrel as it is the effect of such man-pressures on the gun itself; it varies the vibration of the firearm during that definite time period between firing-pin fall and bullet exit.

Quite evidently, keeping such butt pressure identical is easiest when there is no contact at all. It is not too difficult when, as with a hard-kicking rifle, the contact is very solid indeed. It becomes most difficult when the feel of butt against shoulder

In this down-looking photo note that the shooter's cheek only barely touches the stock comb—some shooters avoid even this —and that the trigger hand is only lightly on the grip and trigger. The photo also indicates the lightly controllable tension between buttstock and shoulder; with some shooters and some rifles, there is no contact at all, just free recoil.

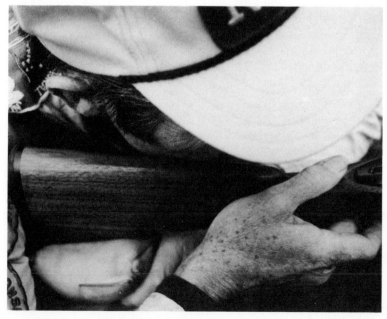

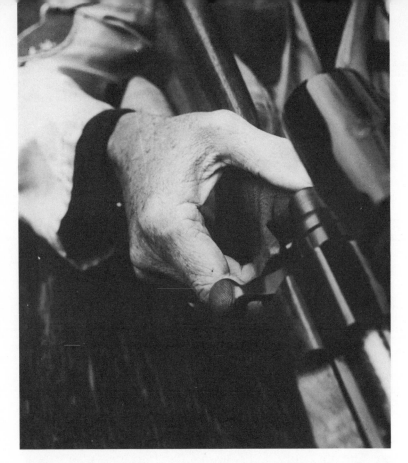

Another view from above reiterates the point that on a bench rest rifle the triggering hand does not grab the grip but merely rests on it lightly, to have minimal effect on rifle vibration yet offer control of the ultra-light trigger. Rarely a bench rest rifle needs to be shot from a tight hold, but with hard-kicking sporters, with their stiffer triggers, a full, firm squeeze with the trigger hand is a necessity, and force is exerted to settle the rifle to the shoulder.

is light but discernible. Since some people like to do things the hard way, and I'm one of those, I have for years used a light pressure with bench competition pieces. And every now and then I know bloody well that it was a personal variation in that pressure, some slight misattention or distraction from established practices, which tosses a shot out of the group.

On a bench rest rifle, the shooter's cheek touches the stock with, if any, the most delicate caress. But it usually bears with considerable firmness on the .30–06 you're sighting in for a Montana elk hunt. Bear in mind that competition rifles—at least most of them—recoil lightly, so you need not worry about scarring your ugly mug with scope cuts. Hence with the varminter-class jobs the only problem is that of holding your eye in decently steady alignment behind a high-magnification target scope. At the risk of repetition, *don't* alter this touch upon the stock, whether it is light or heavy. Do so, and the resulting target will look like a paraphrase of that childish song about old MacDonald's farm—here a shot, there a shot.

The right hand—we're assuming now that you have fed a round into a clear chamber and are in general ready to fire—may be needed to pull a big-boom hunting rifle back into your shoulder with appropriate force, but with a competition rifle it has only one job, that of controlling the trigger. Note I said *controlling*. A great many match rifles have their triggers set from a half pound to in the neighborhood of two ounces—this is normal for the Remington 40X match triggers, for example. Such pull weights would seem to be what laymen call a hair trigger. But never forget that with a trained finger, even so light a setting can be controlled off, neither flicked nor jerked, with considerable finesse. With match equipment, while a few accuracy bugs pinch off the trigger against the trigger guard, most winning-level shooters rest their right hands lightly around the grip section, or in the thumb hole as the case may be, so lightly that gripping action is minimal, and the only force exerted is straight back against the trigger.

And that brings us to what, I am sure, is cause for more "lost" shots than anything save the invisible forms of mirage: side pressure by the right hand. This is steering again, a clear violation of the uniformity principle and guaranteed to blow one for you. Even in working with the hard-kickers, as in developing a load for your trusty .300 Winchester magnum, your right hand must not move or push on the rifle sideways, only straight back into the shoulder.

Pow! Your shot went off. Automatically you shoulder the rifle back into prefiring position on the sandbag, immediately looking through the scope to see where the impact was, at the same time quickly observing whether or not the light, wind, and mirage conditions you thought existed at the instant of let-off really were that way. If, after all the care in observing the ideals of solidity and uniformity, that shot did not go quite where you expected, there must have been some reason. If you cannot account for it you are not progressing.

Yes, that's what it says here. Look and learn. The only trouble is that some of us, conspicuously yours truly, don't always learn what we should. There have been times on the Fassett range, and once or twice at Midland, when I was so mystified by the mirage goings-on that all I could do was mutter "Gosh darn it!" or "Oh, fudge!"

It would be delightful indeed if, at this point, we could say, "You now know everything. Sally forth and win the next match." But life at the bench isn't that easy.

First there is a matter of breathing. As with all rifle shooting, the proper procedure calls for one or two undoubtedly deep breaths to oxygenate the lungs, with the last one half exhaled and held at a point of comfort for the shot. True and easy enough in any test work or sighting in from a bench, except that in the seven minutes allocated for a five-round string in a varmint class match, when you've diddled around on the sighter target trying to dope the conditions until the range master has already called the two-minute warning, you're not likely to waste much time on breath control. But when you can, shoot in rhythm. In competition you quickly learn to adapt your rhythm, at least during the earlier minutes of a match, to those of your neighbors so you don't let off a shot just as the hombre on the next bench has blammed away with his short-barreled .308!

Breath control is fine, but what I'd like to know the secret of is heart control, because after four shots have gone into one hole that's only slightly off round, my personal blood pump begins to whomp and bounce like a sixteen-year-old's at his first burlesque show. Yours doesn't? Well, greetings, Mr. Robot. Some hearts thump even when the hole isn't that small!

In earlier days, when competition rifle barrels were often bedded well out into the fore-end, it was axiomatic that the fore-end must rest on the front bag at the same position for each shot. This is still basic advice in working out with hunting or varminting rifles, but now that the average competition rifle has metal-to-wood fit only in the action or sleeve areas, with the forward section of the barrel markedly free, it seems to be less important. Yet it is still a sensible idea, because lining up a tape marker with your front bag, for example, also means that the rear end of the whole assembly is positioned the same way for your upper body. Some rests, by the way, come with adjustable stops against which the fore-end fetches up when the rifle is pushed back into firing position. These have merit. But if your technique calls for considerable pressure forward between shoulder and buttstock, adjustable stops will cause a wild flyer if that pressure, transmitted up the rifle to the stop button, lifts the rifle off the bag slightly or if the fore-end hits the button slightly off center. I abandoned the stops some time ago, but there are those who swear by them.

Since bench rest shooting is in the final analysis a process of taming the human frame so that it, as well as the rifle, does precisely the same thing for each shot, it is probably superfluous to caution against marked shift of body position during a string or, heaven forbid, against getting up from the bench between the second and third shot. Once in a while it may be

The rifleman's stern should give him a firm and comfortable foundation, on a seat of correct height to permit a reasonably straight spine and solidly placed feet. Angle to the bench and the question of rib contact with the bench are a matter of personal choice. With rifles of heavy recoil the shooter should position himself more nearly facing front, toward the targets.

absolutely necessary to get up during a sequence. You brought the wrong ammunition block, or perhaps you've managed the abomination of unchambering a round which had a bullet deep-seated enough so as to pull the case off the bullet, thereby spilling into the action 22.6 grains of Dupont's best—or even worse, some of Mr. Olin's ball powder. If that necessity does occur, it will prove worth while to waste one or two shots into the sighter target before continuing the string, to resettle you and the rifle into the proper groove.

The same sort of caution applies, I feel, to testing hunting rifles. While sighting in a rifle for a hunt, there may be every good reason to stretch out the firing, to get off each round through a cold barrel, as presumably happens for the first shot during an actual try on game. You are then interested in first-shot impact rather than in grouping. But if you are testing the piece, working up a handload, or evaluating its performance potential, getting up between shots will do nothing for your group. In fact, if the rifle is consistent enough to merit such tests, if it does not tend to walk its impact with heating, you'll probably get tighter clusters firing consecutively even a .300 Winchester magnum or some such large-cased buster than by intermittent shots with inevitably a fresh hold each time.

6

Testing
Hard-Kickers

In working with violent or large-recoil rifles, of course, while virtually all the principles involved in shooting off a bench remain the same, the practices are inevitably different.

The differences are primarily caused by the need to tame that violent recoil. If, for example, you shoot a $7\frac{1}{2}$-pound .30–06 or an 8-pound 7 mm. Remington magnum in precisely the same manner as you might a target-scoped $10\frac{1}{2}$- or $13\frac{1}{2}$-pound .222, by letting the rifle sit on the bags of its own weight and then, with your shoulder a half-inch or so behind the butt, pinching off the trigger, the chances are excellent that within seconds you will (a) be blinded by a copious blood flow from a new scope cut in your right eyebrow, (b) be conscious of a sharp pain in and around the shoulder area, and (c) discover that the rifle has jumped off the bench, certainly off the rests. And the bullet has very likely gone to a point remote from the impact normal with a proper hold.

The hard-kicking rifle, then, must be supported with firm shoulder pressure, with the cheek firmly on the stock and the right-hand grip firm behind the trigger. Close but not unduly tight, certainly never tight to the point of discernible muscle tremor.

Since with the very low rifle position favored by some accuracy nuts, Mike Walker and I among them, the right arm is verging toward flat and the shoulder joint is in a lousy position for recoil absorption, common sense indicates that for rifles of significant recoil the bag set-up should carry the musket higher. By the same token, whereas with 13½-pound rifles shooting varmint-type cartridges it is quite practical for the body-and-shoulder angle to verge toward parallel to the stock, with the busters the upper body position must be not only higher but also more and more behind the musket. The greater weight of your own beef you can get behind the gun butt, the more mass there is to swallow kick; the more nearly straight up your body is, the further down your spine toward your sitzplatz the recoil can be distributed.

It is for these reasons that if some outright cannon of the .458 Winchester–.460 Weatherby tribe is due for checkout, the most comfortable position, the one least likely to inoculate you with a miserable flinch, is leaning into a parked car, over the hood or over the top as the case may be. I have on several occasions fired such elephant slayers for group, as well as for sighting, and the jar is not really all that bad. And after all, how many shots do we need to drop an elephant? Of course, I do remember one buffalo that was apparently made of solid rubber ... hard rubber.

I can and have shot off bench rests virtually every extant caliber up to the various forms of .375, but don't profess to find much fun in it when the hole is bigger than .30 or the bullet weight much over 200 grains. When bullet weights go markedly up beyond that to the Elmer Keith level, or when velocities are hiked enough to have great effect on subjective recoil—not the numbers you read in tables but what you actually feel—I see no shame in increasing the absorption effect of the high and square position by resorting to a folded-up Turkish towel under the shooting coat. Or how about one of the strap-on buckskin-and-rubber pads made near Little Falls? Or is it really a sin to use a sissy bag?

The sissy bag, despite its name, is the shooter's friend where recoil is concerned. Essentially it is merely a $4 \times 3 \times 6$-inch sack of sand or even of fine shot—make your own choice as to shape —which can be placed between gun butt and shoulder in a

For either heavy-recoil sporters or .30-caliber varmint-weight rifles, the "sissy bag" as shown here between butt and shoulder will eat up recoil. It pulls the eye back from the scope, inevitably, but also acts as a massive pad, and in effect adds its own several pounds of weight to the weight of the rifle.

position which avoids binding the stock toe. It has two effects. First, the sand is to a small extent compressible, so will swallow some rearward thrust. Second, in a manner of speaking the bag, since it must be moved backward by the recoiling firearm, thereby adds its own weight to that of the rifle. And everybody since Newton (the gravity Newton, that is), knows that a 12-pound magnum jars you around less than would the same cartridge out of an 8-pounder.

In testing hunting rifles, excessive recoil destroys shooting abilities then and thereafter by setting up in most humans a tendency to flinch, an illness fatal on either game or targets. It has quite a different result in accuracy competition. Here it puts into the human computer a fatigue factor which partway through a long day can have a competitor shooting when he shouldn't, changing his hold shot for shot, and committing all the other sins. Where your hope is only for 1½-inch sporter groups, for example, most of us can accept the setback of an

8-pound .270 Winchester rifle without apparent error. If the goal is .25-inch spreads, however, then even a 10½-pound .308, termed a sporter or a light varminter by bench rest rules, can beat many people to a pulp in short order.

There are happy exceptions. Donalee Stekl, who certainly does not weigh over 100 pounds wearing her stoutest overshoes, is one bench rest competitor of record-establishing and aggregate-winning qualities who has been known to sit behind a .30 caliber all day and punch as small holes at four o'clock as she

As is all sports, individual techniques vary but principles are basic. This represents my basic position for working with light-recoil accuracy rifles like the 40XB–BR 6 × 47 positioned on the sandbags. Note the hidden left hand does the aiming, cheek contact and shoulder contact are minimal, trigger hand rests lightly, and the position can be held for long periods without strain. The rifle here is one of the modern "glue jobs" in which some 5 inches of the barrel are epoxied into the stock, and action and rest of barrel are left free to vibrate. Hence the odd scope positioning.

did at nine o'clock. I do notice, of course, that the lady has of late abandoned her trusty .308s for rifles chambered 6×47, a cartridge which delivers only fleabite recoil. That may be indicative of late recognition of hard fact.

One side effect of violence in hunting rifles, when shot off rests, has always impressed me but as far as I know only me. That is, when a blaster (say a .300 Weatherby magnum sporter, which no one ever accused of being subtle in its violence) is

With a sporting or hunting rifle of fair to heavy recoil, the shooter position should be more facing forward, and higher, in order to ease absorption of the recoil jar into more upper body. Rifle height has been increased here by adding an extra sandbag—sporters seem to shoot better off fairly soft rests—and by screwing the tripod to peak height. Had the rifle been a .458 instead of the 7 mm. Remington magnum by Champlin shown in use, even further steps would have been taken to increase the high, square-on hold. The trigger-hand grip with hard-kickers must be firm, and that hand must also keep the rifle solidly against shoulder or the shooter may lose his bridge-work.

fired off a hard front sandbag, the rifle not only bounces out of control but also, in my experience, does not shoot quite as well as the same rifle and ammunition can off a softer, better-padded support. It is difficult to do enough test firing under identical conditions with a big .300 or any similar "active" piece to satisfy the statisticians, but I have made enough experiments, with and without a couple of layers of sheepskin across the front rest, to satisfy myself on this score.

Further, although the late great Colonel Townsend Whelen and I disagreed to some extent on the point, I am equally convinced that the hardness of the front rest affects impact. Or to put it another way, most rifles shoot away from a hard rest whether contact be at bottom or at side of the fore-end. Hence, in order to duplicate the firing situation you're likely to get during a sheep hunt or a trip after Wyoming elk, for example, your rifle should be sighted in either over a padded rest or off your left hand. And this has little to do with any tendency of rifles using slings to lower impact when the sling is tightened—darned few people actually use a sling as much more than a carrying strap during an actual hunt anyway.

The hunting rifle, then, should be fired from a bench with observance of the same principles as the ultra-precise models but with rather distinctive variations in technique. Where many bench rest testers of field arms—including several of the notables in the arms-writing field—fall short is in failure to recognize the truism that just because a deer rifle will not, or so it seems, shoot any better than 2 minutes of angle is no reason to violate with it all the practices normally employed when handling a real precision job. Who knows—by holding according to the uniformity rules, by paying attention to the wind, light, and mirage factors, as is usual with a tackdriver but too often forgotten with the "just a huntin' rifle," you may turn that 2 inches into $1\frac{3}{4}$ or even $1\frac{1}{2}$. At least you will have given the rifle a chance. I have watched in action one well-known scrivener who regularly pooh-poohs small-sporter groups as freaks. Frankly I think that if he got a tight sporter group it would indeed be a freak. And that does not need to be, fellow devotees of rifle precision. There are *hunting* rifles, much less varmint jobs, which will shoot to the 1-minute mark. Not many, and perhaps not all the time, but some, and with enough regularity to encourage the rifle-precision search.

7

Where the
Action Is

If not the soul, then certainly the heart of any rifle is its action, the "works" of receiver, magazine, trigger mechanism, and bolt or other breeching system which do the basic jobs of feeding, lock-up, fire control, and final clearance of the cartridge that the rifle fires. Frailty or failure of the action in any of those tasks immediately condemns the whole rifle, and the style of action—whether bolt, lever, slide, self-loading, dropping-block, or break-open—is more intimately related to the actual use area of the rifle than any other element of it. The properties usually associated with such actions lead varmint shooters and long-range hunters to prefer the bolt action, for example, or induce whitetail hunters operating in brushy country to plump for the lever, slide, or semi-automatic. Similarly, the circumstances of modern military use make the self-loading automatic or semi-automatic piece basic in shoulder ordnance for the infantryman, but the sniper picks a specialized bolt-action.

It is frequently said that as far as sporting equipment is concerned the quick-firing rifles used by the whitetail hunter—or by people anticipating longer shots but too lazy or too slow to function a turning bolt—give lousy accuracy. The average saddle carbine working on the lever principle, 'tis said, won't regularly hit your hat. This is both true and untrue.

First off, by and large the cartridges for which quick-firing rifles are often chambered are not, in their commercial forms, capable of markedly better than the old *British Textbook of Small Arms* requirement of 3 minutes of angle anyway. No loading company is likely, for example, to spend the care and money needed to produce .35 Remington fodder that will stay inside a demitasse cup at 200 yards for the simple reason that not once in a blue moon is the kind of hunter who buys a .35 Remington rifle called upon to shoot at 200 yards and never at a demitasse cup. If it will hit said demitasse cup at 50 yards that's just dandy in a practical sense. And until very recently there has been no pressure on the makers of fast-firing rifles to design or finish them in ways leading to better than 3-minute specifications.

They will, however, often do better. During those halcyon days when I was called upon, by the demands of my columns for *Field & Stream,* to test-fire every rifle that came onto the market, including some that probably shouldn't have, a high percentage of the "new" types were repeaters on other than turning-bolt actions. I quickly discovered that a 3-minute spec-ification, assuming decent ammunition, was not really a tight requirement and that 2 to $2\frac{1}{2}$ minutes, for such pieces and out-of-the-box ammo, was more reasonable. Often they beat it. I had one Browning self-loader that shot like a house afire; the second Remington I tried in the 740–742 series was excellent; a Model 100 Winchester in .243, once I had doped out the right tension on the forestock screw, shot better than a self-loader had any right to. And every gunscribbler has had similar expe-riences with individual lever actions, or discovered that a hand fit-up on the Remington 760 slide rifles will shrink their groups like boiling water.

But with very few exceptions the style of action most likely to produce accuracy of target quality, or even really superior varminting and hunting quality, is the turning bolt. The reasons therefor are simple: first, relative rigidity of the action proper and of assembly with the barrel and the stock; second, relative speed, simplicity, and controllability of the firing pin fall; third, precise breeching that can support the cartridge completely and in the same way for each shot.

A Shilen-designed action—this one made by John Dewey—shows the basic characteristics common to most accuracy types: massive, cylindrical receiver; large-bodied bolt, in the Shilen a multiple-lug type; minimum-pull adjustable trigger; large guard assembly, serving essentially as a means of pulling the action down into its bedding; simple recoil lug, fixed when the barrel is screwed in.

The quick-firers usually fall flat on the breeching and firing pin speed requirements and leave much to be desired on the point of rigidity, so we can expect not necessarily poor accuracy for their purpose, which doesn't really demand the ability to shoot the heads off flies, but poor accuracy against absolute levels, which do indeed involve decapitating said fly. The dropping-block single-shots, many of which are tackdrivers in practical varminting terms—my Ruger SS .222, Serial No. 13, is a case in point in that it delivers from .6 to .75 all day long with "mated" handloads, and I once owned a Hauck that would do almost as well—fall flat on the firing pin speed demands, and since they normally use two-piece stocks and short threaded sections for barrel insertion, end up not quite of competitive or fly-beheading quality because they suffer "bedding" problems which are really basic lack of rigidity. The only dropping-block action I ever saw win bench rest matches was a Martini which Walker tried for a season or two, and being a sensible man, eventually abandoned. The king of the accuracy hill, until something else comes along, is the turning bolt.

All actions commercially available in the United States today are either grandchildren or grandnephews of the European Mauser/Mannlicher military developments of the past century, and I don't think I'm out of line in saying that as of 1973 it is hardly feasible to design a completely new turning bolt, the so-called "new" design usually ending up as a batch of old ideas assembled in a new combination. Which is all right, too, since if a mechanical idea is good enough to stick around for fifty or a hundred years it must have some basic merit.

The first actions used in accuracy shooting competition were identical to those employed in the great burst of custom and near-custom rifle-building that followed World War II—they were Mausers of one form or another, usually the proven 1898 type. I have no intention whatever of commenting on the merits and demerits of all the Mauser and Mauser-descended, and Mannlicher and Mannlicher-descended, military actions that were turned into sporting equipment in this country between 1945 and 1965 or so, since I doubt strenuously that there is or was significant difference in pure accuracy potential between the Czech VZ 24 and the Loewe-built 1893, once the customizer got through with them. A longtime maker of accuracy rifles like Ted Boughton of Rochester, New York, with whom I have talked and corresponded at length on the subject, might be able to differentiate among such actions but it is today a pointless argument.

Early accuracy rifles used Mausers primarily because they were cheap and readily available. U.S. gunmakers were not about to peddle actions alone at a time when they could sell every rifle they could make, and the small toolroom action builders operating today hadn't set up shop. Early on it became apparent that the "untreated" Mauser or Mauser-descended action (which would include the Springfield, M70, etc.) failed of peak accuracy desires on two scores. One, like any siderail action, it wasn't really stiff—the front receiver ring was connected to the back or bridge only by relatively flexible strips of steel, open by virtue of the necessary magazine cut. When a heavy barrel was hung on it bedding problems became acute in short order. Two, the firing pin fall on all this family of actions—and this is a necessity because the military understandably demand absolute reliability of a solid whack to the primer—has all the solidity and majestic slowness of closing a Cadillac door.

But they were still cheap and available, and while the firing pin fall problem wasn't really cured by "speed-lock" approaches, the stiffness problem could be attacked by the simple device of fastening a hunk of railroad iron to the underside of the action where the magazine had been—a strip, slab, or chunk to personal choice. I have a rifle made by the late Barney Auston on a beefed-up FN, which never did win a dime. This same attack was used in early attempts by FN, Sako, and Winchester (for Fort Benning 300-meter trials) to stiffen their bolt-actions' for one accuracy purpose or another. Pennsylvanian Orin Bellows tried a half sleeve on the top side; Crawford Hollidge, stoolshooter, had a topside stiffener called a "strong back"; and by the middle 1950s full sleeves were being tried.

The first American-made commercial action that showed the route to real accuracy potential was probably the Remington 722. In the corner of my rack as this is typed stands a venerable rest rifle, caliber .222, about 18 pounds, in a cord-of-wood laminated stock by Harris, with a fat barrel in it screwed into a perfectly ordinary M722 action. In the earlier days of bench competition we shot for money, anteing into a kitty when we laid down the entry fees, and that ancient musket has won its price tag time and time again. It once came home from a Johnstown shoot with over two hundred bucks at a time when a dollar was real money, not the price of a candy bar. And that bloody great barrel is simply hung onto an ordinary open-bottomed 722 action, yet it is free-floated all the way.

It was a 722 action, by the way, that Boughton fitted with an aluminum sleeve—it was at the time thought impossible to mate steel and aluminum for this purpose—by the simple device of using epoxy-based Devcon, and so began an historic trend.

The Remington 40X actions, which are by all odds the most-used single type in accuracy competitions today, are essentially only that primary 722 significantly stiffened by the simple device of eliminating the magazine well, shrinking the area cut out for feeding and ejection, and slightly enlarging the diameter, all in order to achieve a higher degree of stiffness than is possible, or at least as easy, with noncylindrical actions. The weight is 2 pounds $3\frac{5}{8}$ ounces. Two conventional lugs, full case head shrouding. The trigger mechanism may, of course, be

Here I have one of the earliest 40XB–BR models and one of the very earliest Remington-made target scopes, fitted with a muzzle-length barrel mirage shade. The rifle barrel is left in the white on most bench rest rifles, the bluing of stainless being difficult, and in any event unnecessary for such use. Note the action is cylindrical, and uses a regular Remington bolt. The trigger is a 2-ounce type.

titivated a bit as compared to that of a standard M700 sporter, or it might even be equipped with a 2-ounce optional trigger—which believe me you do not slap off but soon learn to squeeze as controllably as if it pulled two pounds rather than ounces—but these are nonessentials. This action's recoil shoulder simply screws between barrel and receiver ring when the barrel is fitted. It happens that the firing pin time is 3.2 milliseconds, which rates very favorably indeed. The fastest lock time recorded is the Model 788 at 2.8 milliseconds.

If you skim the reports of major shoots, it becomes grossly evident that this basic 40X, alone or sleeved, is a popular choice. Eastern shoots would average something like 60 percent. Its smaller brother, the M600 or M660 series action, in sleeved form is another top choice—at one recent Fassett shoot in the light-varmint class the two combined to make up 75 percent of the rifles in use. At the Tulsa 1972 NBRSA matches, these Remington-made actions, sleeved or unsleeved, were picked by 87 of 115 sporter competitors, 87 of 128 in the light-varmint classes, and 93 of 150 in the heavy-varmint group.

Sleeving a full-sized 40X in steel, of course, does increase its weight to make that a real consideration, so in the 10½-pound class these are frequently shot as is, occasionally sleeved in aluminum. The lighter 600–660 types, however, are generally fitted with a sleeve regardless of which weight class the rifle is intended for.

Bob Hart of Nescopeck, Pennsylvania, has probably been making specialized custom bench actions longer than any other person, early small-shop operators like Ralph Pride and Sier-wart and Weber having admitted the commercial unfeasibility of so specialized a trade some time back, and there are a con-siderable number of Hart actions in use.

All of Bob's actions start with a Remington bolt for the fast firing pin. He is completely committed to the principle of the cylindrical action for stiffness and bedding ease. He makes a family of four action types priced between $160 and $200 at this writing. The so-called plain action, #1, is 1.400 in diameter, 8.125 inches long, weighs 2 pounds 9 ounces. Version #2 goes to 3 pounds, since at the forward end a short 1.625-inch sleeve section is fitted which branches into a three-pronged cantile-vered extension which takes the forward scope base and keeps it off the barrel. The #3 type is much the same but longer, going to 13.750 inches and using two guard screws forward of the

Bob Hart's "heavy varmint" or 1.4-inch style of action, weight 3 pounds 2 ounces, shows the characteristic Hart system of fastening action into stock, and the sleeved-on three-legged forward extension to keep the scope mount off the barrel. Hart makes a lighter sporter action with one forward guard screw, similar extension; a plain action; and a full-sized multi-screw sleeved unrestricted type. All use Remington bolts and triggers.

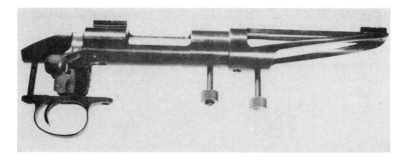

trigger. The #4 action is a full unrestricted type, 15.25 inches overall, three midpoint and forward guard screws, and sleeved to an outside diameter of 1.725. These actions come with either the Remington 40XB triggers or the 2-ounce version, for an extra forty bucks. All of them have a full inch of threading for the barrel shank. Bob Hart has made up hundreds of competition rifles on such actions; he is careful to avoid any chance of action warpage by doing all the metal tempering before final machining.

The Shilen action has gone through several stages, Ed having made up some before associating himself with John Dewey in the Shooters Service venture, more there while in the Clinton Corners, New York, shop, a few more after his move into the Southwest, and then more recently having gone into a Mark II type at the Irving, Texas, shop. There have even been articles written about which actions were made where and when, but this has always seemed to me academic since the basic concept of the Shilen action has not significantly changed.

Action No. 164, which apparently belongs during the SS&D period, is the basis of a heavy-varmint rifle in .222$\frac{1}{2}$ which has for me been involved in several national and regional championships. Just over 9 inches long, including the recoil lug, between barrel shank and receiver, and 1.340 inches in diameter, it is massive enough to make sleeving usually unnecessary. The weight of such a Shilen action runs some 3 pounds. The trigger can be either Canjar or the aforementioned Hart 2-ounce; the trigger guard follows common modern practice in accuracy equipment in being one piece the whole action length with three screws, in this case Allen-headed screws so that a torque wrench can readily be used in establishing constant tension, at tang, midpoint, and recoil lug. The Shilen bolt likewise follows modern practice in being large-bodied (.841-inch diameter on mine) but is fluted to reduce weight and any binding tendency. The bolt's business end uses four lugs in pairs on each side, all lapped into even bearing, a simple spring extractor, and is deeply recessed for the case head. As is true of many bench rest actions, there is no ejector, none being needed, the case being picked out by the forefinger for replacement in the loading block.

The only reason for sleeving one of these actions would be either to extend the bedding area or to extend the action length in order to keep the forward base of a conventional target scope

Comtemporary Shilen practice calls for sleeving virtually any sort of action to give stiffness, scope support off the barrel. The action here is encased in the lightweight square-bottomed aluminum sleeve used on light varminter and sporter types. The rifle could have lost half a pound at least by using one of today's short scopes in the 19-ounce class.

rig off the barrel. My heavy-varminter has no sleeve, the scope is tied to the barrel, and while that assembly may not be the theoretical ideal, it has worked more than satisfactorily on this particular rifle, as witness its record of national victories, and the fact that it will shoot .25 or better all day long when conditions are good.

Shilen is, however, an advocate of the sleeve on principle, and a great many of his rifles utilize fitted aluminum sleeves, either cylindrical or flat-based. The latter style is frequently used with the smallish action that starts life on XP-100 handguns or M600 Remington rifles, and for the past several years I've used one on a light-varminter. Ed's argument is that the flat surface, with the recoil bearing at the rear or tang end, is not only quick to bed, but readily permits sure bedding control. Of fifty rifles using the flat sleeves, he recalls need for rebedding on only two. Opponents argue that to mate a flat to a flat requires all the care used by a toolmaker in making a set of Johanssen blocks, and that to expect a sizable flat area in wood to remain flat is asking too much. I don't know the answer. There probably is none, individual experiences having provided the base for both points of view. There are, however, especially among Western shooters, a great number who swear by Shilen-made rifles, of either sleeved or unsleeved type, so Ed obviously does a lot of things right.

The "strong-back" idea pioneered for bench rest rifles to stiffen actions can also be applied to sporters and at the same time offer flexibility of scope mount position. This style, made by John Dewey, gunsmith, is bored for a variety of scope block combinations. This is perhaps unneeded on sporters but helps varmint rifles.

Toolmaker and bulletmaker Clarence Detsch has made a number of accuracy actions but is hardly in the business of producing them. The same could be said of Homer Culver, Eldon and Ralph Stolle, Baucher, Tirrell, McMillan, and a dozen others, who as superior machinists make their own actions, sometimes one or two for their friends, relatives, or some gent more persuasive than the rest of us. These designs all differ, but all agree on the basics of stiffness, large bedding area, positive and precise breeching, and fast firing pin fall, and I haven't the foggiest idea which one is "best." They all win matches. Shooters interested in these more individualized actions must expect to make a personalized approach, however, by going to matches, making friends, and eventually finalizing a deal either by arm-twisting or the brandishing of considerable folding money.

John Dewey of SS&D, however, along with all manner of precision loading gear, builds accuracy actions for profit, his design being virtually identical to that of the earlier Shilens, and he's a mite easier to approach!

The name "Benchmaster" for the accuracy action has always seemed to me a fortunate one, but I have never used a rifle built around one of these, as made by Charles Williams of

Garland, Texas. Without going into all the details of design, this one in effect combines the sleeve and the action in the first place, the receiver body in some types being as long and large as the usual cylindrical sleeving. Williams made an experimental quartet of aluminum to lessen weight, with steel inserts at all points of wear or bearing, but has since gone to all steel. His present model is 9 inches long, $1\frac{3}{8}$ inches on a square side but with a 45-degree angle out, giving the top of the action an octagonal appearance. The recoil lug is integral, at the front end.

The bolt, however, can be had all steel or as a composite to save weight. This action hasn't been around long enough for great numbers of rifles to be made up on it but would seem to have considerable possibility of satisfying all the accuracy requirements.

Champlin Arms of Enid, Oklahoma, has a three-lug action with large fluted bolt body and fairly heavy receiver, that without a magazine cut or with sleeving has potential for competition accuracy. Good varmint rifles for field work are presently being made on it, but the chief problem for the bench rest gunsmith minded to experiment is the high original cost of the Champlin action.

The barrel-block idea is capable of application to varmint-weight ($13\frac{1}{2}$-pound) rifles if the blocks used are aluminum and the stock reasonable in weight. Note scope-supporting bar atop the blocks. Remington's latest "glue-job" style of rifle assembly achieves the basic effect of the barrel-block system without use of the blocks, yet fastens the rear segment of the barrel to the stock with total rigidity.

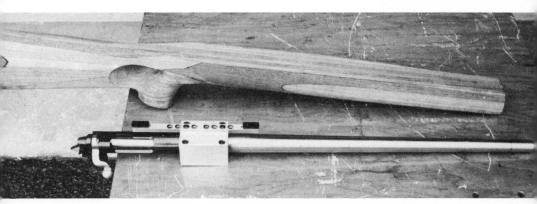

It is to me a marvel that more varmint rifles intended solely for field use are not built up or even commercially produced on actions which have the attributes several times mentioned in this chapter as being desirable for competition actions—utmost practicable stiffness, minimal lock time, large bedding and scope-carrying areas, and precise breeching. In point of fact, a 40X, for example, will shoot rings around the "normal" varmint rifle built on a conventional magazine-equipped sporting action and a somewhat fancier stock. It costs relatively little more than the more conventional varminter, surprisingly little more considering the accuracy differential; it can be equipped with sling swivels and such if need be; it is less likely to alter zero markedly one month or one set of conditions to the next than is the more conventionally bedded "normal" varmint piece. And certainly on a chuck, crow, or ground squirrel rifle any need for repeat shots from a magazine is wholly academic. Matter of fact, in a lot of years of bothering such targets I don't recall ever having seen any rifleman shoot varmints out of a magazine anyway—the rounds are fed one at a time and are carefully picked out, kept for reloading, after extraction.

Shilen is moving into this area with the one-shot varmint rifle built on his latest action design; so is Champlin. Remington could make the 40X prettier if they were minded to. Why other small and large gunmakers haven't tried such a piece bothers me in that it suggests that the shooting public, or at least too much of it, really does not appreciate the benefit of accuracy at the $\frac{1}{2}$-minute level rather than $1\frac{1}{2}$ minutes when it comes to picking off pasture poodles at trans-pasture distances.

Back in the days of the 18-pounders, Taylor & Robbins built some very competitive rifles that were both precise and handsome, every one of them a beautiful piece—big overall, perhaps even to the point of being massive, yet they were anything but ugly. In that sense they were like a 6-foot Las Vegas showgirl, the one in the back with the front and the long plumes. There is no real reason, after all, why a rifle built solely around accuracy performance factors may not at the same time be in its way aesthetic.

8

Straight-Shooting Barrels

Any gun-lover attending his first bench rest shoot will currently notice one oddity: the barrel of virtually every rifle on the firing line will be in the bright, unblued. I've heard as an explanation of this apparent mystery the tale that bluing is avoided because the bluing compounds might work damage to the bore; and I've also heard the even odder story that the heat of modern bluing techniques could upset the heat treat of the steel. The four real reasons are simpler: most competition barrels today are made from billets of high-chromium steels, one of the numerous metallurgical mixes called "stainless," and so are not really in need of much anti-corrosion protection, which is what bluing is; there is little point in reduction of any metallic shine or glare on a range rifle; accuracy nuts are likely to screw barrels in and out so fast, searching always for the perfect tube, that they don't want to waste time or money on a blue job; and finally, bluing is inherently complex, a two-stage procedure, on stainless steels.

The shiny tubes do not absolutely have to be shiny, anyway. Dave Hall treats his to a squirlygig pattern like Damascus, and if you want yours colored blue or black you can have it colored.

Just don't waste money on any engraving—if you're an avid shooter you'll wear out the barrel long before you're through admiring the decorations. If fancy work you must have, put it on the action or the action sleeve, either of which will outlast a bushel of barrels used at the bench.

And how long do barrels last, where accuracy is a requisite? Frankly, I do not exactly know.

There are two basic controlling factors: the metallurgy of the barrel, and the way in which it is fired—big charges or small loads, high pressures or low, fast with the shots in close sequence or slow with them widely spread. The factory or laboratory tests for barrel life ordinarily involve a sequence of a standard loading with five shots, or in some cases ten, fired fast enough to heat the barrel thoroughly. That procedure is repeated after the barrel has cooled back to normal room temperature. In either event that procedure is fairly close to what happens with a bench rest rifle at a match—a string, followed by complete cooling and cleaning, then another string.

But very evidently, if you have two barrels of like inside diameters the one using the larger capacity cartridge, the magnum for example, will get its throat washed out faster; or if both are chambered for the same round and one is loaded to 40,000 pounds and the other to 52,000 pounds the hot-load job will wear out first. And by the same token, if one barrel is of carbon steel and the other of one of the so-called stainless or high-chrome alloys, the nonrusting type will stand the gaff longer, all else being equal.

The reason for the relative longevity of the stainless or high-chrome tube is not its hardness. In fact, the so-called stainless steels would show a lower rating on the Rockwell scale than either old-type carbon or today's conventional chrome-moly mixes. But the steels with a high chrome content resist the higher temperatures better, their very rubberiness being an asset here.

"Wear" is, of course, a misnomer. In the proper sense of that word, barrels are worn only by misuse of cleaning equipment —as chamber throats are worn egg-shaped by an unguided rod that is allowed to pick up grit. "Washing" or "erosion" more nearly describes what happens: the blast of superheated gas, driving tiny fragments of unburned or still-burning powder ahead of it, simply chars and eats away the surface of the barrel metal just ahead of the chamber. That area takes on under magnification the chunk appearance of dried mud in a lake bed or a slab of alligator hide. Ultimately some of those chunks break out and create an unevenness that chews at the bullet and lets gas escape. If the throat becomes significantly so burned or washed, accuracy suffers. Sometimes, quite often in fact, accuracy can be revived simply by cutting off the rear section of the barrel and rechambering in the fresh metal, since the forward segments of the tube are not truly "worn" at all. Wear usually means more than the .001 to .002 of enlargement sometimes observable in accuracy bores past the 3000-round mark.

Sporter barrels chambering hotrock cartridges can be washed out in as little as 750 rounds. I have one small-caliber magnum whose bore looks like crocodile hide for a couple of inches ahead of the chamber with less than 1000 rounds of test-firing and load-checking through it. Conversely, a .22 rimfire will last for 50,000 to 100,000 shots before somebody wears it out, usually with a cleaning rod. Solely in hunting use, I doubt that you'd wear out a sporter in a lifetime. As for bench rest shooting, including test days and competition, we hear tales of .222's that still win matches at 5000 rounds, but I'd figure 3000 to 4000 rounds as a more realistic figure. Double the size of the cartridge by going to a .22–250, however, and the accurate life will be cut by perhaps 50 percent.

Probably more important is knowing when a barrel has started to go. A borescope will usually spot it quite positively; proof on the targets is harder to read. But the groups from a badly worn barrel do show a general enlargement. They do not show the vertical dispersion that might mean either a bedding problem, an ignition problem, or a load too high or too low on the pressure curve. Nor do they give the zero-vertical, lots-of-horizontal type of group which is either bum holding or at times a bedding fault. They just open up all over. Needless to say, before jumping to the conclusion that a given barrel has been washed out, the rifleman should take steps to eliminate all the other reasonable possibilities of fault in sights, bedding, holding, bullets, or loads that might give similarly bad results. And he should also treat the tube to a serious scrub-out, since the fault might be simple fouling.

All modern rifle barrels start as a hole approximately of bore diameter bored through a round-forged bar of the selected metallurgy. Usually, except in one method, the bar is somewhat longer than the finished barrel is expected to be. This primary deep-hole drilling is very likely the toughest problem facing any maker of barrels, whether he has a one-man shop or a mass-production factory, since to keep a hole dead straight and dead center for 30 inches or so is a tough go. Minor variations of hardness in the metal, lumps as it were, cause the bit to slide off line. Even with metal of butter-smooth working qualities all machine work operates on tolerances, and very evidently only a minor tolerance error in the set-up, or at one end of the hole, can lead the bit well astray at the other. Of course, there have been barrels with crooked or off-center holes that shot fine groups—I recall owning one Husqvarna hunting rifle, a .30–06, which had somehow sneaked through final inspection with its barrel hole very decidedly off center at the muzzle, yet it not once but usually stayed under the inch mark and on one or two occasions under the half-inch. But this phenomenon was the exception rather than the rule. And needless to say, any brutal outside turning to make the hole seem centered is not likely to be very helpful, which is one reason why accuracy barrels are if turned at all turned very carefully, on precise lathes, and with a minimum of tricky taperings or curves.

Once the hole is drilled and reamed the barrel is rifled by one of four methods: the classic system of scraping out the grooves with a hook cutter, repeatedly pulled through in a cam-controlled twist one groove at a time; broaching, an inexpensive method used for tubes not expected to be particularly precise, in which a multiple cutter does much the same in cutting the rifling grooves all at once; button rifling, in which a knob of tungsten carbide or extremely hard tool steel; carrying the rifling depth and pitch, is either pulled or pushed through the bore hole to squeeze or cold-form the walls of that hole into their proper rifled form; and hammer forging, in which multiple machine hammers pound the billet over a mandrel which represents the bore, rifling, and sometimes the chamber in intaglio. In this last scheme, which can be used for all manner of barrels, even including shotgun tubes, the original machinery costs are vast. Yet many manufacturers are coming to it because the device produces a very nearly finished barrel, shaping the outside contours as well as the inner, leaving only a bit of clean-up turning, threading, and cutting off before installation. It also produces a tube in which interior surfaces are, or should be, free of tool marks and slightly work-hardened, so desirable for super-accuracy work. But there are also other problems of straightness and internal stress, as well as the tremendous original set-up costs, which limit this system to the large-quantity producer.

Hook rifling seems to have gone out of style since the middle 1950s, probably because it inevitably leaves a lot of tool marks, both the crosswise scratches of bore reaming on the land tops, and the lengthwise scrapes of the cutter in the grooves. These have to be polished out or they will pick up metal fouling in use. At one early stage, however, the best accuracy barrels then available, the redoubtable Gregoire tubes which in the East for a few years took home all the silverware, were hook-rifled and, so the story goes, were made on some pretty crude equipment. They were also, 'tis said, made of such easy-milling steels that your .219 Donaldson Wasp was washed out in the throat by the time you had your best load established. Of course, that may have been a rumor whispered by Gregoire's competition. In any event, he was apparently a master workman, precise in every way, and that is what counts in barrel work, I suspect, more than does the rifling scheme employed.

Today's accuracy barrels of the custom or near-custom sort, and most of the target-rifle barrels from the major manufacturers, are rifled by the button process. The original steel buttons have given way to modern carbide, and there are different systems of hauling or pushing the button through, as well as considerable super-secret shenanigans regarding the lubricant to be used, but the procedural differences all achieve the same end, which is to say a cold-formed rifling pattern which is slightly work hardened, with a high level of possibility that the internal bore dimensions will be, if not identical, at least extremely close throughout the barrel's useful length.

In this day and age I do not believe it possible for any barrel marker of pretension to check bores by the ancient system of ramming through a lead slug .003 to .005 oversize and noting by feel whether or not it meets uniform resistance all the way. The inside of a modern barrel must meet demanding qualifications as read off an air gauge. That instrument divides diameters to $\frac{5}{100,000}$ or .00005 inch. A gauge head of precise caliber is bored so that as it is moved through the tube varying amounts of the compressed air fed into it from a constant-pressure reservoir slips out, the leakage acting as a measure of space or distance. Dimension can be taken at any or all points the whole length of the barrel. For a practical .30-caliber rifle meant for hunting moose, for example, which is to say an average hunting musket, one major manufacturer keeps the groove diameter at .3085, plus or minus .0005. But the hole in a first-quality .30-caliber barrel made for bench rest competition would be more like .3081, plus or minus .0002.

In point of fact, of course, the accuracy gentry are less concerned with absolute actual dimension than with consistency. It is often possible to fit bullets, in this day of hand-swaged projectiles, to the individual barrel, and tubes measuring .2242 or .224 or .2239 will shoot equally well given correct bullets. But a straight and *uniform* tube is vital, no doubt about it, if $\frac{1}{4}$-minute performance is called for. One barrelmaker once remarked to me that a very slight squeeze or choke toward the muzzle benefited accuracy, but his barrels seem to win something less than their share of silverware, and nobody, theorist or practical shooter alike, disagrees with the idea that a belling muzzle, or a tight spot back in the bore, does anything but harm to grouping ability. I'll take mine straight all the way, if you please.

Over the years there have been many million words of discussion, much of it hot air, about how barrels are made or should be made. A fair amount of this persiflage has concerned itself with "secret" prescriptions used by those barrelmakers who at the moment seemed to be winning most of the matches. Since they'd be the first to hoot at any ideas about secrets—except for those small gimmicks of personal procedure every mechanic develops to save himself time or to make a complex task easier or to get the best out of his familiar machinery—I wrote letters to a couple of prominent accuracy-barrel producers, asking some basic questions. I got about what I expected in reply. The creation of a match-quality barrel is less a question of individual gimmickry than it is of devotion to precision, to the concept of uniformity which is the basis for all accuracy work.

First of the two to reply was Clyde Hart of Lafayette, New York. Clyde may not in some opinions be the best barrelmaker in the world, but he is in my opinion obviously one of the best, since rifles using his tubes whether in the sporter, varminter, or unlimited classes have been winning a very large share of matches for roughly a decade. In any shoot located in the East, Hart barrels usually take home the lion's share of the cups, bowls, patches, bolo ties, or whatever may be handed out at the shoot. A bit slower to react was Ed Shilen, once a New Yorker but for some years now a confirmed Texan with his shop outside Dallas in Irving. Ed started in the barrel trade a mite after Clyde, but obviously is doing a splendid job at it, since his tubes win some Eastern matches and usually clean up in the Southwestern do's. On the record, these two make the majority of today's winning barrels, with Remington Arms in the next spot on the strength of their 40X and 40XB-BR rifles, and such names as MacMillan, Douglas, SS&D or John Dewey, Atkinson & Marquardt, Apex, and one or two others contributing to the list.

Stripped of the personal elements, and very mildly edited, Clyde Hart's comments ran like this:

The manufacture of a rifle barrel is no deep dark secret limited to a selected group. It is instead application of simple machine-shop practices to arrive at an end product that is uniform in size for the length of the finished barrel, free of defects in the steel, free of tool marks, and within reasonable tolerances in groove and bore dimensions of a given caliber. These tolerances may vary from one maker to another, as does their primary application. Obviously the maker of target barrels would or should have closer tolerances than a maker of production barrels intended for hunting or plinking, where a minute or even 2 minutes of angle accuracy may suffice.

Target accuracy today is a lot more demanding than it was twenty-five years ago, and is implemented with advanced techniques, better metals to work with, and most important, the abilities of the shooters themselves.

The first thing to be considered in attempting to make an accurate barrel is the steel to be used. It must have physical properties which give an ample safety factor with the pressures it will be subjected to by the modern high-intensity cartridges. The machinability is also very important, for if you are unable to get a good reamed surface you do not wind up with the barrel free of defects or tool marks that you are striving for. It is not necessarily true that a barrel containing tool marks or defects will not shoot well, but I will say that I feel that a barrel that is uniform in size and free of tool marks or defects will shoot far better, all other factors being equal.

The steel must also be reasonably stable in all machining operations, especially turning. Even though most barrel-steel blanks are supposed to be normalized or stress-relieved when you receive them, we have found that many times this is not true. In view of this we have our steel blanks stress-relieved twice—once before we start any machining and the second time after they are rifled.

I do not intend to discuss at any length the methods of rifling, whether they be cut, broached, buttoned, or forged. If the end result fulfills the criteria listed above, is uniform, free of defects, and reasonably stable, one rifling system will shoot as well as the other. Each barrelmaker must determine how he can obtain best results with the equipment that is available to him and still produce a competitive product. While others may be able to achieve uniformity and finish without lapping, we have been unable to do so. Our last operation on a blank is the lapping, despite the claims of an uninformed few that lapping reduces barrel life. When a blank drilled and rifled to proper size is lapped, the finished dimensions meet acceptable bore and groove dimensional specifications.

There are a few misconceptions on rifle barrels that I feel warrant some space in clarification. Generally speaking, rifle barrels do not wear out, they burn out, which is why some types of steel produce a greater life span accuracy-wise than do others. This is the reason why machinable stainless steels, with their higher content of chrome, are currently being used by a number of target shooters.

Usable accuracy life in a practical sense, and assuming similar firing rates, is determined by the amount and type of powder being used. Large-capacity cases with their longer periods of high pressures and heat take their toll on barrel life and accuracy. The high heat to which the throat and breech section of a barrel is subjected has a nitriding effect on the surface of the steel, causing it to be harder than the steel under it. This difference in hardness eventually creates minute cracks in the surface which progressively get worse. As long as the surface stays intact, there is no apparent change in accuracy, but as this process continues it eventually reaches the point where the surface starts chipping, especially the corners of the lands. It is at this time that accuracy usually begins to be affected.

This is one area in which I believe a positive statement can be made without fear of contradiction: the more powder you burn, the shorter the accuracy life can be expected.

Another popular misconception is that one type of steel will produce better accuracy than another. This I cannot subscribe to. All things being equal, one type will shoot no better than another.

Barrelmakers are constantly asked to guarantee a specified degree of accuracy. That is impossible, for there are many factors which make up an accurate rifle. Assuming the blank has the required properties which make it capable of top-quality accuracy, all these may be nullified by the gunsmith when the barrel is installed if the throat area is damaged, and more important, if the barrel is not properly crowned.

The step-by-step procedure in our shop of making barrels is as follows. The steel as received from the mill is tested for hardness to *see if it is within our specs. It is then sent to heat-treat for stress relieving at a prescribed temperature and duration. Then it is deep-hole drilled for different calibers, allowing from .007 to .009 inch to be reamed out for final finish bore size, with finish being checked every few barrels and corrected if found wanting. The next operation is rifling, which in our case is done by the button method. After rifling, the blanks are again returned to heat-treat for the second cycle of stress relieving. The barrels are then stored in racks until orders are received and are then turned to the size the customer requires. They are then lapped to final bore and groove dimensions and the bore meticulously examined the full length for any possible faults in the steel or tool marks. The final step is measuring on the air gauge for finished size and uniformity throughout, data on which is recorded in the work log. Every barrel we have ever sold has this information recorded to form a reference should any changes be required in future demands of the trade.*

To sum up briefly, the requirements of a good barrel are quite simple: that it be uniform in bore and groove dimensions, free of tool marks and defects in steel, and within reasonable tolerances, in our own case .0005 inch from the minimum to the maximum on groove diameter. We feel it makes little difference whether there be four, six, or eight grooves. We also feel that each finished rifle should be checked for the load which will give best results in it, as the size of the chamber, depth of throat, size of the bullet, capacity of case, and variations of the powder being used all have some minor effects on the degree of accuracy of which any particular rifle is capable. This can be arrived at in only one way—through careful testing by a skilled rifleman.

—CLYDE HART

Shilen's remarks were on this order:

Barrel steel must have high tensile strength to withstand the pressures generated by modern cartridges, be resistant to wear and erosion for long barrel life, yet be easy to machine so a smooth machining job can be done on the rifling, chambering, and crowning. Unfortunately the steels most resistant to wear and erosion are also the toughest to machine, and a compromise must be made between erosion resistance and machinability. It is a misconception, by the way, that button rifling or hammer forging "irons out" tool marks left by bore drilling. That is only partly correct. Buttoning or hammering will iron out only very minor tool marks. It is also believed that tool marks can be lapped out. Here again, lapping will remove only minor imperfections. To get a perfect barrel the bore must be extremely smooth and uniform before it is rifled.

The steels most commonly used today are 4140 chrome-moly and 416 stainless, as they have proven themselves over the years to be the best compromises. However, just because a manufacturer states he is using 4140 or 416 is only half the story, as there are many variations within the steel types, and topnotch barrelmakers pay a premium price for both chrome-moly and stainless in an effort to get the best. Good steel is correctly heat-treated and stress-relieved, and properly alloyed so there are no pits or inclusions in the bar.

I definitely believe stainless is a better steel for rifle barrels than chrome-moly. Stainless presents unique problems and consequently stainless barrels are more expensive than chrome-moly. Stainless is more difficult to blue, and the cost of the steel itself is twice the cost of chrome-moly. But we believe it is more than worth it since stainless delivers longer maximum accuracy life than chrome-moly.

Very, very few barrels have perfectly straight holes in them. There are so many factors that keep a deep-hole drill from drilling a perfect straight hole through a barrel that a "dead-straight" hole is a matter of happy chance. The question then is: How straight does the hole have to be to deliver maximum accuracy? In the Shilen plant we have never been able to determine that a crooked hole in itself will hurt accuracy, but after a hole gets to a certain degree of crookedness it becomes impossible to do a good job of rifling, lapping, and chambering.

Some manufacturers still believe a crooked hole of any degree is an evil, so they straighten the barrel. This is wrong, I believe. As the re-bent barrel heats up during firing, some of the stresses put in during straightening are relieved and the barrel starts to return to its original shape, to result in the change of point of impact commonly called "walking." Also, in a barrel in which the hole has been drilled slightly crooked, the crook may be in the form of a very uniform gradual curve, but the straightening process puts an abrupt bend or kink in the barrel which can be a deterrent to accuracy.

Our specification of a perfect barrel calls for stainless steel, reasonably straight hole, no straightening to be done on barrel, rifling to have a very uniform twist (no gain or loss within the length of the barrel), surface of the bore to have a very uniform lapped finish its entire length, and bore to have no pits, inclusions, or cracks (these are defects within the steel itself) and to be absolutely free of tool marks (mechanical defects caused during manufacture). The barrel should be thoroughly stress-relieved after rifling; groove diameter kept within .0001 inch the entire length of bore. The chamber and throat should be cut to minimum dimensions, and be parallel and concentric with the bore. The throat of the chamber and the crown of the muzzle must be cut perfectly clean so there is absolutely no burr. We have never seen a barrel that met such specifications that would not deliver match accuracy.

To achieve the consistent degree of barrel whip/vibration needed for top accuracy requires also bullet to achieve consistent velocity within the barrel each time it is fired. Just as important is the concept that the bullet have a very consistent acceleration rate in the barrel. With uniform bullet acceleration and velocity the bullet exits the muzzle with the same velocity each shot, and the barrel is at the same point of vibration/whip each shot.

Fluctuation of acceleration and velocity in a barrel results from failure of the bullet to meet a constant amount of friction while it is passing down the bore. Powder or bullet-jacket fouling is most often the culprit. Even in the very best of target barrels the bullet is leaving a smear of burnt-powder residue and bullet-jacket material on the surface of the bore as the bullet passes through it. This smear progressively builds up with each shot fired, but not uniformly, piling up thicker in some areas than in others. This results in an uneven friction within the barrel, changes the rate of bullet acceleration, and so changes the whip/vibration pattern of the barrel. Groups start getting larger, usually at the twenty-round mark. By cleaning every ten to fifteen rounds excess fouling is easily removed, and maximum accuracy is maintained for the life of the barrel.

Uneven or premature jacket fouling may arise from a rough spot in barrel, in the form of a pit in the metal, a tool mark put in during manufacture, or a nick or scratch made in the barrel during cleaning. However the rough spot got there, it will pick up an excess amount of bullet-jacket material every time a bullet passes over it. When the pickup becomes excessive enough it will change the friction at that part of the barrel, actually impart a "bump" to the bullet as it passes over it, change the acceleration rate of the bullet, and so cause your "flyer."

Uneven bore surface finish in a rifle barrel can likewise produce fouling. Premature opening up of groups develops because of uneven amount of jacket fouling. Yet after looking inside of barrels with a 6X bore-scope for many years we believe a barrel can be _too_ smooth. A very smooth finish such as you may get with button rifling tends to pick up fouling quicker than a lapped finish, which is not as smooth. Apparently, the lapped surface has a lower coefficient of friction than the glass-smooth buttoned surface.

Tight and loose spots in the bore, taper in the bore, and an uneven twist in the rifling—all these may do the same thing—offer an uneven amount of friction to the bullet as it goes down the barrel.

As a final comment, generally speaking we cannot see any difference in accuracy if the barrel is held within .003 inch the same size either way as the bullet. The many exceptions seem rather to prove the rule than to deny it.

—ED SHILEN

These two statements should be read as complementing rather than opposing each other, because as has been remarked before it is not so much the minor differences in viewpoint or technique that have contributed to the progress of barrelmaking as it is the agreements on basic necessities. And no matter how you interpret the comments of these two craftsmen, it is evident that they agree totally on the need for uniformity—in metal, drilling, reaming, rifling, and all heat-treat procedures—in the manufacture of accuracy barrels. They are really conventional barrels that have been handled with utmost care, utmost quality control.

Aside from the relative availability of the button-rifling procedure, which has apparently contributed much to the modern barrel's accuracy capability, or at least to the relative ease of making that barrel uniform, there has in recent years been one major advance in the accuracy barrel. This lies in the explosion of the ancient myth that barrel *length* is a serious factor in accuracy, a myth that had its genesis in black-powder days and was supported for years by the need, with iron sights, for an extended sight radius. It deserved to die earlier than it did as the optical sight, with an infinite sight radius built in, came into use.

Our first-generation bench rest barrels were all anywhere from 28 to 32 inches long. This made life easy for other shooters on the line, by carrying the muzzle racket farther forward from their ears, but was far less significant in matters of grouping ability than was then believed. It is quite possible, in fact, that early or pre-1965 aggregates—not necessarily the happy freak of a single five-shot group—were not even in the same ball game as today's level of average performance because of, not in spite of, the length of barrel used. The longer, flippier tubes were almost surely more sensitive to variations in time-up-the-barrel, for the simple reason that the amplitude of their muzzle movement had to be greater. Furthermore, in the past half-dozen years the evidence has become increasingly strong that assuming enough length to burn the powder decently it is not the length of the barrel but its *stiffness* which determines its grouping ability.

Every recent move in accuracy rifle design seems related to that concept. The bedding-block system which dates back to the mid-1950s—a massive set of steel or aluminum blocks paired around the barrel to clamp it into position on rather than in the stock, with the action free to vibrate behind and barrel equally free forward of the blocks—is in many ways a limitation on the effective length of the barrel in respect to vibration. Present-day sleeves have a similar effect. Remington's scheme of epoxying the midsection of the barrel into the stock, leaving the action and muzzle free to vibrate but over very limited amplitude, is in the same line of thought. All these were perhaps originally worked out as solutions to the bedding problem, but they also tie in, it strikes me, with limited muzzle movement as coming from either a short or a stiff barrel.

In point of fact, in the sporter and light-varminter categories of both NBRSA and IBS competition and to only a slightly lesser degree in their heavy varmint classes, the evolution has been toward barrels that are both short and stiff and shoot like a house afire. In fact, it is in the first two classes, the $10\frac{1}{2}$-pounders, that the most rapid progress toward the ultimate one-hole group has of late come.

Under the rules of both NBRSA and IBS, barrel dimension is for these "practical" rifles restricted. That is, the basic diameter at the action and for no more than 5 inches ahead of the bolt face is 1.250 inches. At that point a straight taper may begin which would provide a diameter at the 29-inch point of .900. Since the minimum length under the rules is 18 inches, to be more than safe in complying with federal law, this makes for a very chunky barrel indeed, still keeping rifle weight around the $10\frac{1}{2}$-pound mark including the scope.

But it is the extra-chunky barrel that has made today's super aggregates possible. And that stiffness or amount of barrel metal has in turn been made possible by one other element in the rifle, its sight equipment. (Stock weight is necessarily pretty well standardized, since less than $2\frac{1}{4}$ to $2\frac{1}{2}$ pounds in a wooden stock means almost inevitable bedding instability; action weight is controlled by the long-proved need for a stiff action, even one reinforced by a weight-adding sleeve.) The short-coupled scopes of 20X or more being made today for bench rest use by Remington, Unertl, Lyman, and Leupold, run with their mounts, bases, and screws somewhere between 19 and 21 ounces, at least a half-pound lighter than, for example, a $1\frac{5}{8}$-inch Lyman Super target spot. All that half-pound, plus any other extra ounces than can be scrounged, goes into the fat barrel of the modern bench rest sporter or light varminter. Remington's 40XB-BR sporter in 6×47, as exemplary of this new breed, normally has a 20-inch barrel of $1\frac{1}{4}$ inches at the action end, .955 at the muzzle. Used to be that even so-called bench rest rifles were slimmer!

The effect of this superstiffness in the barrel has been marked, particularly in the $10\frac{1}{2}$-pound categories. At the 1972 NBRSA Championships, which were fired in Tulsa under hardly ideal conditions, the three-gun aggregate winner Jim Stekl, a New Yorker using rifles of the 40XB-BR configuration, averaged .4027 for all four days. More to the point, to stay in the "top twenty" listing for the three-gun required an aggregate figure starting with .4 for all but the last man, No. 20. That so many stayed *under* the half-inch mark for four days, for 570 groups or 2850 shots, is, I feel certain, due not only to the shooting expertise of the gang in Tulsa—possibly the greatest collection of wind and mirage experts ever assembled in one place—but to the high percentage of short- and stiff-barreled rifles on the line, especially in the lighter classes.

Very evidently this same line of thought about scope weight and barrels is applicable to the heavy-varmint category, and it could apply to the unlimited bench rest rifles where there are no legal restrictions on barrel diameter, provided the barrelmakers are willing to mess with extra-fat blanks. The old percussion-cap "hog rifles" of the last century had multisided barrels over 3 inches in diameter. In the hunter rifle category, which attracts much activity in some areas—the Snowball Shoots in Millerton, New York, fired in midwinter, would be hard-pressed for shooters without a considerable invasion of 10-pound hunter-class competitors—it's going to be harder to fit such a stubby barrel to the requirements for a rifle which looks like a rifle, is very limited in use of the sleeving scheme, and must have at least 18 inches of barrel in diameter no more than 1.250 inches 4 inches ahead of the bolt face and taper to no more than .750 inch diameter 26 inches from said bolt face. As compared to the average factory or custom sporter, that's a heavy barrel indeed, and it is possible that the hunter-class scores, which are a matter of hitting center rather than of grouping, would improve with a move in the 40XB-BR direction. I have not seen it seriously tried so far, however, nor have I seen the stiff-barrel approach used on any arm meant solely for hunting in the field—as opposed to varmint shooting. Thank heaven for small things, because however effective the chunky barrel may be, it ain't very purty, and somehow or other I feel that a true hunting arm should be both effective and artistic.

No barrel, of course, is any better than the bullets put through it. A good barrel will shoot bum bullets only slightly better than a bad barrel, will handle good bullets better than any barrel, and shoot best those bullets which are both perfect and mated to it in diameters. Nor is it any better than the bedding job, or the chambering job. Buying a match-quality barrel for installation by a gunsmith whose forte is fixing busted automatic shotguns is an invitation to bitter disappointment. Have the work done by a professional of known qualifications, who understands the necessity of dead-straight chamber alignment and precise fit of barrel shank and shoulder, if you're serious about wanting a tackdriver.

9

Suitable Stocks

Probably no basic section of the rifle intended for accuracy has been as subject to freewheeling experimentation as the stock. True hunting-rifle stocks, while they vary from the classic to the rococo California style, from the simple to the strained, are for the most part still relatively conventional. No one very seriously or very long, for example, contemplates using any far-out material for the true sporter handle. I still have a .300 magnum wildcat made years ago with a stock of infinite layers of walnut veneer, more glue than wood, bonded together under heat and pressure in a pattern like a marcel wave. That experiment lasted all of two months when the blanks actually came to be put onto the market. Yet no such restraint exists where the accuracy stock is concerned. There handsome is as handsome does, and if matters could be improved by using a stock made of either Jello or solid ivory somebody'd be sure to try it.

Many full-weight bench rest rifles, of course, are not stocked at all. That is, the barreled action is supported in a return-to-battery rest which is essentially a machine. True, varied systems exist for fastening the barrel and action into this "Iron

Mike" device, and the several schemes for equipping the sliding section with sights are subjects of mild debate, but it is a mite silly to say that such a rifle is actually stocked.

By the same token, prior to the point at which it came to be accepted that the sporter and varminter classes of rifles must look like real rifles, not flying shingles, even in these so-called practical-rifle categories there was wild-eyed experiment. I personally think that realistic considerations as to what kind of stock actually shot best were more vital in killing off these experiments than were any set of rules, because the experiment-minded bench rest shooter has one thing in common with the NASCAR auto racer—he goes right up to the edge of the stated rules and then pushes a little.

At one stage of the lighter rifles' development, balsa wood seemed like a life-saver because its use would obviously permit rifles of far heavier and so presumably stiffer barrel and action components. Every now and again one of these balsa-stocked jobs would shoot a hot group, or less often come up with an aggregate, but by and large the use of balsa or any other super-light wood, even, in fact, conventional woods like walnut if in an extra-light and hence soft grain, has been abandoned.

The reason brings us to a basic requirement for the stock on an accuracy rifle: it must in all events be dense enough to retain its dimension during firing. Wood that is too soft, or has become softened by overdosage with oil or solvent, gives under the hammering of firing, or squeezes too readily under the pressures of guard screws, so that it simply will not retain its bedding pattern but will change from one day to the next, even one match to the next.

I owned, still own in fact, a rifle handle made by Bob Stinehour for a 10½-pound 6×47 with Remington action and barrel, which was in its day a triumph. In the early 1960s the rifle won for me all manner of tinware and kudos. It was made of laminated walnut, seven pieces wide across the 3 inches or so of the fore-end. But in the latter 1960s something went sour. Rebedding neither of the original tube nor later of a replacement worked very long. The 6×47 was sharp today, but all over the paper tomorrow. The evident bedding inconsistency should have tipped me off earlier. Through my own fault, the fairly common one of slopping solvent-soaked patches in through the action so that the wood around the rear tang was constantly oil-wet, I had so softened the wood there that nothing would stay put. We tried hogging out the action area and bedding in so-called glass. That bettered matters, but the wood was still soft underneath and no synthetic bedding compound can accomplish miracles.

The moral, of course, is first to avoid soft wood and always to avoid softening good wood by over-dousing in oil. The same comment, incidentally, applies even more to hunting rifles than it does to accuracy jobs. They are not fired as many rounds, ordinarily, but cleaning a sporter is a fetish with some people—it gets scrubbed whether it needs it or not—and too many hunters figure that if a little oil is good a lot is better.

The failure of balsa has not deterred other wood experimenters, although their present experiments are with woods at least comparable to walnut in density or weight per cubic foot, strength, and cutting ease. Mahogany, which is even in grain, workable, and less heavy than walnut, has received favorable attention. I have seen stocks in cherry that seemed both handsome and stable. A very blond wood from Japan which is significantly lighter than walnut should merit some attention, especially if its action cut-out area is stiffened with glass. Walnut impregnated while still green by the Crane Creek process has a high stability quotient but runs heavy. So do most tropical woods. Fancily grained woods like the curly and bird's-eye maple, myrtle, and mesquite are not only likely to be heavy but probably more important are so complex in grain structure that they're hard to work. Stability may also become questionable, though I must admit that I own a hunting rifle stocked in mesquite that is rocklike all year round. It's also on the heavy side, as it should be for a .375 Weatherby barreling. Despite the experimenters, however, the overwhelming choice for stock wood, either hunting or accuracy rifles, is walnut, be it European (French), Asiatic (Circassian), or American.

Once upon a time, Clair Taylor and Don Robbins of Rixford, Pennsylvania, made bench rifles that looked like real rifles beefed up, and had to be called handsome in anyone's terms. Taylor and Robbins frequently used oversized blanks of one-piece walnut. More recently, however, the laminated blank has become basic to accuracy rifle builders. When the wood strips are properly cut and bonded so that their grain lines tend to oppose one another, and when the original walnut is of appropriate density and tight but simple grain to start with, the laminates do resist warpage from humidity change better than do single-piece blanks. They also seem to hold a higher stiffness in the cut-out regions around the action. How many strips to the blank is very much a matter of opinion. One Terre Haute shooter named Yenowine, a craftsman who could indulge his love for exotic tropical woods because he owned a sizable trucking line, used to glue up complex multiple-piece blanks that after shaping looked like Scotch kilts. At one stage rifles were built from three-strip blanks in which the two outer strips, all that was visible after the rifle was finished, were matched dark walnut of fancy grain. I still have what in the early 1950s was called a full bench rest rifle—about 18 pounds—with a stock of that description. Today, however, the trend seems to be toward multiple strips between $\frac{1}{4}$ and $\frac{1}{2}$ inch wide, and if they happen to be in contrasting colors, the stock shaped from such a blank can appear pretty fancy.

But as remarked before, fanciness is not the idea with an accuracy stock—stability is. In the hope of augmenting the stability even of choice wood or laminates, three approaches have been followed. One is in the bedding procedure and the action design, either or both, the theory being to spread the bearing of metal and wood over a large area so that it is critical in no one point, a concept which will be enlarged upon in the chapter concerning bedding. Another is the usage of so-called "glass bedding," whether of actual glass fibers or of metallic powders that set up into a kind of plastic metal, to reinforce and stiffen the area of relatively complex cutout below the action. The third, more recent, is the use of stocks wholly of synthetic material, hence presumably inert over any reasonable changes of temperature or humidity.

Stocks of this last sort are being made by the Brown Precision Co. of San Jose, California. Brown lays up fiberglass and epoxy into a mold, then joins the two halves, with the larger hollow spaces filled with polystyrene to avoid the emptiness and to some extent the clamminess often associated with plastic stocks. No checkering appears and the raw stock is a mottled muddy hue but it can be painted to suit the owner. For some obscure reason the users of these interesting stock conceptions seem to go for loud pinks and baby-carriage blues, shooters having long since discovered the folly of trying to mask synthetic substances with the grain and hue of walnut. These fiberglass stocks do require precision bedding, of course, and also seem to need a bedding touch-up now and again, so perhaps the stability is not 100 percent, or there are other reasons for variance. But as a method of achieving the absolutely stable accuracy stock, I suspect the idea has considerable future, as long as the intrinsic beauty of wood is not considered essential.

The design of the accuracy stock—that is, its outside contouring—seems to have settled down into a choice between two basic concepts. Where up to ten years ago many bench rest handles used rounded fore-ends, probably to settle into their own valley in the relatively soft front sand bags used by many at that time, today, regardless of class, the fore-end is always flat. Under the rules of the varmint or sporter classes, of course, the fore-end is limited to a 3-inch maximum width and may not be concave or fitted with any sort of guide rail. But flat is the nearest thing to concave, and something like a rail effect at the corners may be achieved by using one of the sausage bags made by Tuller, set transversely on the tripod, lashed or strapped down very tight indeed at the middle. The stock corners then wear grooves in the rising sides of the V of the hard-packed bag.

Considerations of the bedding system aside—whether or not a bedding block or a sleeve is used doesn't alter this point—the accuracy stock varies chiefly behind the action.

Probably the majority of such stocks—and this would be particularly true of Remington's 40X and 40XB-BR series—are full through the action section but are quite conventional in the butt area. They may or may not use a Monte Carlo or stick to the straight-topped high-heel target style favored for the 40X type. Some, and I would say a distinct minority, boast cheekpieces. The tightness and contouring of the grip are a matter of choice. In some such stocks the "pistol grip" as such doesn't exist and the right thumb is expected to lie in a groove along the right side of where the slim of the grip would be, had it not been avoided in the interest of stiffness.

The 40XB-BR series of short-barreled accuracy jobs is remarkable in another way. They're short-stocked. The trigger-to-buttplate distance on these rifles is only 12 inches, from $\frac{1}{2}$ to $\frac{3}{4}$ inch shorter than most shooting irons. The short stock saves wood weight and almost guarantees that the bench shooter will shoot his 40XB-BR "free," letting it recoil for a definite distance before making contact with jacket, shirt, or shoulder. Since I am one of those who likes discernible, though not heavy, contact at the shoulder during the whole firing procedure, I find the 1-foot stock short, but the free-recoil clan think it is just dandy. Make your own choice. If you should try to extend one of these stocks by replacing the simple butt cover with a thick Pachmayr type of pad, by the way, expect to run over the class weight limit, since even with holes in it rubber is heavier than wood.

A smaller but considerable number of shooters use butt-stocks of the thumb-hole variety, and maintain strength through the action area by swells which carry the fore-end edge line back into the butt. The thumb hole is favored by a good many target shooters of all breeds, as far as I can make out on two basic grounds. First, it eliminates in all the normal target firing positions any cocking of the right wrist to accommodate grip and trigger position. Second, it aids in what might be termed straight-line trigger control, in which the simple process of squeezing between the thumb and the first finger, with virtually no other muscular activity to confuse matters, develops the trigger release pressure.

There is much to be said for this second aspect of the thumb-hole stock. Modern accuracy rifles are fitted with 2-ounce triggers or the equivalent, not exactly set triggers (a multiple-lever set-trigger system is not well thought of because of the delay between primary or first-lever release and ultimate firing pin fall) in that they are meant to be controlled, to operate on a squeeze. It may sound absurd to think of squeezing and easing and squeezing again as the conditions seem to change, on a trigger releasing at 2 ounces or so, but this is precisely what most good shots do. Two ounces is actually a fair amount of pressure to a trained digit. The control is indeed easier between thumb and forefinger with the holed stocks.

If, however, the second, third, and fourth fingers of the firing hand are not permitted to lie very loosely indeed about the grip, if for example they are allowed to exert sideways pressure, the thumb-hole design can mean trouble. Any tension in those extra fingers must be straight back. "Steering" one of these stocks by trigger-hand pressures so far below the line of thrust or the center of gravity seems to play hell with good grouping. In stock design as in most things you do not get something for nothing. It took me two years of shooting with a thumb-hole-style light varminter which Ed Shilen made up, a real tack-driver in either his hands or those of his partner Allan Hall, to find out what I was doing wrong with it. Even now, since

I am more accustomed to the conventional rifle handle, I have to make deliberate and conscious effort to shoot it as a thumb-hole should be shot.

Since weight saving by using low-density or punky wood is too risky with rifles designed for consistent accuracy, the rifle-man shaping a stock to stay within class weight limits has only two other alternatives. First, he can eliminate all needless pro-tuberances. I see no possible justification for a large cheek-piece, for example, and there's even some risk with it if the lower edge sweeps well down along the butt. That edge may, now and again, touch the rear sandbag and so vary your hold. Second, he can rout and bore to remove excess wood. Since modern small-group rifles are almost without exception free-floated, there's no reason why the barrel groove shouldn't be routed out underneath, with perhaps a solid spreader section left midway, if care is taken that the stock not be "shelled" to the extent that stiffness is lost. Certainly no reason exists why the buttstock shouldn't be drilled. After such weight-shaving, any device you can contrive to seal the exposed wood in the barrel channel and to seal hermetically the end grain under the buttplate or pad will pay off in future stability of the lightened stock.

Many accuracy-rifle stocks, particularly if designed pri-marily for sandbag competition, use a distinctly rising line of the fore-end between trigger guard and tip. This taper cannot, of course, be parallel to the rise of the underside of the butt-stock, but it does ensure that with a minimum forward push after firing the whole rifle rises up into battery position, in line with the target, rising at both ends as it were. Hardly a neces-sity, this has always seemed to be a small nicety in design that makes the rifle handier and more comfortable to shoot.

In essence, of course, and disregarding for the moment all those matters of basic stiffness, wood stability, and bedding detail we have discussed, that idea of being comfortable to shoot is a vital consideration in stock design. It has been said that a man is so adaptable he can accustom himself to anything, from a shrewish wife to a diet of seal blubber, but I doubt that our species' inherent flexibility extends to rifle stocks, espe-cially accuracy stocks. If your position or relation to the rifle is in the slightest strained, it is inevitable that the ability to hold and shoot exactly the same way each round will be lost. Only with that ability, of course, is the one-hole group possible.

10

About Bullets

If Rudyard Kipling had been a shooter, he might have extended his comment about "East is East and West is West" to the separate worlds of target shooting and hunting and observed that accuracy bullets are accuracy bullets and hunting bullets are hunting bullets and never the twain shall mix. And such a poetic generality would be in good part true, though not necessarily true in all instances.

The expanding hunting bullet is designed to do precisely what its name implies: to begin at or soon after impact a controlled expansion which will enable it to destroy the maximum amount of vital tissue and create as much killing effect as possible, to penetrate as deeply as the structure of the game animal requires, and to deliver as much of its kinetic energy as is possible for that rate of expansion. Thus the bullet must suit the game, and in the past manufacturers commonly designed bullets for very specific purposes. The 130-grain Western Open Point Expanding bullet for the .270 caliber was created to expand very quickly and very violently at or soon after impact, hence to blow up the lung area and seriously unhinge the nervous system of lightly framed animals like antelope or perhaps deer. On the other hand, the Peters 220-grain .30-caliber round-nose with outer-belted construction was designed to expand very slowly, indeed, never to break up, to retain virtually all its weight in one chunk, and therefore to be capable of very deep penetration indeed on muscular critters like large moose or brown bears. Shoot a whitetail deer in the chest with this tough .30 and it would whistle on through much as would a solid. Bang an Alaskan brownie in the shoulder with the .270-caliber quick-opener, and he'd be hurt, in no sense crippled, and probably madder than hell.

On the assumption that today's riflemen and hunters no longer have sense enough to select bullets for specific purposes —and that assumption is probably correct, I must sadly say, even among those segments of the hunting public who reload and can so take advantage of the great variety of projectiles today available—most commercial expanding bullets are meant to be multipurpose. They're supposed to be capable of coping with every impact speed, every range, every degree of animal toughness. I can't honestly feel that such perfection is possible, after a quarter century of hunting hard and professionally nearly all the world's beasts, yet I must admit that the manufacturers do amazingly well.

Simplicity and a wide range of expansion control don't go together too well, however. The German-made bullets which have been for many years the standard in expansion control, the H-Mantel type, are hardly simple. The crossbar of the H is formed by crimping the bottom section of jacket into that form, and the lead cores are soft above the crossbar and hard below, as a basic step in assuring both quick expansion and continued penetration. In many designs of this sort there is an outer jacket belt which slides back as the bullet flowers, to control the rate of its opening. The amount of tip lead exposed is another control, and even this may be covered by a thin protective shield (à la Silvertip), which has little to do with expansion but is chiefly protection against magazine battering, a guarantee that the bullet will retain its intended point shape and so its ballistic coefficient. What all this amounts to is a projectile made up of four or even five parts.

Val Forgett once produced for me 100 each of four or five calibers and designs of these H-Mantel types. Their accuracy denied all reason. My son's Model 725 in .280 Remington, switched over to southpaw operation by Erven Barber, shoots a 160-grain type, jacketed in mild steel, to hunting perfection, inch spreads being as good as the rifle has ever shot or should be expected to shoot. It pays no attention to the fact that those projectiles measure a flat .283 on any man's micrometer. Further, the most complicated bullet of the batch, essentially a 175-grain boattail with a belt outside the H jacket crimp that serves as both driving band and expansion girdle, was so sharp in one of my 7 mm. magnums that I shot all of 'em up, save one that dispatched a trophy black bear on my last journey into the Yakutat, proving and reproving their accuracy. Those slugs miked very close to .285. I did have to back the load to avoid high pressures, but that was to be expected. Hard to figure the grouping, though. Perhaps complexity need not destroy accuracy if it is handled carefully enough, yet I'm inclined to think that my experience with those bullets constitutes the exception that proves the rule.

Our own Nosler design, which has been my field favorite for general hunting use, especially in .28 caliber, ever since they came out, is a three-piece bullet. It has cores forward and aft of a partition, and while these cores are the same in metallurgy, the forward jacket section is both relatively thin and tapered, the stern section comparatively thick. The front half of the Nosler will flower or even break up soon after impact—at a point about 6 inches into the chest of the average animal, judging from my experience—and the butt half, usually about 60 percent of the bullet's original weight, will continue on, with or without some residual strips of forward jacket, either clear through the target or into the offside hide. We get much the effect of the H-Mantel with a slightly less complicated, but still not really simple, bullet.

Except for special and relatively costly bonded-core bullets like the Bitterroot series, most of our other commercial hunting projectiles are of the two-piece sort, the chief exceptions being the tri-part Winchester-Western Silvertip, the Peters Protected Point, CIL's nylon-nosed model, and peg-points like the Remington Bronze Point. Others use only two pieces, jacket and core. The jacket may be drawn with a taper, and usually is, in order to thin the nose section; it may be drawn with lengthwise fracture lines or folds to expedite opening; it may be drawn with an integral belt or thickened midsection to slow expansion and help hold the core in. But it's two-piece.

One would therefore think that there should be a major accuracy difference between the two-piece and multipiece hunting designs. If there is, I've never been able to locate it. All the H-Mantel bullets I've been able to latch onto in shootable quantities have shot up to the requirements of hunting accuracy, even though as I have remarked, their diameters were not stable at our .284 norm for the 7 mm. caliber. The middle Europeans seem to be very casual about making their 7 mm. bullets anywhere between .283 and .285, and frankly, still in terms of *hunting* accuracy, I could never see it made much difference. Nosler bullets of whatever weight and caliber have always shot well, with the exception of one batch when Nosler was fiddling with a cheaper production method. Something like that must be said for virtually every projectile commercially available, whether from big company or small, providing we talk about *hunting* accuracy, which is to say from 1 to 2 minutes of angle from a scoped bolt-action sporter, regardless of whether two bits of metal or three went into the bullet. There are variations, which are probably greater between manufacturing lots than between manufacturers or designs, and some bullets won't shoot for sour apples in some rifles. I've never had a 7 mm. magnum regardless of twist that would really shoot the 160-grain boattail by Sierra, which for everyone else is a fine bullet, yet I used to own a .280 that would shoot cloverleaf groups with it. It's a rare hunting bullet that isn't accurate enough for the hunting job, however. The demands aren't all that great.

There are certain conclusions that may be drawn, it strikes me. First, an accuracy bullet really must be made for that difficult task, and if it happens to accomplish any other—for example, most of the .224 and .243 pills made for groups also work quite acceptably on varmints, though tending to be on the tough side—that's a happy circumstance. Second, we must not expect hunting bullets to be designed and certainly not to be assembled with the quality we properly expect of accuracy projectiles. They may be good, but they're never good enough. The levels of performance expected are simply not in the same league. Nor need they be. I seriously doubt that the ability to deliver half-inch groups, instead of just over an inch, say, controls how well I do on a kudu at 200 yards or a bear at 125. And I believe it is relevant here to add the converse: we must not expect that merely by switching to what is generally accepted as an accuracy projectile, say the 70-grain .243 sold by

Pennsylvanian Detsch to match shooters, our hunting rifle is suddenly going to be transposed into a super-rifle, a quarter-minute tackdriver. Its performance may improve, but not all that much.

As of this writing, the bullet sizes of serious concern to accuracy experimenters are only .224, .243, and .308. Periodically some inventive gent seeks to put to use the undeniable ballistic qualities of, for example, the 6.5 or .264, because a bullet of .441 ballistic coefficient (as compared to the .269 figure for the 53-grain .224 or the .260 of a 70-grain 6 mm.) very evidently has advantages in velocity retention, hence in the bucking of wind effect. He's right in theory, of course, but even with hand swages there seem to be problems of making 6.5 bullets precise enough for competitive use. Or somebody seeks to revive the .25, as happens periodically, although the .25 Donaldson Ace and certain .25-caliber attempts by Wallack back when the accuracy battle wasn't really quite so tough got nowhere at all except for one lucky record group, Dinant's .1075. We hear about various .28-caliber *Wunderkinder,* but none of them have made a dent in any bench tops, save among 1000-yard shooters.

In short, we do apparently know how to make excellent .224 bullets and fair to very good .243-diameter types, and also how to make, at the commercial level, .30-caliber projectiles of remarkable consistency. The reasons for the wide jump are, I think, obvious. First, the easy size to start with, whether in rifles, cartridges, or bullets, was .224. Second, the rule calling for a "sporter" of larger than .23 caliber was easily met with the .243-diameter, a size which at the time had just struck the consciousness of the shooting public. It did permit very minimal recoil and yet showed some distinct ballistic advantages in theory, so men went to work making .243-diameter pills of superior balance. The .25 got lost somewhere in here. Now why the .30 instead of some intermediate caliber? I believe simply that the .308 or 7.62 NATO became official military equipment and normal 300-meter Olympic or ISU equipment at roughly the same time, so that it got a boost far beyond any afforded 6.5 mm. or 7 mm. items that might, in theory at least, do those jobs better. Bench rest nuts, who had been looking for a larger caliber that would barrel through wind with minimal effect, but couldn't take the recoil belt of the full .30–06, therefore jumped onto the .30 caliber and the .308 case. That they then turned around and proceeded to load it up with H380 or 4320 to give .30–06 velocities is merely typical of human nature.

At any rate we now have a considerable number of first-rate .30-caliber bullets. Probably the most widely used in the bench clan is the 168-grain Sierra boattail, right out of the box, although the 168-grain and 190-grain Hornady and the Finnish Laputa match-style bullets have been winning friends. The paradox is, of course, that occasionally at shoots where wind-deflection effect is far less a problem than mirage somebody picks up all the marbles with a .30, or at a *Schuetzenfest* where the wind shift is enough to move bullet holes from one side of the 200-yard target clear off the other edge, the top money will go to a .22. As I've suggested in the chapters about bench shooting technique, it takes a peculiar sort of person to cope with the belt and blare of a .30 all day long; hence I believe that reaction to recoil with these heavy slugs is as important in deciding results as is their undoubted resistance to wind drift.

11

The Supremely
Accurate Bullet

In the past generation vast progress has been made in gun-building: in stiff actions of minimal lock time, in minutely precise barrels, in improved bedding methods, in sighting gear better mounted and in several ways superior for its task, and so on. But few of these improvements in rifles could have paid off without improvement of the bullet. It had to be more nearly perfect, more nearly homogeneous and balanced, more nearly identical in every dimension and every factor of weight and uniformity, or none of the current competitive levels could be reached. That riflemen can today come so very close to the ultimate zero-size group is an indication not only of the *quality* of the bullets now available, but of the *quantity* of superior bullets available.

As late as the 1954 edition of *The Ultimate in Rifle Precision*, since 1949 the bible for bench shooters, much space was given to hand-operated bullet swages that used two-piece forming dies. Emory Tooly won an aggregate in 1958 using bullets from two-piece dies, and such bullets are still widely used with fine results by devoted varmint shooters. But at the present time, I know of no serious competitor in the accuracy game who puts his money on pills made in a two-piece die. These bullets are almost always identifiable by a little ring or swell at the point near the ogive where the two sections of the die join. Since such bullets normally have to be run through a simple sizing die to eliminate any bulge up there, the possibility of jacket spring-back inevitable in any sizing-down process apparently scares off the perfectionist. In 1953, after all, of 105 competitors twenty shooters using one-piece dies went home with two-thirds of all the prizes, including all the aggregates.

Contemporary accuracy bullets come from two sources. One is hand-operated swaging equipment, like the $250–$450 die sets today furnished by MacMillan, Sherman, Detsch, Rorschack, Pindell, Simonson, etc., all of which operate on the expanding-up principle established earlier by Biehler & Astles, whose precise equipment very probably contributed more to the art of bulletmaking by hand than any other. The other is a short list of "factory" or volume producers. These latter believe that having one or two supremely accurate bullets in the line, even at a loss, helps sell the hunting-style projectiles, and the list of sizable competition bulletmakers includes outfits like Hornady, Speer, Sierra, and in recent months Remington.

Relatively few individuals working with manual-press equipment operate commercially or sell any great quantity of their bullets, although a few, fortunately, continue to supply friends. C. J. Detsch of Št. Marys, Pennsylvania, is probably the one great exception, and a great many 6×47 shooters, including yours truly, rely on his 70-grain bullets. Like custom stocking of rifles, making bullets by hand is no road to riches, because the labor time involved is great, the difficulty of obtaining a consistent supply of top-quality jackets is greater, and the problem of dealing with finicky customers even greater yet. No wonder the price tag is high!

For the volume producer, the problems are much the same. He must be absolutely ruthless about quality controls (must discard dies and punches, for example, at the very beginnings of wear long before they would become unusable for bullets of hunting quality), must establish and stick with extreme standards of dimension and metallurgy for jacket material and finished jackets, must maintain a constant test-shooting program to be certain that no fault has crept into his finished bullets that has not appeared in the usual exacting quality checks applied during manufacture. Bullets of this quality, in short, demand more of the volume producer than any other item in his line.

For practical varmint shooting the regular run of .224 and .243 bullets from all volume makers are amply good, since any rifle worth tinkering with will end up shooting quite adequately at least one of these commercial items, though it may take some trial-and-error fussing to locate the right one. A certain amount of basic common sense is indicated. The 55-grain Sierra spitzer, originally meant for use with cartridges of the .220 Swift and .22–250 persuasion, is a poor bet for a .222, which would be better suited by the 50-grain, or better yet by the SX bullets made in the Hornady plant; and conversely, blowing the thin-jacketed types out of a Swift with full loads won't nail many 300-yard chucks because the tender bullets probably won't get that far. But somewhere or other in the normal commercial list there is a bullet suiting your varmint rifle—and half the fun of this brand of riflery lies in locating the right combination anyway.

The pills, usually of 52-grain weight, which are labeled as bench rest bullets by these manufacturers will also work on woodchucks, though they're rather expensive for the purpose. They are definitely made with care, albeit under volume conditions. All are good; some rifles shoot one better than the others. Until Remington got into the accuracy bullet act, it appeared that Sierra users won the greater number of matches. Tom Gillman, bench rest Hall of Fame member and a tough competitor in any league, was a confirmed shooter of Sierras, even in 6 mm., and one prime mystification among the accuracy clan was what, if anything, Tom did to select his match bullets! Speer and Hornady have also done creditably, if less well, in winning a respectable number of matches. The long-awaited Remington bullets, so far in a 52-grain open-pointed soft-swaged .224 only, with a .243-caliber to be ready only when the .224 pipeline is well filled, were in their first full season during 1972. They have already won enough matches and aggregates, including one two-range heavy-varmint victory by yours truly, that there is little question as to their present excellence. The last factory test reported from Ilion on these production bullets, as fired in a return-to-battery rifle indoors, so that neither wind nor mirage was of much account, indicated that thirty five-shot 100-yard groups had averaged .2, ranging as tight as .12 for three-group tests.

Since most people who get into the accuracy act are frustrated machinists anyway, certainly men who like to work with their hands, a very high percentage of winning matches are fired with handmade bullets. The procedure is rather more exacting than complex.

A basic need, of course, is a beefy loading press of H, O, or strong C framed design to minimize springing, the forces in-

The need for ultra-precise bullets to get ultra-precise rifle accuracy has stimulated vast ingenuity in the designing of forming dies, core-swaging equipment, and such. This equipment was created by toolmaker Ferris Pindell. It indicates the lengths possible with the basic swaging press itself to gain

volved being considerable when .30-caliber bullets are being formed, for example. In some cases the press needs a special ram to handle the punches, etc., supplied by the swagemaker. Regardless of the diemaker, the working equipment otherwise involves a lead wire cutter, to chop wire of correct diameter for the intended caliber (.1875 inch for .224 bullets) into chunks slightly over core weight; a core extruding and forming die,

identical swaging of forming forces, each process checked by gauge. In practical terms most shooters who make their own bullets achieve satisfactory results with more common commercial presses of the O or H types, the RCBS designs being favored.

which ensures core weight consistency by bleeding off excess lead and may also shape the core to fit the jacket cup into which it will eventually go; a core-seating die and punch, to make certain that the core fully fits the jacket; and the swaging die itself, which in today's practice knocks out the finished bullet by an ejection pin, pushing against or into the hollow point of the bullet, and is either worked by hand or operated automatically by a frame device as the loading-press ram is dropped. Dimensionally, all dies and swags in a set of tools are made under the expanding-up theory, so that the finished bullet is greater in diameter than was the original jacket cup. Some lubrication is of course needed, the trick here being to be certain that no component, whether cup, core, or partly assembled bullet, go unlubricated but none ever be lubed to excess. That can mean bubbles, malformations of the jacket, and dimen-

Commercial rarities, horizontal presses like this one favored by Pindell, shown during use on his bench, are also used by the ordnance crews experimenting for Fort Benning's 300-meter Olympic shooters. They are massive and powerful instruments of precision.

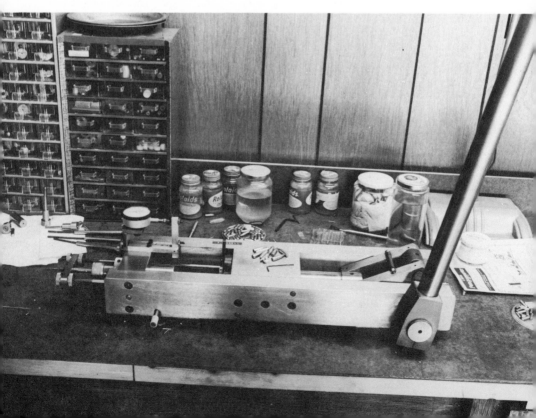

sional variation. Every diemaker seems to have his pet ideas about correct lubricants, so deal with your die man, not with me.

Incidental other equipment involves a proper micrometer and the ability to use it, the usual run of tools (which if you get very far into the mysteries of bulletmaking will eventually fill a small room), an ability to perform each action of the process in precisely the same manner, a willingness to throw out any questionable production, and perhaps a bit of patience, since there is some evidence that the best bullets are made when following each step the components are "rested," especially the formed cores, and so to some extent stress-relieved. Of course you need a large supply of good jackets. The ultimate ideal would be cups that on a Starrett ball mike show no more than .0004 of variance or run-out in wall thickness and are of just the right metallurgy or hardness.

It is not difficult to make bullets. It is difficult to make significantly superior bullets. There have been how-to articles in every publication dealing with accuracy rifles, but frankly I think that direct personal advice from someone who is demonstrably making a better bullet is worth far more than print on a page. And the bench rest game, after all, is entirely populated by men who are willing to help any beginner with advice, even demonstration. That's one of the nice things about it.

At this point we insert a summary of the niceties of the art of bullet-making, compiled by M. H. Walker and Emory Tooly of *Precision Shooting Magazine*'s technical staff:

The first readily available dies for handmaking bullets came into being in the early 1940s. One of the contributors to this article owned a set of RCBS dies in 1945. These were of the two-piece construction where the top of the die was removed and the bullet-forming pushed the bullet up out of the lower half of the die. Bullets from such dies made ½ minute of angle accuracy possible for the first time.

Two types of jackets were used. Commercial jackets were scarce. As far as we know, the only known source was from Huntington of RCBS. Most shooters of the period were drawing their jackets from .22 rimfire cases, made from gilding metal. Later on, rimfire cases were drawn from brass, and the accuracy deteriorated in handmade bullets. Commercially pure $\frac{3}{16}$-inch lead wire was used for the cores. During this early period, core forming or squirt dies were not in the picture. Some shooters, however, took the effort to draw the lead wire to a slightly smaller diameter to improve its uniformity and hence the uniformity of the cores cut from the wire.

The drawing was done by drilling a hole in a relatively thin piece of steel and polishing it with a good lead. The lead wire was then lubricated often with soap and water, and was pulled through the hole in pieces no longer than 18 inches.

Lead cutters in the 1940's were essentially the same type as used currently. Two pieces of steel were bolted together with a hole. Usually a metal tube was attached to act as a guide. The second piece had a cut-off notch with a screw and plate for adjustment of piece length. The round plate acted as a large screw head. The lead wire was fed through the guide, through the hole, through the chop-off notch to the plate and then cut off. This is a relatively fast operation. However, uniformity is dependent upon the consistency of diameter of the wire. Cores cut from wire directly off the roll varied as much as $\frac{3}{10}$ grain, plus or minus. By using the draw method explained earlier, cores could be held to plus or minus $\frac{1}{10}$ grain.

Hardness of the lead was tested by many methods. The one most usually used was the business of cutting off approximately a 2-foot length and lifting it from one end. If it readily bent, it was considered soft enough.

During the drawing of the wire it becomes hardened, and typically an hour or more of "resting" at room temperature is required before the stresses are relieved. Lifting the drawn piece was not a good test for softness.

Lead wire for bullets needs to be clean, commercially pure, and without seams, laps, or inclusions. It must be free from nicks or roughness and reasonably straight before cutting. It can be easily straightened by rolling between two flat, smooth surfaces. Two pieces of maple wood will do the trick.

At the present time, squirting each core in a die is the accepted method of obtaining weight uniformity. After cutting to a weight of $\frac{3}{10}$ or $\frac{4}{10}$ grain over the finished weight, the pieces are lubricated, preferably with lard oil or lanolin, by rolling or tumbling in a cloth, or by rolling on a grease pad. Very little lube is required. In fact, the smallest film is best. Excessive lubricant will cause roughness in the squirted core, albeit some lubrication is necessary to ease the job that the press has to do in squirting. When no lubricant is used the extra pressure required causes the press to spring and results in poor uniformity. A weight uniformity of plus or minus .05 grain is desirable. This is difficult to arrive at particularly if the lead is not uniform before cutting and the full plus or minus $\frac{3}{10}$-grain variation is prevalent in the cut wire pieces. It is also extra difficult to hold the .05-grain tolerance if the press used is not of very sturdy construction, since a weak press will spring during the squirting operation.

Just before the core seating stage in today's die sets, the cores should be degreased with white gasoline or equivalent. Be careful with toxic degreasers like carbon tetrachloride. Use them out of doors. The cores must be completely free of grease if one wishes uniform results. There are some proponents of lubricating cores for bulletmaking, but the practice is not recommended due to the fact that the amount of lube is so very critical. Too much will allow the core to shift during the pointing or forming of the bullet.

Over the years the bulk of the good jackets used for homemade bullets have come from Sierra. A few jackets were available from Campen and other sources, but were not widely used. Uniformity of metallurgy, hardness, weight, and wall thickness are the most important criteria on jacket quality. Tube wall micrometers to measure jacket will thickness are a necessity. If it can be avoided, do not buy a lot of jackets which vary more than .0005 in wall thickness. The limit of .0004 is generally accepted by benchrest shooters for competitive shooting.

Once a good lot of jackets is found, the operation of core seating can begin. The jackets, if they do not have lubrication on them, need to be lubricated on the outside, preferably with lanolin, and tumbled in a cloth leaving just a slight film of lube. The lanolin used should be of the hydrous type. The anhydrous type is much too stringy and difficult to use.

If the jackets are not clean, by the way, or have laid around until they have become oxidized, they can be cleaned by first degreasing and then by soaking them in white vinegar for thirty minutes. After this, they should be washed in water containing dish-washing detergent, rinsed and dried in the oven.

Core seating is a critical operation. The jacket should be filled with core to the point that it perfectly fills the die, but no more. Too much pressure will cause the die to expand. When the pressure is released, the die will contract. This makes the core become loose when the cored jacket is removed from the die. Usually one can determine when the die is perfectly filled and the core-seated jacket is precisely at the die size. If it is too small the jacket will come out on the punch, rather than stay in the die. The use of a micrometer should be one of the musts at this point to be sure of the above and to check uniformity of size.

The punch size used for core seating should be such that a very small amount of bleed-back occurs when the core is seated. If no bleed-back occurs and the punch actually rubs the side wall of the jacket, it is possible to trap air beneath the core.

Lubrication of the core-seated jackets, before the pointing or bullet-forming routine, is of paramount importance. This should be done by tumbling in a lint-free cloth with only enough lubricant to barely wet or coat the jackets. Too much grease will make the bullet under-size and will also create base run-out in spinning. For these reasons, the least amount of lubricant that will uniformly cover the jackets is best.

When setting up the final or pointing die, the bullet is properly formed when the ejection pin will, on every occasion, push out the bullet without entering the hollow point, merely by pressure at the jacket mouth. This can be adjusted by feel. Increase the depth to which the punch enters the die until the ejection punch is felt by pressure to contact the point. The size of the point is not exceptionally critical. Most shooters like to have the point small enough to give a good ballistic coefficient, but not so small as to actually enter the ejection punch hole.

The size of the bullet, obviously, should be as uniform as possible. Checking diameters for the first ten or fifteen bullets run through the die is the best practice. If too much or uneven lubricant is evident, the size will not be uniform. When measuring with standard micrometers the diameters should be definitely uniform within .0001.

Spinning is sometimes a useful activity. This is done by placing the bullet in female centers with an indicator on the side of the bullet. This allows one to determine whether or not the lubrication is uniform and also whether or not little enough lube is being used. Too much will allow the bullet to spin out more than the accepted .0003 or .0004. The spinning rig should have female centers, at least at the base, not greater than about 30 degrees included. A greater angle than 30 degrees picks up on the nonuseful part of the base corner. This will give erroneous readings not commensurate with the actual accuracy of the bullet. Bullets should be miked at approximately $\frac{1}{10}$ inch ahead of the base. All flat-base bullets will normally show a pressure ring from .0002 to .0004 larger than the body of the bullet.

Although carbide dies are by far the most expensive, they will last a lifetime. For up to 20,000 or 30,000 bullets, steel dies work as well, but will develop an especially large pressure ring at the base after this many bullets are made.

For bullet diemakers, one may look in Gun Digest's Directory of the Arms Trade.

Bullets can be made from almost any reloading press. However, the easiest-to-use and the strongest presses are those with the closed yoke, in other words, supported on both sides of the ram. Alignment of the ram and the upper section is important, as only a certain amount of misalignment can be accounted for in the mounting arrangement for the punch. A double toggle press is also recommended, as its potent leverage eases considerably the jobs of lead squirting, core seating, and bullet forming.

—M. H. WALKER AND EMORY TOOLY

These systems are basic, whether the pill is made in Texas or Maine, in Rorschach or Biehler equipment.

Most bullets made by such procedures today—or their commercial equivalent—are multidimensional. That is, the swaging process normally bulges or bumps out slightly the butt on the bullet to leave an obturation ring a few tenths greater in diameter than the shank section just above the base. For example, on a match-grade bullet I have just picked at random these two diameters are .2243 and .2240. The point at which the ogive begins is practically indeterminate, and the point section carries the delicate longitudinal lines of fold normal to the shaping process. None of these elements represents a fault.

There is question among shooters as to how closely a bullet should duplicate groove dimension. I have never heard any suggestion that an exact match was not conducive to accuracy, nor the idea that the bullet must be significantly larger, or significantly smaller, for competitive accuracy. In fact, most such data is full of contradictions and remarkable exceptions. I doubt that there can be much quarrel with the idea, however, that by and large, in .224 caliber, bullets no more than .0002 smaller than the true groove diameter or more than .0002 larger will mate well to the barrel. Larger bores permit greater variance, some .30s shooting .309 bullets. Since ordinarily an air-gauge measurement is stamped on the butt end of the barrel blank, your gunsmith should know the figure for your tube. That should be borne in mind when you order a swage so that it may be polished out to a correct figure.

Very evidently, for each bullet to go through the hole made by its predecessor it must duplicate its predecessor. Even with the ultra-care of the handmade bullet procedure that could mean selection by weight, selection by some other physical measurement, or sublime faith. Being lazy, I am inclined to the last-named, which may be one reason why I have never been one to win matches with single super-tiny holes, only an aggregate now and then.

However, either a well-made commercial bullet or a carefully put-together homemade job rarely shows enough weight variance to make or break its competitive standing. Some years ago, for example, I received from Ed Shilen for use in the heavy-varmint rifle he'd built up for me some bullets of which the norm seemed to be 51.3 grains on my scale, about .3 either way. A very few showed a top just under 51.6 plus, low barely over

51. That would be equivalent to a 1.2 percent error, so I painstakingly lotted out about half of 'em into three batches. With the much larger middle or norm group the rifle won a heavy-varmint aggregate. With the few in the "light" batch a few weeks later it placed, or I placed, respectably well up but not in the money. I arrived at the IBS Nationals without the bottle of selected bullets, just the run batch ranging from 51 to 51.6, yet won the HV aggregate. Whatever was right or wrong about the bullet weights was small potatoes compared to whatever was wrong or right about my estimations of conditions on those shooting days, no?

If you turn up a batch of .224 bullets that vary as much as say 2 whole grains, or 6 mm.'s that vary 3, or .30s that go over 4, the chances are good that they're so sloppily made otherwise they wouldn't shoot anyway, even if those weren't beyond reasonable weight variations.

By the same token, it is rare to locate significant diameter differences in a batch of either handmade or commercial bullets labeled as of bench rest capability. There is, however, one vital dimensional area where error can be trouble.

That is in the relationship of the base to the center line of the bullet. It must be dead square. You will recall that the great Dr. Mann in studying the bullet's flight between muzzle and target conclusively proved that where a misshappen point created little or no error a miscut or slanted butt brought about major dispersion. His work was with lead bullets moving at velocities half those of 1972, but the principle applies to our jacket projectiles at 3000-plus. It may well be that a nicked or misangled base permits powder gas to spurt forth minutely early in the bullet's departure from the muzzle hole, so as to tip the bullet and send it off yawing slightly; or the misangled base may really be only an external symptom of an internal imbalance which makes the bullet intrinsically inaccurate. Not important. The fact that a bullet with a cocked base shoots outside the groups is easy to demonstrate.

As a preventive selection process there was devised the bullet spinner—examples were made commercially by John Dewey and also by Bob Hart—which in essence permits the finger-turning of the projectile in a fixture so that any base misalignment can be read as wobble on a dial indicator. Zero is dandy, .002 is good, .004 too much for .224 bullets but acceptable for 6 mm.

These spinners were quite the vogue for a while. Beyond any doubt they would turn up an out-of-round bullet or one with a burr on the butt edge, but grave doubt existed as to whether they really selected good and bad bullets otherwise. Many-time champion Paul Gottschall, a finicky machinist and one of the most serious and devoted experimenters the bench rest world has so far known, fired endless groups with and without such selection, and really came to no clear-cut conclusion. Since it was evident that the meaning of the indicator readings related directly to the contour of the base, whether the forming punch left the bullet sharp-cornered or with a fatly rounded contour, the whole scheme lost favor when Clarence Detsch began swaging his 6 mm. bullets with a semi-boattail effect so that the spinner wasn't really measuring much of anything.

Probably another spinning test, which checks the straightness with which the projectile is seated in the case and the precision with which it is centered when it slides into the chamber, has more merit. Conventional bullet-seating dies, particularly if the case is not well into the die body when the brass and bullet are pushed together, tend to set up faults in alignment; run-of-the-mill cartridge cases are rarely even in wall thickness around the neck; yet multitudinous experiments have shown that a bullet misaligned in the chamber tends to impact slightly off center on the target.

Hence we turn case necks to keep them perfectly even in wall thickness, and use either straight-line seaters or carefully cut hand-seaters of great precision. Super-careful shooters spin their loaded rounds against a dial indicator and in some cases carefully feed them into the chamber so that the high side is always up, as it were. The cartridge spinners now on the market usually also have a bending device, so that an off-line bullet can be nudged back into line, but whether this treatment is wholly desirable in accuracy equipment remains to be seen.

Very evidently, however, while there are rebels like me who leave case and necks dirty and primer pockets fouled and long ago gave up spinning bullets and still, like the Frenchman's old dog, manage to sniff out a truffle now and then, the plain fact is that leaving no stone unturned is a vital part of the accuracy search. It has to be, even if it really pays off only in the mind.

12

Sight Efficiency

The iron sight, where precision riflery is concerned, has disappeared from the shooting scene. True, a high percentage of competitive rifle events, from rimfire gallery work to 300-meter matches under International Shooting Union rules, still demand the use of metallic sights of a highly refined sort; but in these instances the basic philosophy is that the very real precision needed to be competitive in these events is simply made the more difficult by having to achieve it with iron sights.

There is nothing new or different about the two-way device of making competition both more difficult and presumably more even by artificial rules or limitations. When the solons who run motor racing at Indianapolis Speedway were scared stiff by the amazing performances of turbine-powered race cars, they promptly slapped limitations on the new power concept that for at least a time made it noncompetitive. Nor is there much fault to be found with the idea of forced iron-sight use in certain styles of rifle match—"possibles" are common enough even with metallic sights so that with more efficient equipment perfect and near-perfect scores could become so inevitable as to destroy the competition. It might, of course, be just as sensible to permit the most efficient sight available but legislate smaller and tougher targets!

There can be no argument, however, about the demise of metallic sights on bench rest rifles, varmint rifles, and sporting rifles meant for open-country or long-range use. The optical sight of power and objective size best suited to a given shooting purpose is many miles ahead of the nearest equivalent for any of such uses, as we'll hope to suggest in this chapter. Meanwhile it is this efficiency factor which now ensures that all modern rifles are from the start designed to accept and use telescopic sights properly; that the market offers an almost bewildering variety of scopes and mounts from which to contrive useful combinations; that with each new sporter offered in that market the trend becomes stronger to stop wasting money even offering iron sights as factory equipment. Daily it becomes more common to offer them as extra-cost options, for the minority groups among shooters who seriously feel that they must rely on metallic sights only, or must have them handily available against the real or fancied possibility of optical failure. We might also note in passing that the decreasing importance of the metallic sight on hunting equipment may be one reason for the outright junk which is today fastened on the barrels of low- and medium-cost rifles, shoddy equipment that won't adjust properly, gives a crummy sight picture, and is weaker than a drunkard's will.

There are admittedly special conditions under which metallic sights are desirable to the point of vital necessity. Killing an elephant with a .458 magnum from 26 yards requires no scope, and for fighting an angry buffalo at half that range, sights of any sort are probably an affectation. Yet I have been in both situations on not one but several occasions, always using rifles equipped with low-X scopes (rifles that were built to fit me shotgun-style, I hasten to add), and am still around to tell the tales.

The deer hunter who operates on Oregon coastal blacktail in the sal berry jungles, the whitetail chaser who pokes into Maine cedar swamps to roust out hiding bucks, and the timber-hunting cousins of such men expect shots inside 50 yards, most of the time at running game, and they have some reason for staying with iron sights. The fact is, or course, that much such shooting could be done without any sights at all, shotgun-style;

and a secondary fact is that many of the rifles chosen by the brush-busting gentry cannot effectively be dressed with optical equipment anyway. Witness the top-ejecting Winchester Model 94, for example, still the favorite of hundreds of thousands of deer hunters.

But despite the rationale of Britisher Major Burrard, who felt that telescopic sights were not quite cricket for sporting rifles since they offered the gentleman hunter what Burrard felt was unfair advantage over the game—an interesting concept of the function of a hunting rifle—there is overwhelming evidence of the relative efficiency of glass sights under most hunting and all varmint- or target-shooting situations. The optical sight eliminates all problems of shooter eye focus; it renders the target, whether it be woodchuck or wapiti, larger and seemingly closer to permit finer aiming; it may be zeroed easily; it is of vast assistance in target identification, not only tending to reduce mistaken-for-game accidents but helping to pick out the shootable buck; and it adds, the law permitting, anywhere from fifteen to forty-five minutes of useful shooting time at either end of the hunter's day. The second and the last reasons alone are enough to justify hunting only with glass. If all the whitetail that I have picked out of the timber with dead surety they were bucks, or all the elk and moose that I have managed when iron sights had long since gone blind, were laid onto one cart it would need to be a considerable truck indeed. And the same could be said for anyone else who has spent a quarter-century in serious hunting.

It is not my purpose here to provide a treatise on the proper scope powers for each style of hunting or varminting use. That is regularly done elsewhere, and if you're willing to accept on a hunting rifle an extra 4 or 5 ounces and some added bulk, the contemporary wide-range vari-power has many of the answers anyway. Suffice it to say that for timber operations, $2\frac{1}{2}$X, 3X, and 4X are the choices in about that order; that the hunter of sheep, caribou, antelope—open-country species—should decide between 4X and 6X, with 4X the more practical; that the varmint hunter uses anywhere from 6X to 25X, his practical limit in my opinion being 15–16X, depending on the precision of his rifle and his ambitions as to range. Don't waste a woodchuck's time banging at him from 450 yards with a 6X glass— you can't see him well enough, can't spot your own misses, can't hold closely enough to compensate for drop and breeze.

But don't put a 15X target scope on a little Sako .222 or 6½-pound H&R .17 caliber, either—save that for your 10½-pound Swift.

In terms of sheep precision riflery, of course, the basic rule is the higher the power the closer the holding potential. One very well-known writer on firearms, appearing at his first and as far as I know his only set of bench rest matches down Texas way, during the evening bull session once offered the argument that granted a large enough aiming point for the range selected and for his sights, he could shoot groups as tight with either metallic or low-X optical sights as the same rifle would fire at that range under a high-X scope! In short, said he, the scope power had nothing to do with it, assuming the aiming point was right. He was not thrown in jail, not even, in fact, thrown out of the room, but the shocked silence greeting his incautious remark showed he had lost status among savvy riflemen.

The answer is very simple. Assuming it is well made and optically correct, and that like all such proper equipment of power above 10X and in some instances below 10X it has adjustments at both the ocular and objective ends to sharpen the reticle and to eliminate parallax for the necessary range, the high-X scope has a greater degree of resolution than the low-X. That is, you can see the target better. You can see more precisely where your crosshairs are resting as you approach let-off. Hence you are aiming not by seeing, for example, a "narrow" (and who knows how narrow is narrow?) band of white under the aiming marker but by spotting your crosshairs or dot or whatever not approximately but *exactly* where you want it.

Futhermore, and probably even more important, the higher resolution level of the high-X glass permits you to note more exactly any changes in mirage drift, any grass or leaf movement between you and the target, and to correct for them not in crude terms but in fractions of an inch, even in parts of a bullet-hole width. And since true precision riflery is a game of hundredths or even thousandths of an inch, such resolution factors assume great importance. In fact, as clear refutation of that famous arms writer's rash misstatement, the NBRSA and IBS regulations affecting the hunter class of rifle, essentially quite practical sporting rifles which are fired not for group but rather for center or score, insist that the sight be limited in magnification to 6X.

For bench rest competition rifles, although a few rare birds still stick with 15X or lower (and probably also still wear two-piece bathing suits), every study of match results and equipment usage reveals the same choices of power. One event may show a slightly higher percentage of 30X users than the next, but this is a statistical accident, because it is generally felt among serious shooters that the 30X target scope is (a) too restricted in field to give a good view of the mirage and of such condition indicators around the edges of the target frame, (b) harder to pick up the target with during extreme mirage conditions, when the air is as opaque as a roiled swimming pool, and (c) tiring to the shooting eye unless in perfect focus and made with perfect lenses, which are both more difficult to achieve as magnification rises.

One of the finer things about the bench rest game is that when you enter a match you must fill out a detailed specification card for each rifle and cartridge you will shoot in the events, and this data is usually, or always for the top twenty shooters, reproduced in the club's post-match newsletter. Study of the equipment used in matches shows that magnification choice is a three-way split among 20X, 24X, and 25X, with the 20X's often in the lead simply because there are today more 20X scope types available. There is among such glasses a significant individual difference in specified width of field, and usually a difference in level of resolution, but since the one tends to offset the other in terms of practical outdoor firing, and despite my own preference for 24–25X, I seriously doubt that any vast advantage accrues to the 20X over the 25X or vice versa.

Despite that, I am personally a shade more comfortable with a 24–25X, perhaps because the Lyman Super Targetspot (28 ounces including bases) I have used for some two and a half decades and dozens of rifles, with one factory cleaning and rebuild at the halfway point, is to my eye old-shoe comfortable. After two seasons of regular use I also had my 19-ounce Remington 20X hiked to 24X.

Unertl scopes of 1½- and 2-inch objective sizes were for a time favored by many shooters, partly because John Unertl the elder was himself a rifleman, partly because their mounting systems, recently improved by the Posa system, are generally considered to have an edge on Lyman-style blocks. None of the less-expensive target-style scopes with external adjustment has ever made much of a dent in precision work, however; and the now-discontinued Bausch & Lomb 6–24X vari-power, a rather heavy scope of superb optics but handicapped by its normal reticle and mount, is acceptable to serious bench rest competitors only when rigged with a Kuharsky rear mount or some equivalent noncamming adjustment system.

The bench rest scope question has been confused recently by two other factors. First was the appearance of an internally adjustable high-X glass, the Redfield Model 3200, $23\frac{1}{4}$ inches long, and said to weigh 21 ounces minus rings and bases but often showing up with greater weight, available in 12X, 16X, 20X, or 24X to choice. Brilliant, clear, capable of adequately precise internal adjustments, and offered in at least one reasonably fine crosshair reticle, this scope can be mounted like an ordinary hunting scope, although its overall length poses disadvantages. Assuming that internal reticle movement is positively controllable and reliable under severe recoil, then, scopes of this long-awaited type can eliminate all the troubles real and imagined with the external or target-style mounting rigs.

These were manifold, according to some. The thimbles slipped. After adjustment, shooters neglected to tighten the locking screw provided for the purpose, or when they did tighten it the zero shifted. Dirt got between the scope tube and the "feet" of the adjustment thimbles. The sliding scope tube wore a flat spot or became burred. Or the adjustment knobs twirled when the rifle was encased. Or the simple target dovetail blocks, held only by two 6–48 screws each, vibrated loose. Or the whole blooming complicated business came apart. Or the shooter forgot to pull his scope back between shots, or the return spring didn't shove it back all the way. Or something. The indictments of the conventional target mountings came in great number, a new batch every competition.

Yet a fair number of individuals, whether condemned by penury or hardheadedness to stay by the outsider-adjusting rigs, continued to win matches. They did it by taking extra care with their really rather delicate externally adjustable equipment, by keeping the tube and feet clean and lightly lubricated, by avoiding the sticky nylon feet Lyman once offered, by keeping the thimble assemblies in good order, by consistently, in making adjustments, turning the knobs always in the one direction or going one or two clicks beyond and then coming back, in order to eliminate screw-thread lag. Hence, while the 3200 has made a fine name for itself in the bench game, seeming to be particularly effective on rifles of considerable recoil, .308's and the like, and is very well adapted to the long receivers and sleeved receivers which permit a "straddle" of 8 inches or more between the bases for the 3200, it has not quite taken over the accuracy game.

One new type of scope that bids fair to do just that, however, first showed up in factory form—although there had been a dozen optically hotrodded moves in the same direction—as a Remington product. The 1970 season was its first for wide use, although experimental models had been around for some time. Optically a shortened-up target model in 20X, it is $16\frac{1}{2}$ inches long and weighs $19\frac{1}{2}$ ounces including blocks and Unertl-style adjustable aluminum brackets. The present John Unertl, within a year or so, had his own scope out, his BV20 coming $17\frac{7}{8}$ inches long, $21\frac{1}{2}$ ounces with magnum loops and spring but not including Posa bases. This one focuses not by shifting the objective, which had at first given trouble in the Remington scopes, but by cam movement of a lens ahead of the ocular system. The Unertl scope can make the 19-ounce figure with externally adjusting standard target mounts, no return spring.

Not to be outdone, Lyman, whose basic varmint scopes were being used by the hotrodders like Wally Siebert of Issaguah, Washington, because of their reliable *internal* adjustments, thereupon came up with its own hunting-style 20X, $17\frac{1}{4}$ inches long and only $15\frac{1}{4}$ ounces. By the time this book sees print there'll be others of similar persuasion, I suspect. Leupold has in design one of this sort, which like the others keeps the scope bases off the barrel. As the manuscript is typed, I have more or less switched to fixed-mount inside-adjusted glasses.

The importance of the short-coupled scope of 20X and over, 20 ounces or under, is vast where the precision shooter is concerned. For one thing, such scopes are small enough to make real sense on almost any form of good varmint rifle. While in my opinion they are not as sharply clear all the way across the field as is a really good full-length target scope, in which no shenanigans of objective focal length have been used to gain compactness, they are remarkably good. And their fields of view, though Unertl had to give away a little in his optical formula, are at least comparable with those of other 20X and 24X designs.

Most important in competitive shooting, their light weight, plus the fact they're short enough to be mounted on a conventional rifle receiver with enough spread between the bases, with much more than enough spread on a sleeved or custom receiver, adapts them perfectly to the modern trend in light varmint and sporter rifles, as these are characterized under both NBRSA and IBS rules. It is to be noted that barrel-diameter restrictions appear only in the heavy-varmint-rifle category —no less than 18 inches long, butt diameter no more than 1.250 inches out to a point 5 inches ahead of the bolt face, and thereafter no fatter than a straight taper to what would give .900 diameter at the 29-inch point. The lighter rifles can, then, use the same fat barrels if by some magic they can stay under $10\frac{1}{2}$ pounds gross. They can if we limit scope or stock heft. A scope of some 20 ounces means a stock of reasonable walnut, not a fragile or wabbly shell, and a short barrel of great stiffness and a fat muzzle, say 20 inches and .950 diameter. Hence the 40XB-BR and all its custom variants.

Rifles with such short but ultra-stiff barrels are today both with and without sleeved actions winning the silverware. But they could not exist, under the weight limits, without the pony-style target scopes. Shortly, I assume, these will be used on full heavy varmint or even unlimited bench rest rifles, because any weight gained in the sight can be transferred to where it will do more good toward ultimate accuracy, into the barrel, action, or even the stock. It is such a weight transfer that has made possible today's $10\frac{1}{2}$-pound sporters capable of $\frac{1}{4}$-minute performance.

13

Using the Accuracy Scope

A surprising number of shooters who use optical sights are even more surprisingly unfamiliar with either their principles or their practical usage. Only the other day, in helping a chap get ready for an African safari, not his first but his third, I discovered that he had his hunting-style glass so far out of focus that its crosshairs looked like multiple cobwebs. It had apparently never occurred to him that the glass furnished with the rifle had to be set up for his forty-eight-year-old eyes. There really shouldn't be all that much mystery about scopes, whether on hunting rifles or accuracy equipment.

Nonshooting laymen, for example, are regularly amazed at the tubular scope extensions used on bench competition rifles, extending out close to the muzzle, usually mistaking them for sunshades. They may indeed serve this purpose but are of course unnecessarily long for it, a couple of inches of tube threaded in ahead of the objective lens being ample for that job. The extensions run out to the muzzle because their function is to keep out of the line of vision any heat waves that may lift off the barrel as it is heated by multiple shots. Through a high-X scope—in fact through a low-powered glass if you shoot the rifle hot enough—these incidental waves create a mirage effect which is unrelated to the actual ground mirage normal to little-wind shooting conditions. The mirage coming off the barrel cannot be "read" usefully, so only complicates matters, but it can be avoided by using the tube or even a broad piece of black elastic stretched lengthwise along the barrel.

The extensions are simply made, since scope manufacturers ordinarily furnish a short sunshade tube. Black photographic paper or even target paper can be rolled and taped into a tube over that sunshade, and cut to proper length, just short of but not beyond the rifle muzzle. Full-length metal tubes such as Lyman once offered are fine on unlimited-class musketoons but may add a disastrous ounce or two on rifles used in weight-limit matches, and may possibly have a "loading" effect on the scope tube itself which could introduce an error not to be expected with the lighter paper extension.

A word about reticles—inevitable in any discussion of optical sights. Essentially the aiming device within the scope is a matter of personal choice. I like crosshairs in hunting scopes, hence confirmed timber hunters who learned to shoot with peep-and-post iron sights call me an idiot. Actually, since with the post problems of vertical hold are inevitable at range, and since with the dot problems of correct size for fast vision in good, bad, or downright lousy light are even more endemic, most of us usually come back to the crosshair anyway. That one needs no thought. Your Aunt Susie would automatically dab the intersection on the target, without the slightest instruction; but she must be told how to use a post. One of the great traits of human inventiveness is to come up with old ideas in fresh clothing. A prime example is the German three-post reticle for late-evening pig-shooting, which now appears in the U.S., as the graduated crosshair or step-down crosshair, in one form or another available in virtually all makes of scope. That, in its combination of coarse pointers for bad light and a fine center section for long-range or precision work, now strikes me as the most practical hunting reticle.

The match reticle is something else again, largely because precision rifle matches are fired in good target light, whether natural or artificial. Here we can work from the proposition that the reticle will always be adequately visible. There are two basic aiming points on a bench rest target. One is the center ring or X-ring, which is slightly heavier black than the other rings, can be quartered nicely with a crosshair, or will as neatly surround a dot of $\frac{1}{4}$-minute value. The other, originally designed in for the purpose, is the aiming square, at 100 yards an inch on the outside, the black printed sections $\frac{1}{4}$ inch wide and the whole square proportionately enlarged at greater ranges—2 inches at 200, etc. Here again the squaring procedure can be used, or the shooter who favors the dot can have his made $\frac{1}{3}$ or $\frac{1}{4}$ minute for centering inside the square, with target white showing around it. A small but growing number of shooters are coming to use the corners of the square, fitting one or another corner into the intersection of crosshairs, again with a thin slice of target white visible between hair and maker. Or they aim with crosshairs tangential to the X-ring.

To my own eyes, in severe mirage the aiming square seems to hop around even more violently than does the rest of the target, and years ago I settled on the idea of squaring the X-ring. That moves in mirage too, of course, and to tired eyes it sometimes seems to fade and return, but the centering concept still seems more natural, and since the ring is very close to target center, where the shooter properly prefers his group to form though it's legitimate anywhere within the target borders, it seems to be easier to gauge the amount of holdover for changing conditions. For this purpose, I believe the crosshair must be very fine, fine enough to permit quartering a single bullet hole, which in most paper is .10–.20 when .224-diameter bullets are fired. The actual target coverage of such a fine hair is definitely less than $\frac{1}{8}$ minute.

The dot users work much the same way. To get less than a bullet hole of holdover or "lean" they simply cut the amount of white showing on one side of the black dot. It is for these reasons that there are no reticles other than the correctly sized dot or the fine hair that are acceptable in precision work.

In zeroing a match rifle, incidentally, common sense indicates that the bullet group should be kept out of the black portions of the target, because if you lose your bullet holes you are otherwise lost. Yet the group should form near center so as to help avoid off-target disqualification. Precisely where is a matter of personal habit. Now that score is no longer kept for bench rifles, I avoid shooting out the X-ring aiming point by setting the sights so a still-air group will form just at the bottom of that X-ring.

The late Paul Gottschall, a true precisionist of the bench rest clan and a fellow member of its Hall of Fame as set up by *Rifle Magazine,* used this still-air zero as a basic factor in his shooting calculations. In the belief that any minor impact shift occurring within the rifle itself or with small variation in loading gave a lesser variation than the impact moves caused by mirage, wind, or light shift, he never altered his sight settings to cope with such factors but instead, once he had experimentally established the shifts due to a given set of conditions, held for them. He knew, in effect, the result in terms of impact change due to the extremes of variation in breeze, for example, of a given afternoon, so adjusted his holding accordingly. While this meant that he had to do a considerable amount of his firing using rather vague or indeterminate aiming points, halfway between lines, favoring this way or that a little bit, etc., it also meant that Paul rarely was caught flat by total windshift or mirage change and he could dare to hold fully for an apparent change rather than partway as do most of us.

Obviously such techniques depend on absolute stability of the sighting instrument, plus a markedly high degree of resolution of detail. The perfect accuracy scope has not yet been produced—none is 100-percent foolproof in respect to precision of adjustment in windage and elevation; not all can be changed from one range focus to another by means of simple graduations or markings, without considerable trial-and-error diddling during the process; the mounting scheme giving total stability without introducing "load" factors into receiver or barrel seems hard to come by. Yet the present pony-style bench rest scope is one of the three or four significant advances that bring us ever closer to the perfect bullet-size group.

In the dear days of yesteryear, accuracy-seekers decided that the 7.2-inch spacing between target-scope blocks, which gave the adjustment clicks a sure $\frac{1}{4}$-minute value, $\frac{1}{4}$ inch at a hundred yards, was unduly coarse and could be improved if the forward block were fastened to the barrel to give about a 10.5-inch spacing and a $\frac{1}{6}$-minute value. Some modern scopes (by Lyman) adjust in $\frac{1}{8}$-minute terms. Splendid. Except that every now and then, especially with fairly slim-barreled rifles, something went haywire, a shot landed inexplicably out of the group. Usually thought to derive from an improper bedding contact which let the action unexpectedly shift in its wood, this fluky shot proved at times to come from quite another source.

The barrel of any rifle, even a barrel as fat as a carriage axle, vibrates and whips violently when the gun is fired. Since a conventional telescopic target sight slides forward when the musket is fired and is either pushed back by a spring or pulled back by hand—preferably with a slight twisting action, friends —any minor variation in the return of that scope to the battery position will "load" the barrel, that is to say, set up residual forces within it, differently one shot to the next. At one time or another this varied preloading can, perhaps combined with other factors, flip a shot wide.

I for one thought such reasoning was the bunk, until with a dial indicator screwed to a massive bench-rifle fore-end so that it just touched the barrel, Mike Walker variously pulled the scope back into firing position. It was obvious that the rifle barrel did *not* come to rest at exactly the same place, at the same reading on the dial, each time. The amount that a crow-bar-sized barrel can be bent by relatively small force is amazing. This one factor, the relationship of sight to barrel, is probably the greatest single argument for sleeved actions, or the extra-long action, or even for the action with forward scope extension as has been made by Bob Hart. Getting the forward scope block off the barrel tube proper does indeed help eliminate one possible cause of variation between shots.

The primary step in setting up any optical sight is focussing of the ocular lens system, in the vast majority of scopes accomplished merely by turning the eye lens cone or element in or out until the reticle is sharp and black, not double or fuzzy in any way. Elderly gents who need reading spectacles will find that factory-set rifle glasses need to have the ocular lens backed out from the scope one or more turns, for example. Myopics would presumably need it turned in.

The stunt here is to perform this adjustment without staring through the scope. Since the human eye has a remarkable capacity for adaptation, do not stare but glance through the scope—preferably when it is aligned on open sky or some plain neutral-colored background—and if the reticle is fuzzed take half a turn of adjustment, then glance through the scope again, repeating this peek-and-adjust process until the reticle shows hard, clear. Most shooters go beyond that stage, until it begins to fuzz or double again, then return to the midpoint.

A second focus problem besetting both match riflemen and hunters bench-testing their rifles is that of parallax. Granted that this objective focus error is an overblown bogey-man, it still bothers many shooters who should know better.

The next step, then, is to correct the objective-lens focus. It should be adjusted in relation to the target. If we oversimplify a bit, when that is at peak sharpness there will be no parallax, and the scope will be adjusted for the given range. The reticle will remain both black and steady on the target even when the shooting eye is moved up and down or back and forth across the visual field or exit pupil of the glass. If the crosshairs move with your eye the objective is set for too short a distance; if they move opposite to your head and eye movement the lens is set for too great a distance. Target scopes are usually designed to move the objective lens in and out by means of a series of adjusting rings and lock rings, usually calibrated, but all too seldom accurately calibrated. In going from 100 to 200 or more yards, for example, the objective must be moved back into the scope. On my Lyman 25X, that takes one complete turn; on a Remington pony glass it takes 16 graduations. The wise rifleman will therefore memorize or tape on each scope bell his own settings for each yardage.

In serious target shooting over known ranges, then, the parallax must be completely removed by this method, since if displacement of the viewing eye also means displacement of the reticle as it appears on the target the rifle will hardly shoot where it looks. Furthermore, in accuracy events where a couple of hundredths of an inch is the difference between being a hero or a bum, any such focus error simply cannot be tolerated.

Yet on conventional hunting scopes, which in the low and middle range of magnifications, $2\frac{1}{2}$X, 4X, and 6X, usually come without provision for easy parallax correction, the shooter must not only tolerate the error but adapt himself to it. Most targeting and testing of hunting rifles is done at, for example, 100 yards. Yet industry practice for hunting scopes, likely to be used at distances from under 50 yards to beyond 300, is commonly to set up the scope in precise focus, as far as the objective is concerned, at the 150-yard point. Hence on a 100-yard target it will inevitably have some discernible parallax; and on a 300-yard caribou it will also have some very small amount of parallax, but surely not distinguishable in all the other errors common to rifles and men under such conditions.

Since trying to correct such a scope to be parallax-free at some other known target-range distance may involve jiggering with a sealed-in objective or moving a sealed-down adjustment turret, the smart hunter, unless his scope appears to be grossly maladjusted, leaves it alone. He simply takes care that his eye is always in the center of the scope field during testing. I own one hunting combination, a .270 with a famous-make scope, which for whatever reason shows a reticle shift of almost an inch both ways from center at 100 yards. Theoretically, this means that I might start with 2-inch groups. But by careful cheeking of the rifle and some observation of the crosshairs in relation to the field I can shoot no worse than $1\frac{1}{2}$-inch strings all day, and that is all that could be reasonably expected of the rifle and its ammunition. The stabilized head takes care of gross parallax error.

Delicate, this whole question of sights, isn't it? Experimental rifles with the glassware tied to the stock or offset this way and that haven't proved much so far, but it is evident that for top accuracy the scope and barrel should, like sports cars and teenagers, be kept apart. Yet my Shilen-made heavy-varminter, good enough to win two national championships alone and as many in company with other rifles, a piece good for .25-inch groups or better anytime, still has the forward block out on the barrel. Hard truth has a way of softening at times.

14

Shooting Through the Swimming Pool

Wind and mirage—at once the precision shooter's worst enemies and his greatest friends! All the delicately laid plans of men, the finest of rifles and ammunition and sights, can be whirled into dismay and destruction by a piffling puff of breeze or blip of mirage. And when looking down the range through optical sights is like peering through a swimming pool of slightly turbid water, with no shapely Esther Williams to brighten the view, the good, the bad, and the indifferent among riflemen are set apart—or sometimes only the lucky and the unlucky.

Even the practical hunter can run into wind or mirage troubles. The African safarist frequently curses watery midday mirage, when the light-bending by layers of air of differing temperatures and hence densities—which is all that mirage is anyway—has a herd of zebras walking around 3 feet off the ground, their fetlocks seemingly in a lake. The varmint hunter likewise often spots a chuck or crow that through a high-magnification varmint scope is wading in the flowing mirage of midsummer. Admittedly, of course, the deer hunter operating at 47 yards in timber is troubled by neither, and these swimming-pool waveries are probably of less import in the hunting field than is simple wind, but never forget that wind can ruin what would otherwise be a simple game shot. I have, for example, shot at sheep in a biting mountain zephyr, probably 30 miles of breeze. At 300 yards that much wind can produce 2 feet of drift with certain .30-caliber bullets. You could hit clear off a sheep or goat. There never was a varmint hunter yet who was not bedeviled by wind. Air movement or drift was the chief reason why the Mohawk Valley Chowder and Chuck-Walloping Association, my varminting cronies of early days, shifted from .22 centerfires to 6 mm.'s for the shots clear across the pasture, finding that the .24s were moved roughly half as much as the .224s by the same wind. Just so a generation earlier the likes of Roberts and Whelen and Sweany had gone to .25-calibers to beat the wind sensitivity of smaller bullets. The current interest in .17-calibers has to be a step in the contrary direction!

Wind or air drift by itself inevitably moves every bullet. It has to, because of the same physical laws that prevail when you swim across a stream. The current carries you downriver, off the target as it were. How far it carries you depends on the speed of the stream, its drift, and how long you are in it. Clearly, then, all else being equal, a high-speed bullet should drift or be carried in the wind river less than a slower one.

But at this point swimmers and bullets part company. Presumably you swim at a constant rate; but the bullet inevitably loses velocity through the effect of air resistance—which is proportional to the square of the speed of the bullet—and its speed loss is the clue to relative wind effect. Bullet drift in moving air is roughly proportional to the velocity of the breeze, yes; it is of course related to the distance or range, yes; but it is very closely proportional to the *delay* of the bullet over that range, its lag, which is a rate function of its speed loss. It is for this reason that top-quality match .22 rimfire ammunition is loaded to muzzle speeds *below* the speed of sound at sea level, since the .22 bullet which starts out faster than sound, say around 1200 f.p.s., will drop down through the sound barrier before reaching the target, and in so doing it will lose a good deal of speed at once. So standard-velocity or high-velocity .22 rimfire fodder is always more wind-sensitive than the match loadings. Even so, the match stuff in a 10-mile breeze straight across range (from three to nine o'clock) is drifted 3 inches at 100 yards!

When we operate at speed levels of two and three times normal sound speed (which for the sake of simplicity can be assumed to be around 1000 f.p.s.) it is chiefly the rate of loss or lag factor which determines the wind sensitivity of a given bullet. The pill that is both heavy and well-shaped for its caliber (which is to say has not only a good sectional density but even more important a high ballistic coefficient, the latter involving the aerodynamically important element of form) is less shifted by wind than a blunt, light, speed-shedding projectile of the same caliber. For example, a 180-grain .30-caliber spitzer (ballistic coefficient .435 or thereabouts) holds its speed better than a round-nosed 180-grain with its ballistic efficiency index around .288, if both are started at the same speed. It therefore drifts less. The 180-grain spitzer would also be less affected by drift than would, for example, a 90-grain .30-caliber even though the latter could be *started* at extreme velocities, because the heavier bullet again holds speed better.

Certain brands of target shooter can and do use the formula approach to wind effect. When the M2 .30-06 bullet was standard equipment at Camp Perry matches, for example, they could assume for it that the range in hundreds of yards expressed in units (as 6 for 600) times wind velocity in miles per hour, divided by 10, equals drift in minutes of angle. Hence if we had a 20-mile breeze dead across range, the 600-yard drift for that bullet would be 6 × 20 ÷ 10 = 12 m.o.a., which is 72 inches at that range. Six feet. This is something to be borne in mind, incidentally, the next time you are tempted to blaze away at an elk on the next mountain.

The mathematical game of calculating wind deflections has been played by many, with results not always up to expectations.

In Colonel Whelen's two-volume work *Small Arms Design and Ballistics,* published last by the Small Arms Technical Publishing Company of Plantersville, South Carolina, and long out of print, appears one interesting set of figures:

Cartridge	Bullet	M.V.	R.V. 300 yds.	% loss	Wind drift 15 m.p.h. at 300 yds.
.220 Swift	48 SP	4140	2265	45	.99 feet
.250–3000	70 SP	3000	2190	30	1.05
.30–30	170 SP	2200	1470	33	1.58
.30–06	165 AP	2700	2130	21	.73
.45–70	405 SP	1310	985	25	2.00

From such data we can conclude that the shooters of black-powder days had their problems with wind, too, and that even the buffalo hunters operating with the colossal .45- and .50-caliber Sharps could not forget it! Another set of windage calculations made by that great powder manufacturer ballistician Wallace Coxe is perhaps even more relevant:

Cartridge	Bullet	M.V.	R.V. 300 ft.	Wind drift
.22 l.r.	40 Lead	1070	932	3.29 inches
.250–3000	87 Ptd	3000	2639	1.10
.250–3000	100 SP	2850	2589	.52
.270 Win.	130 Ptd	3160	2958	.32
.30–06	110 HP	3500	3059	1.00
.30–06	180 Ptd	2700	2533	.35
.35 Rem.	200 RN	2000	1753	1.74
.45–70	405 Lead	1360	1158	3.37

Dated or not—and they are dated in terms of modern loads—such tables are helpful to give shooters an inkling of the potential amount of bullet drift by wind, and perhaps to explode a few misapprehensions about wind effect.

There are other less simple formulae, and many tables have been published, but all of them depend on (a) the knowledge of actual wind speed and (b) the amount of the effective wind vector, since obviously it is a most accommodating breeze that blows across from nine to three o'clock, for example. An angular line, say from one-thirty to seven-thirty or five to eleven, is more probable, and of course gives you only a partial drift as compared to the straight-across push.

In bench rest accuracy work, as distinct from hitting inside the 20-inch V-ring of a 1000-yard target—not that Vs don't take a great deal of doing indeed—knowing true wind speed, or even being able to calculate angular drift, is not much help. I have known for many years that 5 miles per hour is a gentle breeze, barely cool on your cheek and likely to be puffy; that 10 will turn over leaves on most trees; that 20-25 will pick up stray newspaper, roll tumbleweeds, and blow your hat off; and that anything above that blows you as well as the bullet. Yet I can't see that such knowledge has helped me much. In accuracy shooting from a bench, whether in testing or in competition, since you are not vitally concerned with hitting in the central V-ring or the animal's heart area, but rather with hitting each time in the same place, the concern is not with how *much* wind but with spotting the *same* wind.

And that ain't easy. In field shooting we can of course observe only the natural effects of air movement—the turned leaves or swaying limbs, the rippling grass, blowing leaves, or drifting silk from milkweeds. On the range we still have all these. If I have heard once I have heard a thousand times the tale of how some smart shooter saved his bacon by watching a stalk of timothy hay that showed in front of his target, shooting always when the grass stalk was leaning the same way. And we also have flags—on some ranges enough flags for the Olympic parade! Obviously to shoot in the same wind we should shoot through the same flag picture each time. But which flags should we watch?

Friends, I dunno. Since rarely is it a game of beating only wind effect—mirage also comes into the picture as a usual

The winds blow free and the mirage runs like a murky river on the plains of West Texas, as this Midland range regularly demonstrates, and it isn't hard to see why. A 35-bench layout, this one could readily be extended.

The Fassett, Pennsylvania, range now has grass over much of the 100-yard berm, but still confounds accuracy seekers by its own peculiar brand of light and quickly shifting mirage, which during 200-yard events has been known to make strong men cry. Prevailing breezes are often mild fishtails from over the shooter's right shoulder, but on some days stronger breezes sweep over the hill from two o'clock and then whirl up the ridge at left.

thing—and since the air movements across a range are controlled not only by the breeze itself but also by the terrain across which your bullet and the air are moving, or in many instances the terrain before the breeze ever got to the range, there is no one answer. In any match you may well find several successful shooters watching different patterns.

But two things are very clear. First, any flag movements or dust drift that occur well behind the target frames can be forgotten. Second, since your bullet loses speed at a faster rate during its early stages of flight, the most vital flags are those fairly close to you, say out to 50 yards when you're working on 100-yard targets. A change in movement of the flag just off the end of the 100-yard butts is in this instance probably helpful only as an indicator of breeze change that is *approaching* the range, a pickup or letup which is coming. It does not necessarily tell what is already happening out in front of your middle bench.

In a wind situation, the time to shoot is during the steady or standard breeze. If you have been firing through a flag pattern indicating a steady movement, but let a shot go as the ribbons droop, you are dead as far as that match is concerned. By the same token, if the flags suddenly pick up into a violently flapping horizontal position, you should sit and wait until things normalize if you can. And immediately before any match, instead of chewing the fat with your next bench neighbor while waiting for the "Commence firing" order, watch the condition for a minute or three to establish what seems to be the standard pattern for that part of the day.

Presumably if the wind goes above about 12 miles per hour mirage will be washed out, disappear. You can't see it, though it may still be there. Now this may be true for the ranges in the eastern part of this country, but as any shooter will attest who has shot at both ends of our fair nation, it ain't so in the West and Southwest. There the mirage may still be not only visible but thick enough to shovel, so shimmery you can't surely see 200-yard bullet holes, while the wind is skying newspapers and blowing tumbleweeds into the fences! I assume the difference is related to the average humidity, but I distinctly recall shooting at Midland, Texas, in enough wind so that my vertical crosshair had to be off left of the target paper by 6 inches in order to punch holes, only occasionally visible through the mirage, in the middle of the safe no-disqualification area. The wind may blow that hard at Fassett, Pennsylvania, for example, but if it does the mirage shimmer has long gone.

I suspect that this difference in the thickness and in the quality of the mirage is even more distinctive, to the point of being individual to the range. Such individualities can drive people nuts. Eastern shooters may go all goggle-eyed at Midland or Tulsa conditions that seem quite reasonable to the locals; conversely the West Texas rifleman who hits Fassett for the first time, where it is not the visible lump of wind or mirage that ruins your group but the sneaky little blips and bloops that nobody ever sees, can push his blood pressure to new records. I distinctly recall this happening at Fassett to one group of top-quality Southwestern riflemen. I saw them driven to the desperation of taking apart and going over rifles that were A-1 in every respect. Yet those same men, a few weekends before, had happily fired little teeny groups in a wash of mirage and dust-carrying breeze that threatened to move Texas into Oklahoma.

Every range has its own peculiarities, no doubt about it. The Council Cup range at Wapwallopen, around seven-thirty in the evening, when everything seems to be absolutely dead, will consistently put pop-ups, high shots, into your night-before-the-match test groups. The mists at Reeds Run have made strong men weep. Tulsa last summer was showing a vertical that nobody could see any reason for. The Camp Fire Club range I used for over twenty years, odd terrain because the ground fell sharply away to a brook at 75 yards which ran almost 30 feet below the targets at 100, a range partially pro-

The Wailing Wall, where the targets are displayed after being measured, is a fixture at every accuracy range. As yet, no shooter has jumped off a tall building after seeing on his target the hard evidence that he had four shots in a little tiny hole but blew the fifth up into the black somewhere an inch out of the group, but this can happen any time. And at Midland, where the sun is hot and the mirage thick as soup, it just might!

tected by trees for part of both sides, normally shows a kooky mirage picture that nobody, not a whole string of championship-quality riflemen, has ever read consistently correctly. Johnstown, pretty much the cradle of the whole activity, is by everyone admittedly a darned sight easier to shoot on the left than on the right, enough so that Sam Clark, back before the days of drawn and rotated benches, always seemed to end up at Bench #1 and as either Shooter #1 or next thing to it. For a time many thought that shooting through a tube meant perfection, zero conditions, but this is hardly true, the mirage conditions in factory or bulletmaker tube ranges often being as bad as in God's great outdoors.

Earlier we said that mirage was the end result of variously heated layers of air, the temperature gradients and to some extent the humidity variations causing parallel differences of density. Anyone who has ever flown knows that the cool air of morning is more dense than the heated atmosphere of midday, hence offers more lift. Humid air is also obviously more dense than dry. The visual phenomenon we term mirage relates the differences in density to the passage of light. The light rays coming to the eye from the target are literally bent or refracted in varying degrees by these variances in density. The refraction of light passing through clear water and air, which causes the image of an oar to bend sharply where it leaves the fluid, is another and more obvious example.

Mirage, then, can exist whenever there is a layered temperature gradient. It can occur in the Arctic, and through a binocular. I have seen ultra-faint mirage across polar ice during the brief but bright sunlight of a May day. It appears to the naked eye, and is more evident through magnification, unless the air movement is great enough to mix up the layers, as it were to homogenize the refraction differences. It is, of course, most strikingly evident on a hot day, when the sun is really warming up the earth, and in a practical sense it concerns the shooter most when the heating effect of Old Sol is greatest.

It is, as thousands before me have said, both a nuisance and a salvation to shooters, a nuisance primarily because of the light-bending or image-moving effect. This may be so colossal as to seem to shift a lake or a mountain range halfway across the Mojave Desert, or it may be so insignificant as merely to move a 200-yard target an inch or so. Insignificant, you say? That's what it's all about! The light-bending effect is sufficient to move the target aiming point illusion—after all, everything we see is to some extent illusion, if only in the sense that the multilensed eyes of a housefly would see it differently—so that when we fire at the picture we see of the aiming point, it has actually been moved or bent in the direction of the mirage movement, so our bullet strikes over to that side of where the target center actually is.

A simple visual demonstration of the light-bending is to set your rifle up on sandbags so that it is immobile, aligned on some target. Then without touching it peer through the correctly focused scope at a time when mirage is obviously present. Notice how the aiming point on the target not only blurs but also hops. Each hop is of course a momentary effect, due to the passage through your line of sight of a bit of air markedly different in density from the next. But if your rifle had been lined up when the air was still, before the mirage began to run, you'd also note that the picture of the target center has been pulled or stretched off a bit in whatever general direction the major mirage flow is taking.

Probably the most convincing demonstration I know of mirage basics in shooting terms was reported by Jim Gilmore, a good and active shooter who writes for *The Rifle* magazine, official organ of the NBRSA. Gilmore described the firing tests of his friends Nick Young and two-time champion Jerry Rogers. Using an unrestricted bench rifle in a return-to-battery rest, which presumably eliminates mirage effect since it can be fired without resighting between shots, in the first series they used the mechanical rest, disdained mirage, and corrected only for flag-apparent wind conditions. They got fancy strings like .432 and .374. In the second they continued to dope the wind as well as possible, but the rifle was resighted and adjustments made for each shot, thus allowing the mirage-responsible target displacement to come into account, and their 200-yard five-shot groups roughly doubled in size, the figures reading more like 1.203 and .758. This does not, alas, suggest that all shooting should be done from machine rests. It does indicate that targets are shifted to a significant extent by mirage flow.

The direction and rate of the mirage movement—and this is where our enemy becomes our friend—are indicators of general air movement at the lower velocities. In fact, they may well be truer indicators than range flags, and if you run into the not uncommon pattern in which the flags go one way and the

I hand over to Arkansas gunsmith Tom Gillman the Field &
Stream *trophy and individual "keeper" bowl, symbols of the
Three-Gun Aggregate NBRSA Championship for sporter and
light and heavy varminter competition. I have won the bowl
twice and been runner-up twice more, but Gillman has taken
it three times.*

mirage the other, the best guess, if you can't wait for things
to make sense, is to believe the mirage.

If suddenly the mirage shimmer seems to rise straight up or
boil, any sideways air drift has quit. In another second or three
it may switch to an opposite direction. During the boil, because
of the let-up your bullet will hit behind the earlier drift (to the
left if the mirage has been running left to right) and it will also,
since the target illusion is now displaced abnormally upwards,
hit high. As an odd example, one year at the range in the St.
Louis area some 50 or 75 feet out in front of the low-numbered
benches was a low dirt berm, left over from some rimfire installation. Every now and again a bubble or boil would flip

upward off that low sun-warmed mound. I got caught twice during the 100-yard sequence and blew myself out of that aggregate for sure. But a boil or upward-running mirage can occur on a range flat as a pool table, and it is usually a fine time to sit back and contemplate your other sins, since it does not usually last long before air drift turns boil into run.

If the rippling or running effect seems to be slanted to the left, then the air drift is predominantly left, regardless of its precise angle across the range. Your bullet will be carried left by the breeze, and will also strike even farther left of where it should on a dead-air target because the illusion of the aiming point has been "bent" left from the light-bending effect. Conversely, a slanting to the right of the mirage lines indicates right displacement from both causes. And at this stage a key point must be repeated: mirage is basically double-acting in terms of possible error.

Let's run through a couple of cases in point. Shooter A started out with his rifle zeroed in dead air to strike center at 200 yards. In mirage conditions and a light breeze predominantly left to right he fired his five-shot string, using a $\frac{1}{4}$-minute rifle, in a pattern of flag movement and mirage drift which was for each shot an exact duplicate. His group then appeared slightly right of its usual impact, of course, but in a cluster of shots of a half-inch or better. That's winning pool any day.

Shooter B, with rifle of equal precision and identical zero point, was less successful in evaluating matters. In fact, he may be one of those people who do not read anything but the newspapers and those not often. His first shots on the sighter target registered an inch or so right of where the rifle had printed for the preceding match, but without attempting to figure the way of that he went up onto the record target, and Shot #1 printed similarly right. All in order, thinks he. For the next shot, however, the mirage had eased a bit, indicating wind easement also, actually a return to the prevailing condition, so that round hit an inch left of #1. So did #3, and #4 went into the same cluster. Not too bad, thinks he, since the total is only about an inch. But while he's thinking that and feeding in his fifth cartridge, without his noticing it the mirage quivers, boils a moment, then settles into a *left*-running pattern. Shooter B fires his #5 and it makes a neat hole $1\frac{1}{2}$ inches left of the #2, #3, #4 cloverleaf, so he ends up with a $2\frac{1}{2}$-inch total spread that puts him far down in the ruck again. He simply did not see, or paid no attention to, the change in mirage run to the right, and most spectacularly he missed completely the switch or reverse to a left-hand run.

So his target is essentially a weather report, as Jim Stekl calls such. It registers merely the differences in wind direction, and the differences in target shift because of light-bending, that under a specific set of conditions may total $2\frac{1}{2}$ inches at 200 yards.

Actually, that much difference between full-right and full-left condition is mild! It could quite easily be six or seven inches. There is one breed of accuracy bug who favors shooting a couple of shots, on the sighter target during the apparent extremes, in order to see what the total effects are. For my money, this is more useful in establishing an alibi than for any other reason. If you don't know what the extremes are, just relax for a moment, forget to watch that shimmer before you shoot, and you'll find out what's cooking out there.

Evidently, then, the safe way to shoot groups—and the system used by most men who shoot for high aggregates rather than for individual match wins—is to observe conditions and to fire only when the same pattern is evident. And in most cases that's the best procedure.

The opposite scheme is to machine-gun, to fire five as fast as humanly possible—and to a few shooters like Allen Hall that's very fast indeed—in the hope of getting off the whole string in one condition. This is fine if the condition holds, but if it doesn't, you're due for a *big* one.

But what if you aren't a machine-gunner and can't wait, either because you're an impatient soul or because you've eaten up six minutes and fifty seconds of your allotted seven minutes getting off the first four shots, and that desirable condition hasn't come back, probably won't. Then you have to hold for the difference. How much? Ah, there's the rub. If I could give you a simple formula for that we'd both be champs forever!

It's like body English. You sort of lean into it. If your rifle tends to hold its dead-air zero, the amount of impact displacement may give you one idea. A shot or two on the sighter will give you another, but before you come to rely absolutely on going to the sighter target to evaluate any given set of conditions, bear in mind one point. That is, in the time it takes you to pick up a cartridge, feed it into your action, close the bolt, resettle the rifle, glance across the wind flag pattern, and resight, the whole mirage picture, the entire pattern of drift, can flip-flop 180 degrees, so that the hold indicated by the shot on your sighter could be doubly wrong in the opposite direction! If you use the sighter, you must above all watch for changes between any experimental shot and the counter on the record sheet following it. And in the final analysis the amount of hold is a matter of individual judgment.

Beginning shooters are well advised to hold over about half the amount they think is indicated. The skilled mirage-reader may hold the full amount, an inch or more, or may actually edge his holding or lean by less than a bullet-hole width. And it is toward the end of minute aiming variation that some shooters today are placing the crosshairs tangential to the inside ring, or to the aiming square corner, not merely centering it.

It is in the evaluation of mirage that certain classes of shooter gain great advantage. First the experienced accuracy bug, for obvious reasons, since he has presumably long since learned how to cope with wind, can use mirage. That's what it says here! Second, the longtime smallbore shooter, who has usually learned his mirage and wind reading the hard way, can handle it. Third, the young shooter can see it when others cannot. This last I firmly believe, because it is rudely clear that young eyes, unworn by years of reading, can often see mirage when older and more tired searches cannot find it, or read variations which to more aged eyes simply do not appear. This past summer I took to his first match a keen-eyed young twenty-eight-year-old. A hunter and sometime reloader, he first heard about mirage, wind, etc. during our four-hour drive to the match. But he could see a shimmer of drift when two-thirds of the older men on the firing line could not make it out at all. By the second day he had picked up the basics and with his extra-sharp young eyes was doing very creditably indeed.

More people are devastated by mirage letup, switch, or reverse than by variation of intensity. It is the sudden slack, usually premonitory of a complete turn-around to movement in the opposite direction, that should ring our alarm gongs. Variations are not nearly as brutal in their effect as full letups or the total reverse.

Finally, there is not nor can there be any substitute for earnest practice in judgment and compensation for mirage conditions. Reading a book or studying this chapter does not provide the answers—only the theory. The man who would practice accuracy shooting should do it not when the air is limpidly still at eventide, but at midday, when it's boiling around in lively fashion, with a new batch of firing circumstances coming in every minute. All you learn by the dead-air firing is to pull the trigger.

One dodge common among shooters at an early stage of their progress is to eliminate mirage by some optical means. Low scope power means less visibility for the mirage, for example, but if we go back to a low-X scope then we lose important degrees of resolution, important particularly to the shooter with old eyes. The sporter class of rifle, for example, was at one time so restricted in scope power (8X) that a spotting scope was necessary equipment to (a) estimate mirage and (b) see holes in the target. Those two reasons, plus the fact that old-timers in the fraternity were having a tough time, and couldn't shoot nearly as well as they could with 20-25X, caused a howl and the adoption of present no-limit rules on scope power. The burgeoning hunter class of rifle is presently limited to 6X, and only the fact that these rifles are fired at a relatively coarse bull's-eye aiming point, with the intention of hitting center rather than into a group, has kept quiet the pressure for higher-power scopes in that class. But as every shooter quickly finds out, just because you can't see mirage doesn't mean it isn't there, still having its light-bending effects.

To carry the elimination reasoning further, since not only lower power but also less light transmission will render mirage less visible, I once got some Bausch & Lomb engineers working on the problem. They came up with a version of their 6-24X variable, which had just come onto the market, equipped with an adjustable iris shutter ahead of the objective lens, working precisely like the aperture adjustment of a camera. They may even have swiped parts from a camera of the right size. This prototype, which cost B&L a considerable chunk of money, clearly demonstrated two points. First, it was indeed possible to lower the visibility of mirage under any or all conditions by getting the right combination of scope power and light transmission. Second—and this suggested that the engineers in question were brilliant in optics, but didn't know beans about practical shooting—the groups from the test rifle were at 200 yards markedly worse when mirage was thus disregarded by being more or less unseen than they were when with the same scope both iris and power were opened to maximum, and the then-visible mirage read as well as possible. This test of at least fifteen years ago proved essentially the same thing that the Gilmore trials of more recent date, commented on earlier in this chapter, also strongly indicated.

Mirage is a damned nuisance, we all agree, hunters and accuracy competitors alike, but since we can't beat it, join it, learn to use it to advantage as a drift indicator.

Changes of light can also make for an amazing difference in impact. You do not need to use bench rest equipment to discover this, since any sporting rifle with a 4X scope will show much the same effects—the rule being that when the light goes up the bullets go up. Simple enough. So expect a low shot when a cloud crosses the sun. How much? Well, friend, a leetle. If I could correctly answer that in terms of fractions of an inch I'd do better than I do. But $\frac{1}{4}$ inch at 100 yards or $\frac{1}{2}$ inch at 200 is not at all exceptional.

By the same token, heading or following winds affect impact. Clearly the true speed of a bullet traveling at 3000 feet per second is not going to be significantly altered by the addition or subtraction of the 22 feet per second of even a 15-mile wind, since that's less than the speed variance common in most loadings, but the wind impact is usually angular on the bullet anyway, and the effect of a breeze on the nose of a bullet, usually yawing during its early flight, is quite different from that of a breeze on the tail.

The rule here is that the incoming wind tends to lower the impact, the tailing breeze to lift it. Again, how much? And the answer is the same except that strong forward or aft breezes can make a rather astonishing difference, particularly if they sweep down over the butts, or swoop up over a hump along the line a full $\frac{1}{2}$ inch or more at 100. This is no doubt why the bane of the shooter is not the nine-to-three or three-to-nine breeze straight across the range, but rather the fishtailing breeze which runs from five to eleven or seven to one and back again. Such a wind has on impact both vertical and horizontal effects. It is also usually light enough so life is complicated further by mirage which is equally twitchy, likely to go from run to boil to reverse-run in a matter of seconds. That can puzzle the best of mirage-readers because the change can occur while you're just thinking about pressing the trigger.

I have long suspected that one reason why people end up talking to themselves on one particular Pennsylvania range is that the winds there rarely blow anything like straight across.

They wash in either from about one-thirty or four-thirty, depending on the day, so that there is always some fishtail tendency. The successful shooters there almost universally fire only when the breeze is strong, has in effect committed itself. Not a bad basic rule at that.

In our age, from a purely competitive point of view the rifle and load are probably less important than is the individual's mirage-guessing ability of the day. I have earlier stuck to the term *read*, and here use the term *guess*, because there can be no doubt but that on any given firing line of a major event there are a whole flight of rifles capable of winning, capable of the $\frac{1}{4}$-minute level, and as well a goodly number of shooters any one of whom is capable of winning on those days when he is handling the mirage well. Probably half a dozen. This has to be. When the typical day's procedure involves making one estimation after another for five five-shot groups, or for ten five-shot groups, or even for the ten ten-shot groups that may be required of unrestricted-class shooters, obviously one guy is going to run a higher percentage of correct estimations than any of his peers. On the day he is guessing right he is unbeatable. Two weeks later he may well be unable to estimate the end of his nose and he couldn't beat his grandmother. And thereby hangs the charm of accuracy competition. Lightning just might strike you at any match!

15

Secrets of the Bed

As in life, in rifles most of the good things and many of the bad things happen in bed. And in more serious tones that merely indicates that bedding, the relationship between the metal parts and the wood of the stock—or the plastic of the stock for that matter—is one of the two or three most critical elements in the precision balance we call accuracy. The best bullets in the world will not shoot into one hole from the stiffest barrel and action, if it is poorly bedded. And, again as in life, bedding is apt to be a changeable thing, subject to the whimsy of the weather, even the tension on a screw.

Grossly evident, for example, are the changes of impact generated by wood warpage in a sporting rifle. In conventional hunting equipment, the action section is let into the wood with appropriate even bearings therein at the forward section of the receiver and back at the tang area, with the recoil lug fitted against the corresponding mortise so as to bear only at the rear. Then the barrel groove is cut out so that out at the fore-end tip enough wood is left so the forestock pushes up against the barrel with pretty fair pressure, enough to require significant effort to separate barrel and forestock tip. The theory is that this pressure will cut the peaks and hollows off the vibrations of a relatively slender barrel and relatively violent cartridge. So far so good, and when all is in order it works.

However, if the wood is kiln-dried and fancily grained or poorly finished or the blank was incorrectly laid out on the walnut plank, as it's likely to be on a commercial production rifle, and if a spell of either abnormally wet or abnormally dry weather comes along, or the piece is left standing in a damp cellar or behind a stove, the water content of the wood changes and it crawls or warps. Any one of the contact points, or each of them, changes, and understandably the fore-end, being relatively light, and connected to the buttstock by a bridge of two thin walnut slabs where the magazine has been cut out, wiggles up into or down away from the barrel or sideways in relation to it. The impact then shifts to a brand-new point, perhaps several inches from where it should be.

Enough to miss game, that's for sure. A New Haven chap named Harry Townshend once went with me on a bear hunt in southeastern Alaska, where it rains more often than not, with a rifle he'd self-stocked in fancy maple. After a week of drizzle and three missed bears Harry checked his sighting on the beach, shooting over a jacket-padded rock at a canned-soup carton. At 100 yards the rifle was hitting a foot under the trademark, more than enough to miss the fattest black bear that ever lived. One eating sedge at 150 yards would be safe as churches. We then noted that the stock had grown all around the buttplate, and the fore-end had warped amazingly. And during the hunt the rifle shifted around at least twice more to our target-proved knowledge.

Fault of the wood? Perhaps. More likely the fault of Harry's sealing. He had left the areas under the buttplate and between barrel and forestock free of any finish or sealant, much less the water-pump grease which makes a good anti-wet packing for that forever-wet region of the world. The kiln-treated wood understandably picked up a gallon of Alaskan rainwater. The point is that with hunting rifles a bedding change can alter the musket's whole character, and with it the character of your hunt.

But we are here more concerned with bedding as a component in true target accuracy, which as earlier suggested in the chapter on stock woods, presupposes elimination of the kind of coarse fault Harry was dealing with.

With modern accuracy rifles, featuring stiff actions and barrels, forestock pressure no longer exists. In earlier days target rifles, especially rimfires, were equipped with screw-adjusted, hydraulic, or electric devices well forward on the fore-end as a means of controlling upward pressure on the barrel and hence its flexing or vibrating action. These have disappeared from the scene. I once owned a massive heavy bench rifle made by Oklahoman Barney Auston which in order to ensure evenness of fore-end pressure used two hydraulic cylinders fed with power from an oil-filled reservoir. There added pressure could be generated by turning in a screw. Great machinery, but the rifle never did shoot, although possibly for other reasons. There hasn't been experiment in such areas for years—and for one simple reason: it is easier and more effective to let the barrel flex as it will, bed it free-floating. At times, in fact, the distance between barrel and forestock is big enough to pass not just the classic test of a matchbook cover, but the whole package of matches.

Bedding today, then, in accuracy-rifle terms—and for many people in hunting rifle terms as well, in order to avoid the whimsical and changeable pressures of forestock bearing— applies chiefly to the action area. When bench shooting first started, since the actions in use were flexible siderail types descended from the Mausers, like the Springfield and assorted military actions from overseas, even the M70, some bearing at the fore-end was almost inevitable, but when these actions began to be stiffened, first by slapping on iron bottoms, then by sleeving, the risky fore-end contact went out the window. Today, actions are either designed to have a large and easily handled bedding area—as for example the Shilens old and new, the Benchmaster, Hart and other custom actions, the cylindrical Remington 40X—or they are fitted with sleeves. These not only stiffen the action proper, but give it enough length to handle the target scope without putting one block out on the barrel, and they also markedly enlarge the bedding area, the contact base between rifle and wood. Most of these actions and sleeves are themselves cylindrical. At least one experimenter, Ed Shilen, has had success, however, with an aluminum sleeving which is square where it meets the wood, flat on bottom and sides, with the recoil lug not conventionally forward at the juncture of barrel and action, but aft, where the sleeve butts against the stock.

In the early stages of such developments there were moves in quite an opposite direction, the no-bedding approach I've always called it. Until 1972 this manifested itself by a simple scheme in which the barrel was clamped just ahead of the receiver between a pair of sizable mated steel blocks 4-6 inches long. The bottom block was set into the stock, or what passed for a stock, and early on the use of glass bedding as a simple and neat way of accomplishing this fit appeared. The barrel was free to flap at the front end, the action similarly free at the rear. And a lot of these unprepossessing "rifles" shot remarkably well indeed.

In 1972 the no-bedding idea went off in a new and immediately productive direction. Since the whole field of gluing or bonding parts together, even pieces of different materials, has broadened like a grassfire in the past half-decade because of developments in quick-setting bonding compounds we lump under the term epoxy—we may yet drive cars that are stuck together, not welded or bolted—the people who made the 40X saw an opportunity. As anyone who has messed with the epoxy glues and substances like Devcon knows, if the metal surfaces are not properly prepared before fitting into an epoxy or "glass or powder-metal bed, adhesion takes place. Tight adhesion. Instead of avoiding this, the "special bedding" 40X puts it to use. What I have jokingly called the library-paste rifles were born. The stock is normal in outside contour, but the action area and the barrel groove are cut more open than usual, made much too loose for any normal bedding job. Likewise, a section of the forestock some 6 inches long forward of the recoil log is hogged out. This section is loaded with Devcon, the barreled action set down into it, with the recoil lug touching nowhere in its mortise, and excess compound that is squeezed out along the barrel is wiped away, and when the epoxy sets the rifle is bonded together more or less permanently.

The barrel, then, is free to vibrate forward of the bonded area; the action is free to vibrate aft of it, and of course the inletting around the trigger section must be free to permit this. At this writing, both Mike Walker and Jim Stekl of Remington's 40X shop are convinced that this is the quickest, simplest, and most reliable way of turning out a $\frac{1}{4}$-minute rifle that exists. And judging from the performance of the rifles they've been quietly trying in 1972, especially the equipment regular winner Stekl has shot, and from the potential exhibited by the .222 heavy varminter and the 6×47 of this construction I started messing with late in the season, they may well be right. This could be the bedding system of the future.

All is not beer and skittles with the scheme, of course. In the first place, a high-magnification scope positioned with its forward base about 6 inches out onto the barrel and the rear base either just onto the barrel or atop the receiver ring may well cause eye-relief problems. We can't use a scope base on the receiver bridge because the whole action flexes a mite under trigger pressure. In the second, how do you fix or adjust the trigger if the rifle has to be disassembled for such a job? It won't come apart by undoing two or three action screws because there aren't any.

Well, if the scheme goes into production, some system of openings for trigger access will be devised, and these rifles can be taken apart. Some will come loose if given a sharp rap after a night or two in the freezer. All will let go if the barrel in the epoxied area is heated with a small torch to about 350 degrees, the flame kept away from the wood by a slotted shield of as-bestos.

Before you wax all sweaty about ruining the barrel, bear in mind that 350 degrees is really rather mild heat and harmless to any steel of the chrome-moly or so-called stainless types— you can come close to it by firing twenty-five or thirty shots as fast as humanly possible, which no accuracy nut is likely to do of course. Even that would have no effect save a minor acceleration of throat wear, perhaps. There is no evidence thus far that such heat has injured a "glue-job" barrel in the slight-est. Nor has such a rifle come apart under recoil, although some amazingly drastic tests have been tried.

So who knows? The no-bedding-at-all system may eventually solve a lot of our problems.

Meanwhile the usual rifle in contemporary use, whether for busting bears or punching holes in paper, is bedded, and suffers all the problems incidental thereto. Do not for a moment be-lieve, incidentally, that the use of glass bedding or the fiberglass stocks now being produced for accuracy and varmint rifles eliminate all bedding woes. They do not. The all-glass stocks must indeed be bedded correctly in the first place, and as pre-cisely as any piece of wood; and laying in a thin layer of glass in the action area of a hunting rifle, in order to cure any ten-dency toward wood movement, reinforces or stiffens the stock

This view down into the inletted area of a 40X indicates that the precision element of a bedding job applies chiefly only to the critical areas—that smooth finish and nice fit are handsome but not necessary except on the critical bearing points at rear of recoil mortise, under receiver and at receiver edge, and at tang. In a "shell-bedded" treatment such as this, chief bearings are at tang and receiver ring.

only to a degree. It cannot eliminate the forces generated when that wood makes up its mind to shrink, grow, or crawl.

Symptoms of bedding change in an accuracy rifle—which is not likely, after all, to walk clear off the paper just because its forestock warps a hair—are these. First, a consistent two-group situation, two shots here and three there, as it were. Second, a tendency to string, usually diagonally but often in a straight vertical. Third, and rarely because this is usually either the fault of the shooter or some wind-mirage problem, horizontal spreading. With a precision rifle which was well bedded in the first place, these symptoms do not have to be coarsely evident.

In all cases what they amount to—and this applies to both practical hunting pieces and full-scale accuracy rifles—is that a misfit between metal and wood or some hang-up of wood and metal creating abnormal friction between them is causing the action or barrel, both of which flex considerably when the rifle is fired, to fail to end up in the identical position each time the rifle shoots. Hence the ensuing shot is fired with a different set of stresses acting on the metal and affecting its vibration or flex, so causing the rifle to poke its bullet into a different spot. The three-and-two group, for example, shows clearly that the piece shot from two slightly different bedding or stress situations.

Once you are convinced that a bedding problem or change does exist, that you are not misreading as a bedding fault failure of your scope to return to zero, failure of yourself in holding or in judging conditions, failure of your load to perform acceptably, failure to be 100 percent certain that all screws, nuts, bolts, and whatnot are properly secure (which, incidentally, does not mean setting up on the action screws until they markedly compress the wood under them and thereby create a bedding fault)—then stand your musket upright on the bench and pick up a short screwdriver sized to the action screws.

And may I say here that for a few paragraphs we are going to be talking about stiff-action accuracy jobs, not slim-stocked hunting rifles save in a general sense, since the lightweight sporter may betray its bedding problems with unwanted pressures here and there that usually show up quickly to an experienced eye even without the use of oil and lampblack. We are also talking about a rifle that was once shooting a lot better than it is today.

If the action has a center guard screw, and if the barrel will move at the fore-end tip—you can feel it with a sensitive finger —when you turn that center screw in and out, the receiver has been sprung, put under tension by either a hump or a hollow at the mid-action area. If the wood is high in the center, this will show up if you take out the center screw entirely and alternately tighten and loosen the rear guard screw while your finger is positioned to sense any flexing of the tang section.

To locate high spots, competent stockers use a coating of mixed lampblack and oil on the bottom of the action or sleeve, setting the action back into the stock and in most cases tightening only the front guard screw when making the contact check.

They commonly use fine sharp half-round chisels for the job and take out thin, small chips from the high areas, rebedding being a delicate job. Ultimately the lack of flex in the tang area when the rear screw is put back in and turned alternately tight and loose shows that any high spot is gone.

Round receivers or sleeves should not be fitted into the wood too tightly at the upper edges, since this may result in binding. A few stockers avoid this, and as well the problem of precisely mating action and wood over from 120 to 150 degrees of a circle, by using parallel ridges or bolsters on which the action rides as in a V.

Two other common bedding faults involve the guard screws, which should not touch wood at any point in their passage through the stock, and the recoil lug common to most action types. This should not under any circumstances—and this goes for hunting rifles as well as accuracy items—contact its mortise at the bottom or the sides, but should be in contact as evenly as possible across its rear side. Usually, to make that contact surely even, the mortise is so cut that the metal bears on wood at the outer edges and across the bottom in a U-form.

The correctly bedded rifle—and this also applies to good hunting rifles—does not put its first clean cold barrel shot into one area, the ultimate group in another. The opening round, unless the barrel has been left oily or doped with bore cleaner, should plunk into the eventual hole or group center. Once in a while we find a rifle which doesn't "settle down" or "warm up" until after a number of rounds and then delivers quality performance, but there's usually something wrong with this one, a crooked barrel or some peculiar fouling condition. The best bench rest rifles I have owned always put the first round to center well enough so that it acted as a meaningful sighter, and gave a true reading as to what had occurred in the way of light shift or mirage or wind change since the last match.

For the benefit of hunters who like to use rifles tuned to their peak accuracy, I will add a few final comments on gimmicks with the sporters.

First, since most such rifles do have fore-end pressure, that push must be straight up, not sideways. Most stockers accomplish this by cutting out the actual bottom of the fore-end groove behind the tip, so that the barrel rests on two bolsters as it were. If in looking between barrel and fore-end from the muzzle end or in looking down on the rifle it appears that the wood is pressing on one side but is free on the other, chisel work in the groove is indicated to ease the pressure, since otherwise the rifle, especially one using a violent cartridge, will walk its shots away from the pressure side and give lateral spreads.

If with tang screw moderately tight, in normal position, alternate tightening and loosening of forward or receiver ring screw reveals barrel movement that can be felt by left forefinger when it is held at junction of barrel and fore-end, the wood at the receiver ring point is low, or there is a hump under the mid-action point. Either will cause the action to flex and fail to return to the same point after each shot.

Second, the siderail-action types will usually shoot better if the pressure between stock and metal in the receiver ring and recoil lug area is carried a bit farther forward out into the barrel groove, say as much as 3 inches, especially if they are otherwise inletted free-floating, open at the tip. The rounder actions, like

When the forward or receiver-ring action screw is normally tight, if the tang flexes as tension is alternately applied and relieved on the tang screw, the tang area may be too low, or more likely there is a high point in the wood under the action which causes the action to bend when all screws are tight. On a Remington action the center screw should be merely tight, then backed a quarter turn.

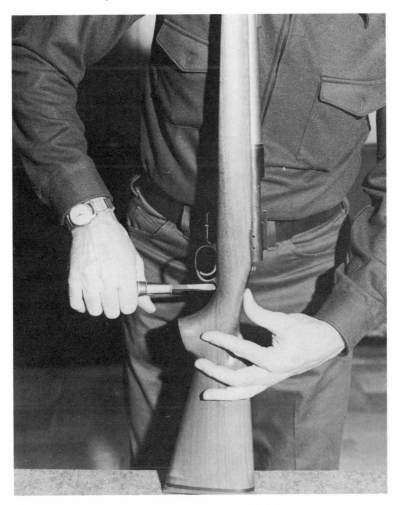

the M700 and other cylindrical sporter receivers, can be free-floated without that added support, and usually shoot well free all the way, which is of course desirable since the sporter fore-end, which is likely to warp a bit anyway, then has a bit of room to shift in before it affects the impact center.

The handsomely stocked rifle that gun nuts always gape at and exclaim over, and term a superb inletting job even before they've taken it apart, may not be that at all. Too much tightness at the wood edge where it meets metal, especially if the close fit results from a slight undercut, may be a fault rather than a virtue if it in any way binds the normal flexing of action and barrel. The metal is going to move some anyway. The aim in a perfect bedding job, on any rifle, be it sporter or bench model, is to minimize the flex while assuring a return to identical wood-metal relationship after each shot.

And one final comment. If you feel you must attempt the stocker's art, must buy a set of inletting chisels and some glass bedding mix from Bob Brownell's store and improve the performance of your musketoons, that's fine. You'll learn a lot about rifles and what makes them tick. But don't start practicing on your best shooter. Work out on your worst. You might even improve it. Certainly if you ruin it there's little harm done. The best pieces? Deal with a qualified stocker on them, if possible a man who has had experience keeping accuracy rifles in tune.

16

Accuracy Cartridges
and Loads

It has long been a secret hope of mine that some iconoclastic character would show up at a bench rest match with a black-powder, lead-bullet boomer firing cartridges big enough to bludgeon a bison, and proceed with it either to beat the britches off the current crop of experts or at least to scare them to death, and I don't mean with sheer noise. It does any world good to be shaken a bit now and again.

But this is not to be. The black-powder item, if it were muzzleloaded or even cartridge-fed with the same brass case loaded over and again, the way Marcy Prescott used to load his one .219 Wasp case over and again right at the shooting bench, would have problems managing the seven-minute time limit, and even if it did, the hard fact is that rifle accuracy has taken huge strides since the heyday of such equipment.

And this is true no matter how we revere the big calibers. I for one have always felt that the .375 Holland & Holland, for example, was one of the most intrinsically accurate calibers we have ever had, for the simple reason that I've never owned or shot a rifle in the caliber which did not, for hunting equipment, perform superbly well. Cloverleaf groups with those big fat bullets seem common as dirt, yet somehow when you measure 'em they come up in ruler fractions of inches, not in hundredths. Fine for hunting rifles, not in it otherwise. And of course there's always the sobering thought that even if we could get one of the heavy-bullet calibers, relatively unaffected by wind as they are, performing up to modern accuracy standards, what mortal man can sit at a bench all day behind such a musket without becoming a mass of recoil-jellied pulp?

No, the trend in accuracy cartridges is, with a few exceptions which we will carefully note, toward smaller and more readily controllable sizes.

We can, it seems, approach a definition of a cartridge created for accuracy. On present evidence it would seem to be the case which, when loaded with a powder of such burning speed as to reach peak velocity for the round, is filled with that powder up to the base of the bullet or virtually so, yet achieves its velocity with minimal charge for the bullet weight and caliber. In a long-winded and cumbersome way, that's a statement of the truly efficient cartridge, one in which neither capacity nor powder weight is wasted, and top speed for powder grain is achieved within tolerable pressures.

Let's get the large-volume exceptions out of the way first. As of today the prime choices for long range accuracy work (out to 1000 yards) are the short magnums in .28 and .30 caliber, notably the 7 mm. Remington magnum and wildcatted versions thereof with slightly longer necks, and the .300 Winchester magnum and its apparently preferred wildcat predecessor, the .30-.338. Loadings for these rounds, which are admittedly supreme at such ranges, can be explained in one word—full. Standard practice is to load powders like DuPont #4350 or #4831 or Norma #205 in the heaviest charges the individual rifle will handle behind the bullets used, in .30 caliber normally Sierra 168- or 197-grain boattailed spitzer match bullets, or the competitive Hornady and Speer-Lapua versions, in order to get maximum velocities.

The super-specialized items like the .30-.378 and 6.5-.300 Weatherby which drew so much attention from original 1000-yard accuracy experimenters like Alex Hoyer, using ultra-slow powders like the .50-caliber machine gun propellant, seem to have had their day, and the better-balanced short magnums are now the choice. The 1000-yard accuracy game, as practiced in the Williamsport area, despite the vast problems of wind and mirage over such ranges, regularly permits $\frac{1}{2}$-minute-of-angle spreads, a "normal" winning group out there going some 11 inches, the record at just over 7 inches.

The other exception to the small-cartridge trend is not really an exception, being the .308 Winchester or 7.62 Nato as it is variously termed, in that there are .30s of significantly lesser capacity that could be tried, like the .30-30, .30 Remington, and a vast litter of wildcats, yet it is one of the lesser .30s as compared to the .30-06, the .300 H&H of Wimbledon fame, the .300 Winchester and .300 Weatherby. As an official military round, it of course offers commonly available brass, and will surely be given much development attention such as the .30-06 has received. The cases are strong, and are held to close dimension even in factory production. The recoil factor of the .308 in $10\frac{1}{2}$-pound sporter-class rifles, for example, is so heavy as to be too much for a fair number of competitive shooters, alas, yet it becomes possible for many with the supplementary or "sissy" sandbag between butt and shoulder, which in effect increases gun weight by its own heft, and also compresses to some degree, for effective kick easement.

In recent times the .308 has come into wide use in the full bench rest rifle classes, where the piece is so heavy that recoil is no concern to the shooter. The idea is that with a return-to-battery rest operative, so that resighting between shots is not necessary and mirage effects can be disregarded, by using the high ballistic efficiency of .30-caliber bullets the wind effect can be, while not disregarded, brought down to manageable levels. Hence shooting one of the unrestricted machines could become a thoroughly automatic procedure. Well, I gave up the big rifles some years back as being too remote from reality, but from what I hear, all is not automatic yet.

Bullet choices for the .308 are: 168-grain Sierra boattail match, the 168-grain Hornady spire-point boattail, rarely the 190-grain Hornady, occasionally the Speer-sold Lapua or Finnish-made match bullet, and quite commonly handmade bullets of 130-grain weight. These are hand-swaged hollow-points made with the lead well back below the opening by using jackets of a length usual for 150 grains or heavier.

The basic loading concept for the .308 in accuracy usage is as with the other large cases—full. As mentioned elsewhere in this book, Ed Shilen has on occasion won matches with a fast-powder combination approximating the forty-year-old 300-

meter loading of only 2200 foot-seconds, but present procedures call for full steam ahead. One point about the use of
H-380, which is essentially a hair slow for the .308 case size,
involves bullet seating. Normal charges of this powder, 47-49
grains, almost fill the case to its mouth, and shallow seating,
so that the bullet is definitely lodged within the beginning lands
by bolt closure, is necessary in order to make certain that the
H-380 creates enough pressure to burn itself properly. The same
injunction applies to using H-380 with the little 6×47. Bullet-
powder combinations commonly used by .308-choosing competitors are: 40-43 grams of Hodgdon's #4895 with 168-grain
bullets; 36.5-39 grains of #3031, same bullet weight; 41.3 of
RelodeR #11 with same bullet weight; and 46-48 grams of
H-380 with 168-grain bullets.

At the present time, while virtually all of those available are
capable of top-drawer hunting accuracy, there are no cartridges
in .28 or 7 mm., .270, 6.5 mm. or .25 that are being regularly
and seriously used in bench rest competition, although periodically an experimenter like Marlin Bassett will go on a binge
of 6.5 frustrations. The reason for this is simple. While there
exist plenty of accurate hunting bullets, there are no bullets
of true tackhole quality being produced in such sizes by any
manufacturer (or indeed as far as I know by any hand-swaging
individual), although there is no technical reason why this
should be impossible if man can make .30s of such quality.
Bassett's rationale, that 6.5- or .264-caliber bullets can have an
extremely high ballistic coefficient and thus excellent wind-re-
sisting qualities without becoming so heavy as to create undue
recoil factors, has much to be said for it as far as theory is
concerned. Meanwhile, with present bullets in these calibers
the hunter has adequate accuracy for his field needs, and it is
between .25 and .30 that the choice of caliber for American
game usually lies.

Since there is every reason, ballistic and otherwise, with the
possible exception of minimal recoil, to dismiss the various
.17-calibers as potential accuracy phenomena, let's turn to the
.224s.

Among the .22 centerfires the downward case-size trend has
been marked, and has now probably stabilized until other
propellants are devised. Old-timers in the bench rest accuracy
game will remember that way back when the .22–250 was making records and winning matches, it was in general behaving

as should a cartridge which had been accepted as tops for most full-range varmint shooting. A .22–250 on the firing line today, however, would probably be an item of curiosity, there being general agreement that (a) no more than 3200–3400 f.p.s. of velocity is needed for such work, and (b) cartridges using 30 to 35 grains of powder to propel .22 bullets are too violent, create too much reaction to be controllable for peak precision.

Nonetheless, following its recent commercial re-entry by Remington, the .22–250 has become one of the very most popular varmint cartridges we have with rifles from virtually every manufacturer. Its performance fills the gap left by the passage from the scene, or the virtual passage, of the .220 Swift, which was killed by the bracketing effect of the .222 clan on the one side and the .24-calibers on the other. Hence the .22–250 is relevant in any discussion of accuracy.

The story of the wildcat has been told and retold a dozen times. Suffice it to say that it was probably conceived in 1912–13 when gunsmith Gebby and designer Newton first talked of a necked-down .250–3000, Newton's interest at that time being in a 70-grain bullet, made by sizing down the .22 Savage Hi-Power projectile. The idea went nowhere until the early 1930s, when at the request of Captain Grosvenor Wotkyns, Gebby made up a couple of rifles. J. B. Sweany also turned out a .22–250 barrel or two, J. B. Smith and Charles H. Morse contributed powder and bullet know-how, and what came to be copyrighted as the .22 Varminter as chambered by Gebby was born. In a sense, it was commercially successful even then, helping Smith to set himself up in the powder and custom-loading business and Morse to establish himself as a bulletmaker. Yet despite pressure from handloaders and accuracy fans it stayed a custom item until Remington seized the opportunity a few years ago of reintroducing a thirty-five-year-old wildcat.

A major claim always made for the .22–250, which would never quite equal .220 Swift performance peaks, probably because the strong-headed Swift case would take higher pressures, was its loading ease and flexibility. Obviously, no one cartridge is significantly easier to load than another, the same procedures being followed, but the .22–250 does digest a variety of combinations.

Probably the most basic load for it is 36 grains of DuPont #4320 and the 55-grain bullet. That's a practical hunting load, death on chucks, and in some rifles may make 3800 f.p.s. The present loading handbooks are stuffed with .22–250 data, however, and the shooter can make his own choice. For years the favorites among accuracy bugs and bench competitors favoring the Gebby round involved somewhere between 30 and 32 grains of DuPont #3031, the lighter charge giving 3625–3650 on most rifles, still somewhat above the 3200 foot-second region which most bench-resters think is a preferable wind-deflection area. For easy metering, small-grain powders like IMR 4895, the ball propellants, and the lamentably discontinued Hercules RelodeR series would today supersede long-grained #3031. My own experiences with .22–250 rifles, and there have been many, though none that expected to be of competitive level, suggest that despite its flexibility reputation the cartridge works best at very nearly full throttle, however.

The .220 Swift, onetime darling of the varmint hunter, but not commercially loaded as this is typed, never has made it in bench rest competition, although rifles in this caliber and in the slightly steeper-shouldered .220 Wilson Arrow form traditionally would beat the minute-of-angle mark when that was a triumph for practical varminting equipment. I recall owning a .220 Wilson Arrow, chambered by the great L. E. Wilson himself, with a Humphrey stock, which despite a siderail Mauser action would hold the 55-grain Wotkyns-Morse cadmium-plated bullet below the inch mark all day long. It created great havoc among the woodchucks. I am also inclined to agree with Whelen in his remark that in its day, the M70 Winchester in .220 Swift was the most accurate combination, in straight factory terms, for both rifle and ammunition. The chambering was discontinued in 1964, however, and only recently has interest in the Swift revived in New Haven. But to my recollection, only one New Jersey shooter for long remained a devotee of the Swift for bench competition, and while he won matches, he has now given it up as an improbable task.

The .220 Swift normally works best with at least three-quarter-throttle loadings. My own presently preferred chucking load, one generally considered a full maximum, uses the 55-grain weight of Remington's plated bullet over 38.5 grains of #4320 for a speed of a solid 3800 feet per second, that bullet being chosen because it is accurate, and will stand the Swift speed yet will surely burst on impact, as we want a varmint projectile to do, though the Swift is usually fast enough to make even the 55-grain Sierra come apart. Other useful loads are: 37.5

grains of #4064, which I have found accurate with some 55-grain bullets; 35 grains of #4895, which has shot well in some rifles with 52-grain match pills; 35 grains of #3031, which is also good; and in the RelodeR series, 38 grains of #21, which is accurate but not maximum by a grain or two. The Swift, incidentally, has probably been responsible for more rifles coming apart at the seams than any other cartridge, or so the arms plants say, so treat it gently, being sure to watch cartridge length.

The last widely employed .22-caliber cartridge to shoot loads at all comparable in amount and yet win accuracy crowns was probably the .219 Donaldson Wasp. Essentially a compacted form of the rimmed .219 Zipper, it was made by necking back, cutting off, and fire-forming Zipper cases, often with neck reaming. The Wasp was by all odds the emperor of the one-hole game during the early 1950s, the heyday of Dubois and Johnstown, then holding a number of records. The inexpensive military actions of that period could be readily adapted to handle the rim, and of course there was no need for placement of one round ahead of the other to get smooth feed, since the rifle was to be used as a single-shot.

The very strong rimmed case made possible high working pressures, so that the Wasp seemed to be a remarkably efficient cartridge, and velocities in the 3600–3700 f.p.s. area were quite normal. It was an efficient round; there were some powders with which loading up to the neck base was possible without dangerous pressures, the powder shook little if at all, and the large rifle primer size usable would light off the charge well, so every last ounce of performance was squeezed out of the case's capacity.

There quickly developed a sort of mystique about Gregoire-barreled Wasps, which persisted until tubes of longer-lived steel than Gregoire used appeared. Perhaps most of this was unjustified; accuracy searchers later found that it is easier to get pinhole results with cartridges of lower density and velocity norms, around 3100–3200 f.p.s. And by the time the Wasp appeared there was already reason to have faith in moderately sharp shoulders, in the 30° region, so it is hardly cricket to claim mysterious abilities for the quotients built into that combination of case size, powder usage, and whatnot.

Relevant here is an anecdote about Al Marciante. In chambering up one bench rifle in .219 Wasp—and characteristically doing it the night before the big Dubois shoot—Al Marciante simply ran his throating reamers in all the way and later left his case necks similarly long after the shoulders were moved back by the die treatment. So he had a longnecked Wasp. He was hot and the rifle was hot, they won all the Dubois cash and cups, so the following week everybody called upon his favorite gunsmith to make up one of those longnecked Wasps.

The basic .219 has also been necked up to take 6 mm. bullets, 6.5 mm. bullets, and even .30-caliber slugs, and in its day was variously malformed by curious reamer-grinders, but I doubt that the original Donaldson form has ever been improved on. I further have little doubt that a .219 Donaldson Wasp, put together under today's criteria for accuracy rifles, might be a winning combination.

Basic loadings for the cartridge in the 1950s were:

With 50-grain bullets,
    27 grains DuPont #3031 M.V. 3600 f.p.s.
    28 grains DuPont #4320 M.V. 3600 f.p.s.
    29 grains DuPont #4064 M.V. 3600 f.p.s.

With 55-grain bullets,
    26 grains DuPont #3031
    29 grains DuPont #3031 M.V. 3715 Max
    27 grains DuPont #4320
    31 grains DuPont #4320 M.V. 3626 Max
    25 grains DuPont #4064

Charges of Hodgdon's #4895 were popular, differing lots indicating loads of from 24 to 28 grains. Needless to say, every Wasp rifle was a law unto itself, and accuracy bugs worked up their loadings within the framework such data suggests. Today, with bullets of the common match weight of some 52 grains and charges of Hodgdon's #4895 up to 29 grains depending on the lot, of the Ball C powders about a grain less, and of H-380 up to 32 grains, first-rate performance can be expected. Of the unfortunately discontinued Hercules rifle series, #11 is a better bet than the #7 type which is now so popular with cases of slightly less capacity.

The Wasp still has interesting features, albeit the rimmed case is hardly desirable for contemporary bench-type bolt-actions, so that it probably rates most use in single-shot varmint rifles like the Ruger or the ill-fated Sharps type Colt proposed to offer. In today's scheme of things there just isn't much need for it, however.

King of the hill in accuracy terms, of course, is the .222 Remington, a rimless number which later spawned two slightly larger brethren, the .222 Remington magnum and the .223 or 5.6 military round. The .222 in either standard or wildcatted form just seems easier to make shoot than anything else, probably because its case size is just about right so that a fair number of powders permit high loading density and give the 3100–3200 f.p.s. which seems to be magic.

I am proud to say that I had considerable involvement in the developmental history of this cartridge, though the basic credit must of course go to Mike Walker, who had for quite some time been working on a varmint cartridge intended to fall somewhere between the Hornet and Bee and the Zipper/.22–250/ .220 Swift class of chuck-poppers. He started with the .25 Remington case, unfortunately weak brass, tried the .30 carbine type, eventually created a new case, and the .222 went into primary production. At that point yours truly got into the act.

First, with ammunition factory-loaded with the 48-grain Swift bullet at 3135, Mike and I sallied forth to shoot chucks. Those hard bullets richocheted, the chucks crawled into their holes, the ballistics numbers sounded to me like the price of a suit at a discount house. Phooey! Appeals and suggestions to certain powers then in the Remington hierarchy brought results; the bullet was upped to 50 grains and made from very thin cups to ensure blowup; the powder was changed to #2405, which is #2400 with slightly heavier coating or burning deterrent, and the speed hit the middle 3100s. Not good enough, as I indicated, but a change to slightly slower #2412 gave the flat 3200 feet per second which, it then seemed to me, gave the new load a certain Abercrombie & Fitch quality, since 50 grams at 3200 anyone could remember. With such a combination the chucks died on the spot and we heard no ricochets.

And the second way? Well, I urged further the chambering of bench rifles in the new cartridge, not that much urging was needed. That the .222 is and was an instant success on all scores, as a splendid varminting round in off-the-shelf form for semi-civilized areas, as a commercial proposition, and as an accuracy form, is a matter of history. For any small contribution I may have made thereto, I give thanks for the opportunity to serve.

These early bench rest .222s were made up on the Model 722 actions still with magazine cuts and normal-size feed opening, the original trigger. They used cumbersome laminated stocks by Harris, untapered barrel of 1.2-inch diameter at the muzzle, weighed around 18 pounds. At its first shoot one of these .222s took second in the aggregate, showing .35 for five five-shot 100-yard groups. By 1953 the cartridge was winning everything in sight, and held the ten-shot 100-yard record of that day at .3268. I still have the heavy .222 rifle which was national runner-up to Sam Clark in the mid-1950s, and it still shoots quality groups.

The caliber has been winning ever since. As why not, since the case is compact, delivers enough speed (3000–3200) with minimal violence, adapts well to a variety of modern powders, lasts forever under bench-loading conditions with minimal neck sizing, and doesn't wear out barrels, 3000 rounds being just a good warm-up for some rifles.

For many years my pet load for the standard .222 case was 20.5 grains of DuPont's IMR #4198 with whatever bullet was then doing well, ordinarily one in the 51–53-grain weight area, which for no particular reason has come to be normal for accuracy .224s. A good many shooters still use #4198, charge weights running from 19 to 22 depending on the case thickness and the individual rifle.

Surplus #4895 from Bruce Hodgdon is on the slow side for this case but up to 24.5 grains has been used in accuracy loadings; DuPont #4320 is likewise slow, 25 grains of it giving under 3000 feet per second. Other powders applicable are Ball, Lot C-1 from Hodgdon, up to 25 grains (and Lot 2 can go a mite higher), and RelodeR #7, unfortunately discontinued just as it was beginning to catch on. The Hercules powder has worked for many shooters in dosages anywhere from 19.5 to a 23-grain maximum, with best results usually in the 20.5–21-grain area. Olin's #748 BR is slow enough so that nearly all that can be handled in the case works out, 25.4 grains being standard for one well-known shooter.

The .223 with its short neck has not in standard form drawn much use in the accuracy clan, but the .222 Magnum has, although many have thought that the so-called magnum case, $\frac{1}{10}$ inch longer than the normal .222 and so of greater capacity, was just about at the ragged edge for sure and full ignition with small rifle primers. Loads for the full magnum case form will, in relation to the .222, usually run about 2 grains heavier with #4198, 2 to 3 grains larger with slow powders like #4895, Ball, etc. I've never noted any mystery about loading the .222 magnum that couldn't be solved by reference to the manuals by Messrs. Speer, Hornady, Sierra, Lyman, et al., all of which should be on any accuracy fan's bench.

The .222½, of which much has been made of late, is precisely what it says it is, a case made from .222 magnum brass that ends up about halfway between the standard and magnum .222 forms. Ed Shilen, whose brain child it is as far as I know, has never told me the why of the cartridge, so, unless it be that idea of limitations on the ignition effect of small rifle primers, I doubt there's any particular rationale. However, a great many master rifles have been built in the caliber, many by Shilen and many for shooters living well west of the Alleghenies—there were forty-five .222½'s in the heavy-varminter class at the NBRSA championships in Tulsa, for example, out of 150. That's nearly a third. I have shot in recent years a .222½ heavy-varminter by Shilen which has won one national crown and assorted other honors, and a light-varminter which has picked up various regional wins has since been rebarreled in the ordinary .222—with no effect that I can see one way or the other.

The .222½ uses the same set of powders, 21–23 grains of Re-lodeR #7, with most votes going for 22 or thereabouts, 21 grains and up of #4198, my preferred load being 22.4 grains of this hard-to-meter powder, 27.5 of #748BR.

The other wildcat .22's made from the .222 family, usually from the .223 case and called the .23–40, .23–35, .23–45, etc., with the second figure referring to shoulder angle, are also users of the same types of powder and in much the same charges. They shoot much the same too, and probably are another exemplification of the many-times-proved adage that shoulder angle beyond 30 degrees is something like a girl's having freckles or not having freckles—it doesn't change the performance much. Many of these rifles are soundly gunsmithed pieces and winners, however.

An interesting pair of "proprietary" wildcat cartridges, created, shot successfully in competition, and chambered for by Hot Spring, Arkansas, gunsmith Tom Gillman, mark the transition from .22 to .24 calibers. Tom's .22 Tom Cat utilizes the .222 magnum case with an overall length of 1.845 or 1.430 inches to the 30-degree shoulder, which is .372 across. The regular loadings call for 29.5 grains of DuPont #4320 or 27.5 of #4895 and the usual Remington 7½ primer. A full case of H-380 has also been used with this version of the .222 magnum. Gillman has picked up two national heavy-varmint crowns with this one, plus light-varmint wins at 100 as well as 200 yards, and shot this cartridge as part of his '64, '66, and '70 three-gun championship run. It still holds as this chapter is typed the 200-yard record of .1923. The 53-grain Sierra bullet is Gillman's choice for it.

The .24-caliber form, not surprisingly called the 6 mm. Tom Cat, uses not the .222 magnum but the .224 Weatherby magnum case opened up to shoulder and body dimensions of .406 and .414 inches respectively, with a .261 neck, length to shoulder of 1.530 or 1.900 inches overall. The normal .224 Weatherby case delivers .22–250 performance with .224-diameter bullets, so relates well to the .24 caliber when the call is for considerably more speed than practical—the more common 6×47, for example. Usual loadings for this 6 mm. Tom Cat, which has taken a fair batch of championship awards for Tom, are 34 grains of H-380, 30 grains of DuPont #3031, or 27.5 of #4895, and Gillman has for years shot the 75-grain Sierra bullet.

Neither the .243 Winchester nor the .244 or 6 mm. Remington is essentially an accuracy competition item, save perhaps in the hunter class of rifle in which the case volume must be larger than that of the .30–30, because both these popular calibers run a bit overlarge, on the violent side for precision shooting inside 300 meters. They remain today what they were in the beginnings, combination game and varmint cartridges.

The story of their immediate origins has been told but might bear repeating at least in part, since it is if nothing else a commentary on the American system of competitive business. The .243 is of course the immediate blood heir of the .240 Page, which was dreamed up, hardly "designed," by Al Marciante and me on a piece of experimental ordnance brass of the type which eventually became the 7.62 Nato. Winchester was first disinterested, when I suggested it, or seemed to be; later they adapted the .240 Page concept to a more slope-shouldered item, merely the 7.62 Nato necked down, an activity in East Alton which I discovered only by accident. The appearance in prototype of what was then called the 6 mm. Winchester, eventually the .243 Winchester, is also a matter of history. And when the .243 appeared, coincidentally with a short-barreled, free-floating form of the Model 70 referred to as the Featherweight, it made its primary hit less because of impressive terminal ballistics and potency on game than because of the basic accuracy of those early combinations. They were good shooters.

The part of the 6 mm. story that is less often told involves a round first called the .244, and its relationship to the Winchester development. I frankly felt rebuffed at the first reaction of Winchester's Research and Development boss to my enthusiasm for the .240 Page—which was really a polite fiction on his part, in all probability—and so promptly presented to Remington, first by letter and then to a round-table group representing the whole factory operation, the .24-caliber idea in the form of the .243 Rockchucker. On that famous wildcat by Fred Huntington I had owned and shot several rifles, both varmint jobs and a dinky sporter stocked by Monty Kennedy. We wildcatters had easily attained ballistics of 85 grains at 3400–3500, and 100 grains at 3100 plus. Remington plumped for the idea but thought in terms of varmint-game rather than game-varmint, so eventually came up with bullet weights of ten grains less and consequently a twist of 1-in-2 rather than the 1-in-10 needed to spin a 100-grain spitzer bullet.

All that next summer there were discussions with both companies. When it became evident the ultimate cartridges were going to collide head-on in the marketplace, I made discreet suggestions that might perhaps have led to abandonment of one or the other project. But they were too far committed, and in any event any such agreement between manufacturers would probably have brought down the wrath of the Justice Department. Ultimately both cartridges were announced.

The .243 was the early victor in sales, the original Model 722 .244 rifle being neither fish nor fowl, too heavy for a sporter, not heavy enough for a true varmint rifle, and the game-varmint concept won out. Remington has since admitted that by speeding the twist in their rifles, building both hunting and varminting models, upping the bullet weights, and renaming the round 6 mm. Remington.

Any difference between the two in accuracy potential is insignificant, I think. The Remington case is a bit easier to load because of its longer neck, probably flows less brass into the neck with high-pressure loads because of the sharper shoulder, and holds a touch more powder and so should, all else being equal, get higher speeds. The differences are probably more academic than real. Both are first-rate long-range varmint rounds when properly loaded and in the proper rifle; both are effective hunting cartridges on game like antelope, deer, caribou, and even sheep but way over their heads on critters like elk; both are loaded to tight accuracy standards by all manufacturers; and both can be loaded to even tighter accuracy by virtually any careful handloader using ordinary handbook data and a dash of common sense, because there is today a very wide range of .24-caliber bullets suited to any purpose and all of good shooting quality. I frankly see no gain in proposing "pet loads" for either.

The smallest 6 mm. in normal use, however, is strictly a bench rest accuracy item. It was developed strictly for that purpose, the original wildcatting here having been done by Mike Walker in 1962–63, although there have been assorted minor diddlings since, notably the sharper-shouldered Hall version. The normal 6 × 47, however, is merely the 47 mm. .222 magnum case necked up to hold a .24-caliber bullet. For use in tight-neck chambers it is normally neck-turned to admit .002 clearance in firing. It is very probably the prime example we have of the modern trend for a small-capacity case using full-up-to-the-bullet loads to give minimal recoil and velocities in the 3000–3200 area. As such it is good enough so that many top-rank shooters use the same rifle to meet both sporter and light-varminter classifications. Yet it is not by any sensible criterion either a hunting or a varminting round, but an accuracy development.

In the early 1960s the usual charge for the 6×47 called for 23 grains of DuPont IMR #4198 and the best bullet available at the 70–75-grain level. For a number of years I had one Huntington measure practically rusted at the setting of 23.5 grains for the Detsch bullets then available. Many shooters still stick with #4198, upping the charge about half a grain to 24 for bullets of 60 grains as made by Sierra, for example. Of late, feeling has developed that #4198 is not only hard to measure with its long granules but in present lots seems to burn dirty, hence there has developed a swing toward other powders.

H-380 works well in some rifles with some bullets, but only if the bullet contour is full forward to permit seating out for solid contact with the lands, over all the powder that can be handled in the case without spillage, 29 to 30.5 grains. The land contact—impossible with some throats and some shapes of bullet—ensures initial pressure levels high enough to burn the slow powder.

Fast-disappearing RelodeR #7 is the choice of many, charges running from 23 to 25 grains with the usual 70-grain bullet. This powder meters well, burns clean. Surplus #4895 needs about 26.5 grains to perform properly, and some shoot 27.5; Ball powder, Lot C works well in the 26-grain area; Hodgdon's #322 is being tried at the 25-grain level, as is RelodeR #11 with 27 grains. Olin's #748BR does handsomely with full-case charges, 29–30 grains.

My own present 6×47 load is 23.5 of hoarded Hercules RelodeR #7, adjusted upward a mite if there seems to be any tendency to string.

One comment about primers should be made before we leave the .222 and .222 magnum and rounds based on them. While RWS and CCI primers are widely used by discerning shooters, the overwhelming favorite here is Remington's #7$\frac{1}{2}$. This succeeded their original #6$\frac{1}{2}$ small rifle primer, is identical to it in pellet size and chemistry, but has a tougher or thicker outer cup to cure the problem noted with some full-pressure loads in which the firing pin dished or punched out the primer center. This does not happen with the #7$\frac{1}{2}$ even when pressures are hiked so high the pockets begin to open up. It cannot be allowed to happen with a precision rifle since a blown or punched primer almost always means a shot out of the group.

The middle-sized 6 mm. clan probably originated with the 6 mm. International, although I recall one earlier experimental form which used a considerably larger short magnum case and would devastate woodchucks halfway across the county. The so-called International is the .250–3000 necked down. It is left full-length in some versions, shortened $\frac{1}{4}$ inch overall as well as in the body in the Donaldson version, and has only the shoulder pushed back to reduce body capacity a bit and to leave a long neck in the Walker version, for which 40X series rifles are presently chambered on order. Intelligent handloaders can easily work up loadings for this round with smoother-metering powders from the original #3031 data, which involves 32 grains for 60- or 75-grain bullets (velocities 3450 and 3390), a 30-grain charge for 90-grain hunting bullets (3160), and 28 grains for 100-grain hunting projectiles (2900).

An area in which accuracy experimentation is still going on is in the hunter class of rifle as sanctioned by the two bench rest associations. In addition to the limits of 10 pounds gross weight, 6X scope power, and a magazine functional for at least two added rounds which keeps the hunter class in "practical" rifle bounds, the caliber must be .24 or larger and the cartridge of capacity at least as great as that of the .30–30. While the category is well established, with competitions for score being regularly fired at ranges all over the country, and while the original idea of permitting a simple off-the-shelf factory rifle to be competitive is understandably pretty much changed to one in which hunter-class shooters, after three or four matches, switch to a musket built specifically to win within the rules, there has yet been no standardization as to cartridge choice. The 6 mm. Remington is common only because M700 rifles are, I suspect, and I look for rapid development in this category within the next five years.

The .250–3000 case left full-length will make the capacity limit and is commonly chosen for custom hunter-class rifles. These start from the M700 action usually, because of its good trigger and pin fall and round action bottom for relatively easy bedding, and acquire a new barrel and a new stock, one well suited for sandbag use, and the necked-down .250 chambering, which burns less powder than either the .243 or 6 mm. cases. DuPont IMR #3031 works fine for bullets in the 70–75-grain range, from 30 to 35 grains shooting well in some rifles, but surplus #4895 meters more smoothly and is used with such bullets in charge weights between 33 and 36 grains.

Please note that this chapter has not gone into exhaustive detail as to powder and bullet combinations individuals consider prime for each case. Nor has it told all as to the "secret" combinations used by consistent accuracy winners. To have done so would have wasted paper. First, there are no "secret" loads. Rifles show individual preferences, and what works for Joe Hotshot may be a dud for you. Second, and for much the same reasons, there is no sense in prescribing exact combinations, it being wiser to suggest areas or levels of loading in which various powders can be used.

Minute variations can be too important in the accuracy game. For example, in a match involving the 6×47 this last summer I changed to a different lot of bullets from the one maker, without adjusting the load, and without checking the dimensions of the two bullet lots, accepting merely that they were of the same weight. And I promptly opened two primer pockets from the first ten rounds fired. Bullet #2 was different from #1 in a matter of a couple of ten thousandths of an inch at various points along its diameter, but the end result was that #2 had almost twice as much shank or parallel bearing area. To shoot #2 properly and safely, then, the charge for #1 had to be dropped a full grain. Yet another rifle, of different interior dimension, might have digested either combination safely.

Your accuracy load, to repeat, for any cartridge must be your own, the one *you* have developed, perhaps with a handbook or other advisory material to start from, which for a given bullet does best in *your* rifle. It may be printed somewhere in a book, but that doesn't matter—it has to be yours.

17

Precision Loading

The problem for the home loader of high-accuracy ammunition is the same as that for any other handloader, only more so. Precision loading is in no sense a mysterious process, and I must confess to feeling that many people make an absurd mystique of certain steps in it. Rather it is one of exhaustive care, and it rests solely with you as to how exhaustive, and exhausting, you want to make it. It has to be clear that the effects of being ultraprecise, having every last element of the cartridge perfectly identical with every other round, can be sharply diminished by a puff of wind or a flip of mirage. Yet essentially he who would achieve the best in accuracy must also load with the greatest care possible for him, and the concerns we manifest for bench rest ammunition must be exactly the same for any other sort of load, even cannon-size hunting magnums, if we want the utmost from them.

It all starts with the case—the selection and preparation thereof. Most shooters working up ammunition for a new rifle, or a new batch for an old rifle, are willing to sort cases by unprimed weight. All we are checking by this procedure is relative capacity, which is another way of saying relative case-

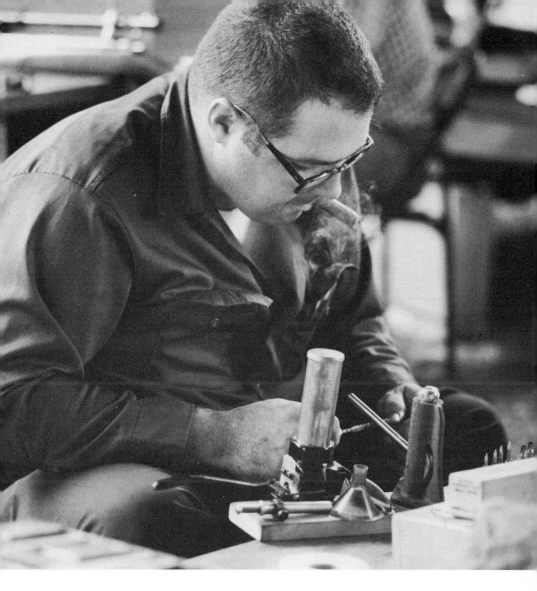

The smoking accuracy bug is not contemptuous of the relationship between cigar sparks and smokeless powder, since it is generally accepted that one famous reloader of the past, J. Bushnell Smith, ascended to heaven on the pillar of flame caused by his tossing hot tobacco ash into a large canister of shotgun powder, but he does have a clear idea of just how flammable powder is and is not. Note he is cleaning necks and the powder measure is empty.

wall and head thickness. With good brass of the same lot and make, weighing usually means little today, but common sense indicates that the precision reloader noting any significant weight difference will put the heavier smaller-capacity cases at one end of his block to be fired together, the lighter and so presumably thinner brass at the other. Such sorting is of course a must if we're working with pickup brass of mixed lots—which no sensible accuracy bug ever does.

Next step with the unprimed brass is to check primer flash holes for consistency. Most loading-tool and die makers offer gauges. Those from Huntington come in a set of four go-no-go plugs; the .081 will enter most .222 flash holes, the .089 size will not. Or you could use a #45 drill and clean all holes to .082, for example. Remember that if you drill out flash holes you also increase the passage of the primer flare and so alter pressures, and might have to reduce printed loads.

Next comes the matter of case neck turning, seldom if ever done with hunting ammunition, which usually is meant for fairly sloppy or near-maximum chambers, but commonly practiced for bench fodder intended for use in very close chambers, where without such turning the jam of bullet and brass in the neck might hoist pressures, make chambering the round difficult, and so on.

Reaming has largely been discarded on the grounds that it doesn't cure but may well perpetuate the unevenness of neck wall which is a primary bugaboo behind the need for neck treatment. Today the necks are outside-turned, either in a lathe, or in a Forster turning tool, or in the simple rigs recently dreamed up by Bob Hart and Ferris Pindell, to achieve uniformity in thickness, and .002 to .003 expansion in firing. If your cases are of a good lot and the neck walls show on a ball micrometer no variation more than .002, and if they apparently do not cause interference in the chamber, leave well enough alone. Too much turning down may so thin the neck walls as to cause them to lose reasonable grip on the bullets. That, someday, may mean powder spilled in the action, and a holy mess that can be, especially with ball powder.

Whereas hunting ammunition is often sized full-length in the interest of smooth feeding, there is no reason to overwork your brass this way for accuracy loads. Actually, the amount of sizing should be minimal. Many shooters use hand or hammer dies into which the fired case is driven with a soft hammer. Then the primer is pushed out and the case itself driven free with a depriming rod. There is no expander plug over which the case is pulled, as on a normal die used in a loading press, so these dies work only the neck section, and seldom all of that. They are one-piece straight-line equipment with no danger of misa-

Everybody but everybody loads their own cartridges during an accuracy match, even the ladies. Here Emily Shilen restuffs a batch of .222½ cases using one of the simple press designs which take the hand out of hand dies except for the priming stage. An accuracy shooter does not need power in a press but precision.

lignment of the case unless the die, which is usually made with the same tooling as the rifle's chamber, is somehow cockeyed. By the same token, in a standard-type $\frac{7}{8} \times 14$ die in a press, only the neck should be sized, usually to about a caliber depth or halfway down the neck, and the die and expander plug should be of such diameters that the resulting case will just hold the bullet firmly. This to avoid overworking the cases and shortening their life. Forty cases for a bench rest rifle will usually outwear the barrel. Since hauling a case back off an expander plug can stretch or misalign the case walls because of the leverage in a loading press, inside cleaning with a bristle brush before sizing is recommended.

The sizing procedure is usually just as critical to bullet seating, by the way, in causing bullet runout or wobble. Few presses are aligned dead zero, but if yours appears to be straight

Reloading equipment can be cheap or expensive, complex or simple, and sometimes a simple and well-made item does a better job than the fancy one. This is a Pindell-designed tool made for the job of outside-turning case necks to suit them to a tight chamber. It does require a vise but little else save common sense to do a job ordinarily requiring more complicated lathe-type tools.

and you still get runout it is probable that you are either pulling the case crooked over a large expander plug or your seater die is itself off-center slightly, the fault normally coming in the adjustable seater stem or punch with its conical hollow face. Valve-grinding compound on a bullet in a dummy load, rotated against that conical opening with the case well up into the die body while the die is held in one hand and the case head in the other, may work wonders.

Repriming cases is a matter of feel for most people, although a few dyed-in-the-wool fanatics use depth gauges to make certain each primer is seated to the precise depth indicated. If you carefully clean primer pockets between loadings, meaningful depth variations are unlikely, however, and it is interesting to note today that men with $1000 rifles and $1,000,000 reputations

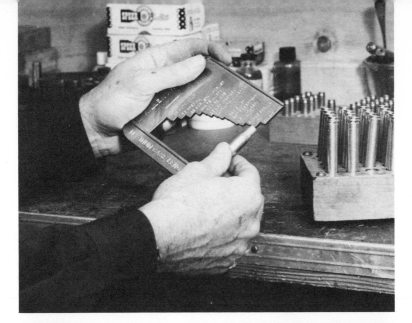

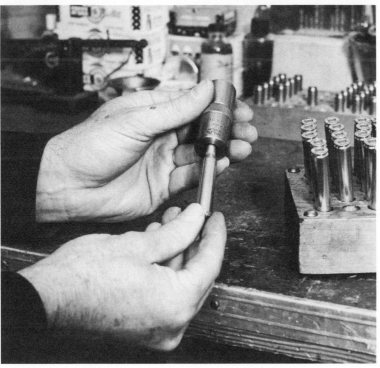

A vernier caliper or a crudely simple case gauge like the Mc-Killen and Heyer type will suffice for a regular check on overall case length, showing up any significant "growth" of the brass under constant use. The Wilson style of cylindrical case gauge, however, which will indicate overall length within acceptable limits and also show the headspace situation, is a superior design, provided you can buy enough for all your calibers.

are repriming their brass with the simple and almost absurdly cheap hand equipment made by Lee Loaders, with which it is possible to "feel" the primer into full seat very accurately. I for one think this is a far better procedure than using a press, and like the other more costly hand priming tools it has the great advantage of letting you sit and gossip while repriming your brass. Bench rest people between matches sound like a ladies' sewing circle.

To the layman, the business of weighing out powder in ultra-precise fashion seems to be a chief requirement in making precise ammunition. This is about 90 percent bunk. In this day and age virtually all powder dispensing is done at the match, by machine measures. No one, or certainly mighty few, owns enough matched cases to go through a whole match, a reasonable minimum requirement being eighty if you skip the warm-ups, or close to a hundred identical cases for the whole course for one rifle; and the once-common practice of home-weighing charges into little bottles, such as dentists get their novocaine in, and using these precise dosages at the match seems to have passed into discard. Perhaps novocaine is differently packed, or the shooters have discovered that even their time is worth something. Certainly more shooters vary their loads during the matches to suit the temperature or to cure stringing, or just for instance.

Further, all the better measures today, first choice among discerning competitors probably being the Lyman measure equipped with the micrometric drum and adjustment system made of brass by Homer Culver, will throw charges correct enough to keep muzzle velocities as close to standard as other factors will permit—provided, of course, that the measure is correctly operated and always operated the same way. The Culver device does throw very clean charges with a minimum of cutoff, but its great advantage lies in the accuracy with which any pre-established weight can be duplicated by setting the micro adjustments, an ability claimed for many measures, achieved by few.

The essential skill in using a measure properly, beyond the obvious need for keeping the powder reservoir at a reasonably constant depth, is to duplicate the speed and force of the movements for each charge, and to use the knocker, if any, the same amount at the same stage in the procedures for each charge. And if a long-grained powder hangs up your measure,

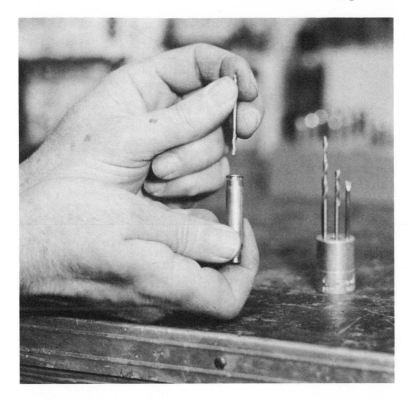

Gauging cartridge case flash holes can be done with a twist drill of proper size. The actual hole size is less important than that all be of identical diameter. Find the drill that will just enter into the largest hole in your lot of cases; then use it to bring the others up to that standard. Remember that larger flash holes demand lessened charges, of course.

dump that charge back and try again. But the weighing of charges is for primary setting of a measure, not for the improvement of accuracy by controlling the powder weight. That seems to be a much less important variable than others in the loading equation.

Bullet seating is certainly one of those. As has been earlier mentioned, with a powder really too slow for the capacity of the case (as H-380 in the 6×47 or even the .308) it is a necessity to seat bullets so that they are in hard contact with the lands, in order to keep pressures high and constant. For a good many years, this idea of pre-engraving of the bullet by land contact held sway among the accuracy clan; and with some rifles and loads, it is still productive of the best accuracy.

More generally, however, the practices of today call for seating the bullet so that the primer force will give it about $\frac{1}{16}$ inch of jump or free forward movement before coming into contact with the edges of the lands. The best system for establishing this with a rifle of unknown throat characteristics involves making up a dummy round with the bullet seated rather shallow. Bolt this into the chamber. It will probably show contact marks, engraving from the land corners. Seat it a full turn of the die more deeply (which will be $\frac{1}{14}$ inch deeper with a stan-

Since loading at the matches is inevitable, standard practice— virtually no one has enough identical brass to shoot the entire series—accuracy bugs tote along considerable gadgetry, tools, components, whim-whams, and unidentifiables. Neater than some, West Coast rifleman Tom Seitz, to whom these hands belong, has already put away his sizing and priming equipment and powder measure and is finishing use of a straight-line seater of the "hand" type now almost universal.

dard $\frac{7}{8} \times 14$ die) and again look for the marks. If they persist, go in another turn, and so on until the bullet is seated below land contact by a full die-body turn, which will give you the $\frac{1}{16}$ jump or so close to it as to make little difference. You can then observe, with a micrometer set at the .223 point, where that point is on the bullet and remember it for future reference, should it be necessary to reset the die. This try-and-set system works well enough but is not advisable with live ammunition. Use a dummy.

Somewhere between $\frac{1}{16}$ inch of jump and actual land contact will probably be the most effective seating situation for your rifle; rarely is more jump called for. Bear in mind that bullets of different lots from the same maker may well have been swaged in a forming die of different point contours, so that a seating check is necessary whenever you change bullets; and that most rifles betray considerable sensitivity to this factor in loading.

Needless to say, bullet alignment is of equal importance, since it is grossly evident that a bullet started cockeyed can hardly end up precisely straight. Simple chamfering of the case mouth will solve a lot of bullet straightness problems, especially with sharp-cornered flat-based bullets, the dovetail type having an understandable ability to funnel themselves in; but on occasion, as mentioned earlier, off-center necks or uneven necks will cock the bullet in relation to the bore. On the market today there are precise straight-line seaters, custom hand forms made with the chambering tools used for a given rifle, and also commercial straight-line seaters operating on the Vickery principle, one or the other of which is highly recommended for precision loading. And there are today a variety of alignment-checking machines in which the loaded case can be turned for a most precise check, even "bent" slightly to correct any error.

Seating of bullets in hunting loads is considerably less critical or complex. Since a repeating rifle would no longer be a repeater if the bullets were set so far out they contacted the lands or jumped a sixteenth or whatever, but would not go into the magazine, common sense here indicates that the primary consideration must be magazine length. Screw the seater in until the full-length round will feed smoothly. Then, if it happens because of an odd-ogived bullet to be in contact with the lands, screw the adjustment in further, since with a hunting load you obviously do not wish, in emptying the chamber, to fill it with powder grains left if the bullet sticks in the throat. The rule, then, is simple: seat back until the lands are cleared and the magazine will feed slickly. But don't seat any more deeply than is necessary to fulfill those needs.

A device commonly used in accuracy loading is the bullet spinner, made by Dewey, Hart, and others. A bullet turned by the fingers between two centers and against a dial indicator shows off any common fault, such as a base not perpendicular to the bullet axis, any deformation of the base especially at the edges from rough handling (an excellent reason *not* to transport bullets in glass jars or metal containers unless padded against any rattling), or variation in the radius of the corner where base and shank meet. The spinner does not, as some believe, turn up bullets which are simply out of round—it probably would, but I don't recall ever having bumped into any such in some years of bullet spinning. It does, however, tattle on the base and the base corner.

That can be important, since evidently if a bullet does not exit from the bore at absolutely the same instant all the way around, or if gas leakage past the edge is permitted by any roughness in the edge or any unevenness in the curve of the corner, the high-pressure gases escaping past the open spot will tend to upset that bullet, cock it, and so destroy accuracy. This is not a novel conception. The inimitable Dr. Mann may have worked with black powders or primitive smokeless and he may have used lead bullets driven at less than half the speed of our present jacketed accuracy pills, but he proved conclusively that whereas a misshapen bullet point had little or no effect on grouping, a cocked, cut, or slanted base destroyed it completely.

The great problem of today has been to develop statistical evidence as to the effect of very minor bullet base faults that are discoverable on a spinner. At least thirty groups must be fired under controlled and identical conditions to prove an error of .01 with acceptable reliability, or so the statisticians say. The result is that not all accuracy bugs spin their bullets to pick those showing less than .004 and usually less than .002 swing variation on the indicator, yet we all might do so profitably where flat-based bullets are concerned. With taper-tails or boattails, forget it, since the spinner then rarely measures what it's expected to.

Probably the hardest part of the precision-loading game for the beginning shooter to accept is the idea of individual load

All that the hand reloader needs and then some, except for the powder measure, is shown here. Actually, even the bottle-capper style of simple press is not necessary. Left to right: primer and bullet trays, a bottle of bullets, the press with a seater base in place, the straight-line seater under the partially loaded cartridge block, a hammer-type neck-sizing and decapping die, a simple recapping tool, a soft-headed mallet, and can of powder. What the rubber band and camera lens ring are for I have no idea.

tailoring to the individual rifle. He has read of this procedure but really has no idea of how demanding a procedure it can be. The concept of waiting always for the best possible conditions for testing loads (as distinct from practicing for competition, where the shooting should be done under rotten, or at least average, conditions) and of shooting enough groups to have some fair meaning, and of changing only one major variable at a time instead of a haphazard jugglery of bullet, charge, seating depth and holding technique all at once—all these demand a patience rare in beginning shooters but necessary in successful ones.

And the one firm recommendation I would make for anyone interested in precision reloading, whether for hunting, varminting, competition, or just to better his own test results, is to go to two or three bench rest matches. You may or may not be moved to join the games. You will certainly be amazed by the variety of the equipment, some of it handsomely homemade by men who are by either avocation or vocation highly skilled machinists. But you will also inevitably find out more about precision reloading in two or three such afternoons than you could by reading several books like this one, and more in a day than you'd pick up dubbing around by yourself for a month of Sundays.

18

Big Guns,
Little Holes

At once the original and the ultimate end product of all this accuracy interest is the big rifle, the ultimate cannon permitted under the rules. It has to be remembered that when modern bench rest shooting first started in the late '40s and early '50s its practioners took a leaf from the "hog rifle" shooters of the last century who had fired ponderous black-powder equipment, with huge bullets of paper-patched lead, from muzzle rests. Hence in the twentieth century they adopted rules which permitted any centerfire rifle, trigger-finger-fired, regardless of weight. In practical terms this at the time amounted to a shooting iron that looked pretty much like a conventional but obese rifle, one weighing anywhere from 15 to 20 pounds. Items much heavier weren't then very practical because we didn't have actions for super-fat barrels, although weights soon got to the point where John Collins built a golf cart arrangement to wheel his "regular bench rifle" up to the firing line. Even so, onlookers at bench rest competitions eyed such equipment with awe, and usually asked questions beginning with "Whazzat?"

Exemplary of the modern approach in accuracy rifles of un-limited weight is this .308 being tested by precisionist Ferris Pindell. The massive piece depends on mated steel blocks as described in the text to fasten barrel and action on the stock, both the forward section of the barrel and the action proper being left free to vibrate. The scope is mounted on the blocks with a bar. Here set up to be fired off sandbags, during such tests this rifle fired three consecutive 5-shot groups measuring .106, .122, and .150, for an average of .126, suggesting that the millennium of every bullet precisely through the same hole is not unattainable.

They had even more reason for such queries when ingenious souls realized that the principles of the machine rest, or more correctly the return-to-battery rest, could be employed so that the relationship between the rifle and its supports could be not merely that of a gun sitting on sandbags but of a shooting machine in V-blocks or their mechanical equivalent. The firing device—and I'll never forget the appearance at Johnstown of a dingbat which for its stability depended on a piece of heavy plate glass, across which recoiled a gun-carrying cradle born of a union between a flying shingle and a Waring blender—went through all manner of complexities. Wayne Leek had one which always reminded me of the Chesapeake Bay Bridge. These did produce as a side benefit the Iron Mike devices now

Pindell's barely credible target, reproduced life-size. What next?

used by rifle and bullet makers in comparison tests. Eventually they settled down into reasonable form and today we have rests of deceptively simple appearance. In these a rifle which is recognizable as a rifle—albeit hardly as a Griffin & Howe .270 sporter, since for one thing it weighs between 20 and 40 pounds, usually about 30—can be fired and then returned to zero in battery position so unerringly that repeat-shot sighting is superfluous.

When fired off such a rest, the so-called unlimited rifle—unlimited as to weight, caliber, barrel size or shape, sighting equipment, but manually fired—becomes in today's usage an *experimental* rifle, as indeed it is. And presumably for the sake of evening-out competition, matches are so designed that such shooting devices can be segregated from those unlimited rifles that are fired off sandbags—that is to say, off a rear rest which does not use any return-to-zero mechanics but instead a nonadjustable rear sandbag, malleable with the fingers.

Some would immediately jump to the conclusion that the return-to-battery rig would nearly always win the potted petunias, since target displacement by mirage is one of the problems facing the group shooter, and obviously a rifle which need not be sighted should in no sense be bothered by mirage variations. But the fact also exists that mirage variation also indicates wind variation, the second of the problems bothering the group-shooting enthusiast, and while the no-aiming combination may handle optical flukes it does nothing for the switches in wind effect. Indeed the full return-to-battery outfit usually adjusts so slowly that holding for wind change becomes difficult.

In point of fact, the sandbag shooters win their share of open competitions. The 1972 NBRSA crown went, for example, to Texan T. J. Jackson, who put together four days of shooting, ten ten-shot groups at 100 yards averaging .3529, and ten ten-shot groups at 200 averaging .4408, for a grand aggregate of .3969, and Jackson shot off sandbags all the way. That he fired a .22–45 (the .222 magnum wildcatted with a 45-degree shoulder) at the shorter yardage, and chose a .308 for the longer, merely reflects a point widely accepted among the accuracy clan that the .30-caliber, provided the rifle develops recoil acceptable to the shooter, as would be the case with the big guns, is less wind-flustered than the .22s. It says nothing about sandbags versus rests. And the life history in big-rifle competition of Ralph Stolle, who has won enough silverware to stuff several closets and as far as I know has stuck with sandbags, is another case in point.

The moral is that no shooter need be frightened off big-rifle competition by the anticipated costs and trouble of the return-to-battery equipment. He can be in the ball game using sandbag equipment closely similar to that preferred by the varmint-rifle shooters.

These big rifles, as you've noted, shoot a very different course of fire from the practical-weight equipment, four times as many shots from the one class of rifle, and believe me, a ten-shot string is far harder to maintain than a five. The rule of thumb has in the past been that a five-round group from any given rifle-ammunition combination usually averages in size 70 percent of a ten-shotter fired by the same combination and under the same circumstances. Part of that difference derives from the likelihood of mechanical variance, which of course increases with the greater number of shots. Much of it, undoubtedly, comes from the simple human problem of doing the same things in the same way and in the right way ten times rather than five. After all, the shooter is exposed to the whimsies of wind and mirage twice as long!

In any event, where the aggregates at the national event Jackson won at 100 yards (for ten ten-shotters now) ranged for the top twenty shooters from a high of .3255 to a low (low?) of .4023, it took some spectacular numbers to win individual matches. Like the .189 Prachyl fired. Ten rounds, into a not-very-bulgy hole.

The costs of competing with such ultra-close-shooting unlimited equipment may run a trifle higher than with varmint-weight pieces because you shoot up roughly twice as many components and probably wash out barrel throats a bit faster, but, as Ferris Pindell recently pointed out in a long letter to me, it is hard to prove any vast differential in original rifle costs. The actions are much the same; the barrels are much the same; the scopes usually identical; and while the stocks utilize more wood, usually enough to keep a large fireplace contented all winter, a high percentage of unlimited rifles use "bedding" systems that permit switching various barreled actions onto the one stock, using just the one scope.

Common is the scheme—the forefather of the epoxy no-bedding system already described in Chapter 15—involving barrel blocks. According to Pindell, these are usually two steel blocks $1\frac{1}{2} \times 3\frac{1}{2} \times 5$ inches, held together with eight $\frac{5}{16}$-18 socket-head screws and then bored to a plug gauge fit for the 5 inches of the barrel immediately ahead of the receiver. The blocks are then lapped to precise barrel diameter, a close fit. Then one block is ground off .010 to make certain of proper clamping on the barrel. It is usual practice to mount the scope on a bar across the upper block.

The blocks should be of steel normalized to 1200 degrees to avoid hole enlargement under firing vibration. With the action and barrel free-floated, the block is held onto or into the stock by a plate on the underside.

Much the same approach is used with opposed V-blocks, with which of course the trial of assorted barreled actions on the one stock outfit is even easier, since dimensions are so much less critical. The only requirement is a straight-sided barrel, untapered at least in the block-supported section.

The almost serene reliability of these big rifles leads many shooters to believe that unlimited competition is actually the best sort of preparation, perhaps with a few years of outdoor rimfire work, for top performance with accuracy rifles of more practical weight or type. The shooter must in each match deal with the problems of mirage change or wind shift not for five but for ten shots, and he can concentrate on these absolutely because the shooting machine he is using will surely respond to each decision by him. In short, if he judges that the conditions warrant his holding left a third of an inch or say a bullet hole and a half, he can so hold in confidence that the resulting bullet print will not have been fouled up by some rifle error.

There's much to be said for this approach, and while it may seem to some to be the big leap, entering the bench game can intelligently be done via the big-rifle route. Another element here, of course, is that the more massive rifles make it easier to prove out technical points, experiments, development ideas, since if with a big rifle you make a change in components, for example, your firing tests will accurately reflect the effect of the change without also suggesting that perhaps your bedding has gone sour or that you're not holding well that day.

The basic purpose of these super-sized rifles, after all, was precisely that—to advance the cause of accuracy by experiment that might later be applied to shooting-weight equipment. The effect of advances with the unlimiteds is already obvious on

An unlimited-weight rifle, here set up on return-to-battery rests for firing in the experimental class, which uses the steel bedding blocks but deviates from most modern usage by the placement of the scope on action and barrel.

the heavy-varmint, light-varmint, and sporter categories, some of which are nothing but unlimiteds that have been slightly miniaturized; and there's no particular reason why much of their experimental indications can't be carried even further into outright hunting, and varmint shooting. They've long since cropped up in target rifles, heaven knows—at the 1970 World Shoot in Phoenix I saw one 300-meter hopeful, an Australian, toting up to the firing line a musketoon featuring the bedding-block system here described. He never saw that on a kangaroo!

19

Cleanliness Is Godliness

Anyone who has ever visited the kind of garage in which racing cars of Grand Prix quality are built cannot fail to have been struck by one aspect of the operation—its surgical cleanliness. And much the same applies to accuracy rifles. If they are to shoot superbly well they must be kept superbly clean.

Many rimfire shooters brag that they never have to clean their rifle bores, the combination of modern priming compounds and soft-lead bullets performing that function to perfection, they say. But the same can hardly be remarked of centerfire barrels for high-velocity loadings. Here the need is grossly evident. I for one may seem to have denied that need in earlier magazine writings in which I made the point that only a really serious rainfall or dropping a rifle overboard would bring me to cleaning a hunting musket during the course of a hunt. My thought was—and still is—that an occasional swipe-through with a dry patch is adequate for any but those most desperate situations, on the grounds that it is the habit of most hunting rifles to throw the first shot unpredictably out of the fouled-barrel impact area, and that the likelihood of rusting was almost nil in the course of the average hunt. Since I still feel that way, and on African safaris, for example, I make sure that the trusty gunbearer Mgugu keeps his mitts off my guns, at least as far as the bores are concerned. Why? First because I do not want them gunked up with some English-style mixture of sperm oil and furniture wax with a resultant wet-barrel shot in some generally southwesterly direction, but also because he may mix up the bolts as did Brandy Macomber's boy once. That can later lead to scrambling your brains.

Competition rifles are something else again. Quite. The simplest of experiments will make this clear. Assuming you have a close-shooting bench or varmint rifle, one reliable enough so its group measurements have meaning, sit down with a block of ammunition and fire several strings of five-shot groups. By all means take your time, so that the barrel does not overheat. It is an odds-on bet that by the fourth or fifth string the groups will have started to open up. Obviously this is related not to barrel heating but to bore fouling. Proof? Clean the barrel by scrubbing it thoroughly with a brass bristle brush of proper diameter—make your passes clear through the tube each way, two to four passes for each wetting of the brush and perhaps eight in all. Then run one wet patch followed by three dry patches through the barrel and start your shooting sequences again. The situation will repeat itself, with normally tight groups until you have fired upward of twenty rounds, then a slow opening of the spreads.

Competition rifles, then, should be cleaned after each match, certainly after any fifteen-round firing sequence, if they are to maintain top performance. Habitually, 90 percent of bench rest competitors clean after each match, which is to say after each six to twelve shots.

Note that I have so far made no reference to the cleaning agent. Frankly, I am not at all sure it makes all that much difference, there being several good bore cleaners and powder solvents on the market. I use Hoppe's No. 9 for two reasons: I always have and I like the smell of it. But if you reckon Gunslick or G-66 or Old Man Mose's Genuine Tiger Milk works better, that's your dish.

There is, of course, one minor nicety about Hoppe's which does not seem to be widely shared. Quite aside from powder fouling, which in a small way is no disaster and is usually handled by normal cleaning procedures, some barrels, for whatever reason of internal roughness, tool or reamer marks, tend to accumulate streaks and lumps of bullet-jacket metal. Such metal fouling can of course be catastrophic, since subsequent bullets passing over any such lumps are themselves deformed, and of course any shot which happens to take out with it the accumulated gilding metal is going to fly off somewhere behind the barn. If you leave your bore well wet with Hoppe's for a night or two, then run a clean white patch through as a check, the patch from a barrel with any significant metal fouling tendency will show grass-green streaks of cuprous metal. A serious scrubbing may solve the problem if it is temporary; if the tube regularly fouls and a harder-jacketed bullet at lowered velocities does not prevent it, the best cure is a new barrel.

There has been hot debate over the use of either abrasives or chemicals to cure the metal fouling problem. I have even heard advocated a touching-up with steel wool. Not in my barrels, chum! Some fifteen years ago a Pittsburgh firm dealing in grinding compounds did offer a paste of jeweler's rouge in oil, and it was quickly discovered that such an extremely fine abrasive, used with discretion, would take out caked powder residues and mild metal streaking without ruining the bore. That gunk came to be marketed among shooters as J-B Compound. It would on occasion completely rejuvenate a barrel seemingly shot out but actually suffering from bad fouling. Nonetheless, unwisely used it could have a lapping effect and bell the muzzle and chamber ends. While today virtually all highly accurate barrels receive a final lapping during manufacture, it seems only discreet to have said lapping done only by the original maker.

The chemical removers—usually functioning with the action of ammonia or something equally as strong and equally as likely to cause corrosion if incorrectly used—will also remove accumulated gunk. At least one shooter of my acquaintance purges his tubes with all the enthusiasm that frontierswomen once applied to dosing their young with spring tonics. He wins matches, too. But the treatment seems harsh, with danger for the careless, and I for one will stick to regular cleaning with milder agents, the brass brush, Hoppe's, and patches.

A first-rate barrel, incidentally, will not throw its first or dry-clean-tube shot significantly away from the fouled-tube impact, so that in bench competition the first round into a sighter target has meaning. As a matter of habit, I usually fire

The sub-small calibers like the .17, which develop virtually no recoil even in a light rifle like this factory H&R model, can be fired from a low rest position. However, since they have a tendency to foul, regular cleaning is advisable. A good .224 will go 20-25 rounds before showing any tendency to enlarge its spread, a .17 roughly half that, in my experience. Match shooters clean even .224s with consistent and standardized procedures after each match, after 7-12 rounds.

The lively little .17—posed here on a shooter's thumb—is of interest in semi-settled areas for varminting but as yet has made no accuracy records.

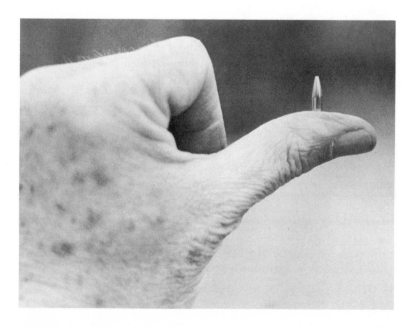

two on the sighter before moving up onto the scoring target, but there are situations when this is a waste of time and powder. The difference between true accuracy rifles and thin-barreled sporters in this respect I assume has more to do with the relative violence of the cartridges and the relative stiffness of the barrels than with any factor of bore quality.

Contemporary accuracy rifles almost uniformly come with 2-ounce or similarly delicate trigger mechanisms, which do not respond well to most oils, certainly not to any gum. On them, the tiniest bit of one of the new space-age synthetics or a very occasional spray with one of the molybdenum types is ample. If your bolt lugs or bolt body show any tendency toward stiffness or galling, chances are that after careful wiping off to get rid of gritty powder residue, the moly treatment or a tiny dab of Rig will cure any problem. Much the same treatment is indicated on the bearing surfaces of a sliding or target-style scope.

It is easy to over-oil a rifle, and let me say here and now that constant dousing of the "works" with a lubricant, any lubricant, will eventually ensure that the wood in the action area, especially around the rear tang, becomes punky, soft enough so that the bedding is in a state of constant change. The rifle will go sour and the shooter sourer. I ruined a Stinehour-stocked 6×47 in this fashion. After soaking, its bedding never stayed constant.

There have been some hot arguments about case neck polishing, primer-pocket cleaning, and the like. I recall deliberately going through one entire competitive season without ever cleaning primer pockets or wiping off case necks, and was unable to see that it made a darned bit of difference in what I did or didn't win. Senseless.

It is absurd to buy a precision-made rifle in which the chamber has been cut so close that case necks of standard wall thickness tend to jam in the throat, one so close that the necks must be turned to permit a very mild but adequate grip on the bullet yet only .001 to .002 of firing expansion, and then to shoot it with brass carrying a thick accumulation of powder crud. The sin thereof lies not so much in raising pressures as it does in possible variance of pressure. Therefore by all means keep your cases clean, with a bit of old toweling faintly redolent of Hoppe's or some like solvent, or even a wipe of crocus cloth; and by all means keep the primer pockets decently clean so that primers are always seated with the same force and to the same depth. Dewey's Crocagator or, if you can find an old-timer and borrow a file, a pocket cleaner-outer made from a small-sized cartridge case will do that just dandy.

You will never, incidentally, see a brass or aluminum cleaning rod in an accuracy fan's work area. He will give house room to only two types: the one-piece steel rod by Belding & Mull, or the imported plastic-coated Parker Hale rods. The reason is simple. Neither has the tendency, common to soft brass, of picking up bits of grit and dirt—remember that glass is common in primer mixes—to scratch the chamber throat. And he will almost without fail realize that chambers can be worn oval by overenergetic use of a cleaning rod, so will always employ one of the simple rod guides made by Bob Hart, Taylor & Robbins, or half a dozen others. These slide into the action much like a bolt and keep the rod dead centered in its back-and-forth movement. I for one have become so accustomed to these that every rifle rod I own comes so equipped, except for a fat steel rod I use on cannons like the .375 and larger, and there's hardly need to clean them often!

20

The Makings of
the Accuracy Nut

The idea of an accurate rifle is readily comprehensible to anybody; and all agree that within reason accuracy is desirable. It is only when this idea is carried to its ultimate conclusion, that no level of accuracy larger than a pinhead is acceptable, that the true nut stays with it. And please believe me, while you do not really have to be mildly mad to become an accuracy fan, it helps. It helps.

You must, for example, be prepared to make profound adjustments with your wife. She must be persuaded to see some sense in your absenting yourself from her chatty society or from the soothing syrup of the television set in order to flap a loading-tool handle up and down, endlessly up and down, in the manufacture of bullets which you'll use merely to punch holes in paper.

And when it comes up a shoot weekend, as I see it you must follow one of three courses. First—and not necessarily the most desirable—you must fill her full of the old togetherness con, persuade her to come to the shoot with you. There she can, after all, share with you the delight of living in a cramped trailer at the range, in a temperature of 116 degrees and no shower, or she can remain at an air-conditioned motel with nothing to do except watch the maid clean the room. If she doesn't shoot, she goes quietly mad trying to knit, snooze, or read while the Battle of the Bulge is fought about 50 yards away. If she does shoot, as her spouse you will have to fret over her rifle and load her ammunition, only to get your britches shot off for your pains when the final results are posted.

Of course, husband-shooter, you can just up and leave her at home alone, in which event you are of course a graceless and selfish boor, forever after the object of disparaging remarks, not to mention a considerable amount of hardly concealed glee when you sneak home from a bench match with no trophy beyond a bumped nose. Gentry who follow this course expect to get nagged a bit. A bit, the man says!

Or you can adopt the craven course and buy her off. You go to the bench matches, but she barges off in her own car with a chunk of travel money from you in her hot little hand, to visit Cousin Geraldine or spend the weekend on Beach Sandy Cliff or worse yet, to spend Saturday on a shopping spree. For every group of .250 or better you fire, she'll shoot $250.

Assuming you can indeed arrange a *modus operandi* with your wife which will permit you to continue shooting and her to continue living with you, you're off to the matches. Now what does it take to win?

First, you must have better control of your emotions than Jack Nicklaus. If you misread the mirage and get caught at 200 yards in a full switch, and so produce a group which some fiendish measurer with a yardstick assures you makes 2.758 inches, you cannot fly into a temper. You cannot cuss and swear and kick trees and bite babies. You cannot threaten to sell all your rifles for 98 cents and do all the other tension-relieving things one really should do when confronted with the horrid truth that he has just, with that one lousy round, shot himself out of the championship. No, you must control your frenzy, it says here. You must gulp and accept the awful fact, and with icy control set yourself to the task of getting .006 next time. That'll balance off your bad guess and you can hope that every other guy on the firing line will goof during the day and fire his own 2.758 group. They won't, but you're supposed to believe they might.

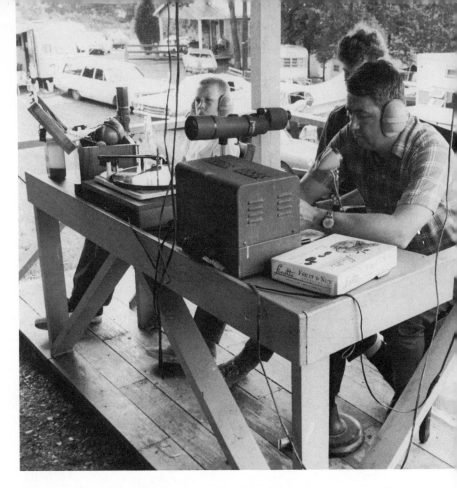

Maestro of the range, any range, is the range officer. In full regalia, with ear protectors, microphone, squawk box amplifier, player for between-match music, and sustenance against possible starvation is Wallace Hart, who almost never gets to shoot at his home range in Pennsylvania, unless owner Bob Hart takes over the microphone job. The spotter is for use on reported crossfires.

You must also be possessed of a fair degree of plain stupidity. For example, all the statistical evidence I have just made up shows that an accuracy shooter reaches his performance peak somewhere between his third and tenth year of competition, usually from his fifth to eighth. He is on his second or third set of rifles then, rifles which are correctly made and in the correct calibers to be truly competitive; he has learned all he may ever know about the effects of wind and mirage; and his eyes are still young enough to be able to see what's really cooking out there. Somewhere within that stage our hero gets hot, his rifles get hot, and he is for a few seasons darned near unbeatable, winning tinware here, genuine potmetal trophies there, and in general earning the respect of all the other gun nuts. Even, sometimes, of his wife.

But that stage passes. After a time some other character with five to eight years' shooting takes his place in the top five and the top ten and then in the top twenty and our shooter friend eventually wakes up to the fact that after two decades in the game he hasn't really learned one damned thing. Lots of experience, yes, and a collection of alibis to cover every situation,

Between matches, during a target change or a backer break-down, the atmosphere on the firing line becomes desultory, almost somnolent. Here during the 1970 Nationals at Tulsa, I discuss and cuss the mirage with a group of Southwestern shooters; Bill Schellert at left, the late Dr. Sam Nadler at far right, and standing center a well-known Texas competitor un-named because of the probability, from his glum expression, that his wife beat him in the last match. The plastic-wrapped lady is unidentified.

but he still really can't say precisely how much he should lean into that wind or this mirage situation any better than he could at the five-year mark. Of course the old-timer catches a trophy now and then, much as an old blind dog locates a truffle under a tree stump. After my first heyday in the early '60s I latched onto IBS national championships, even a three-gun, in '70 and '71. It's just an ever longer time between the now and the then.

I ask you, does a man have to be more than slightly stupid to get himself into that condition? To do so deliberately?

The truly successful accuracy nut must also develop a superior type of forgetter. For example, some six or eight years back at Wapwallopen I had the three-gun aggregate in the hollow

Typical of layouts in the West and Southwest, the Tulsa range uses benches with cast concrete tops and cinder-block legs, hardly the world's most comfortable shooting table but one of the steadiest. Here I am shooting a heavy varminter of conventional design made by Ed Shilen, second shooter to my left.

of my hand. Just one more respectable 200-yard group and I was in. The first four shots made a scattery but acceptable cloverleaf pattern. The flags looked right, the breeze felt right, the mirage looked right, so I let go #5. Bob Hart, who as owner of the range ought to know its quirks rather well, was standing behind me and I heard him sigh as I shoved the gun forward to look at the target. He had a right to sigh. I had the right to commit suicide. Number 5 had flipped off to the left over two inches. "Warren," said Bob, "I was praying you wouldn't shoot, but you couldn't hear me. Everything was right except one thing—when those high trees up back of target five or six begin to turn their leaves that means a breeze has whipped out of the field off to the right there and you'd better not shoot." Obviously not, judging from where the shot—and my chance at the three-gun aggregate for that year—had gone. So where does the forgetter come in? Well, only last summer at Wapwallopen I had fired a nice four-shot clump, then blew it to nearly two inches for no known reason except that—you guessed it—those damned trees were turning over again! A forgetter is very handy. Like what a woman has after childbirth, it eases the pain.

And the serious accuracy bug periodically does need something to ease the pain.

Even with all these sterling attributes, of course, the accuracy fanatic will probably achieve little, seriously, unless he somewhere develops the three-way knack of concentrating absolutely, of being willing to take exhaustive care, and of coming to believe implicitly in his own reading of shooting conditions.

As for concentration, he who in a match worries about the performance of any more than one person besides himself is doomed to lose. If after you've fired your group you run up to the wailing wall, or sweep your scope up and down the target line, in order to see what every other Tom, Dick, and Harry has come up with, the end result can only be utter confusion and the feeling that you are, after one bad group, totally lost. The spouse of the late Larry Rucker, known to all as Katie, used to keep a running aggregate so that anyone even faintly in contention could learn from her where he ranked, but I for one always found this more distraction than aid, since inevitably it brought about tightening, the clutch feeling, and there went the ball game. For whatever it's worth to other competitive shooters, if you feel you must shoot not so much against your-

Life on the range has changed over the years. Once match competitors stayed in motels, loaded in their cars. Nowadays the big rage is the trailer, tent, or camper, and most loading is done on tables set up under awnings. And the whole family comes to the shoot, from the baby to granddad.

self—which is totally defeating to some mentalities—but rather against somebody, then pick on somebody who is in your own relay, who is a friend, and who above all is a consistently competent shot. Then, like the chap who plays tennis with a man one step better than he, you may well outdo yourself.

For the more than twenty years that we have known each other, Mike Walker and I have shot against each other whenever possible. At least I've always been conscious of shooting against him, my reasoning being that if I stayed even or ahead of him I'd rarely be out of the money. That way no need existed to worry about the performance of some ten-day wonder at the other end of the firing line who produced a .184 to win the first match, .175 to take the second, and then with a pair around .8 blew the whole shebang. There are always at least six people who do that at every major match.

Exhaustive care is presumably built into accuracy work. That is, we must not only duplicate hold and firing conditions absolutely for each shot but must also go through agonies in the preparation of our loads, the matching of cases, the total concentricity of bullet and case, etc. *ad infinitum.* The more methodical the shooter is, the better he should do in the long run, because he leaves no detail to vary.

This is necessary as far as it goes, but I have always felt some people carry it to fruitless extremes. It has been repeatedly demonstrated, for example, that with a free-flowing powder

Trailers, tents, mobile homes, and campers have become standard equipment among the competition clan, since most ranges have plug-in facilities and are located well away from motels. Either two or three meals a day are ordinarily available at the clubhouse. A sharp-eyed shooter, incidentally, would note that the U.S. flag is blowing in one direction, the flags on the range front in another. The chances are pretty good the mid-range ribbons are moving in a third. C'est la vie at Fassett.

If the rifles could somehow be silenced a bench rest firing range would be as quiet as a tomb, since the absolute concentration demanded, perfectly exemplified here in the faces of these Pennsylvania shooters, permits very little casual chatter. In some matches, shooters who have finished their string must remain quietly at their benches until the "Cease fire" command has been given.

and a reasonably good measure, weighing out each charge offers no advantage over thrown charges. By the same token, some of us meticulously polish each case neck between shots until the loaded rounds glisten like jewels. That's no guarantee of success, either. As I stated earlier, as a blow for independence I once went through an entire season without ever cleaning a case neck or a primer pocket, and that was by and large a winning season. But sloppiness is just as goofy the other way. It is evident that powder residue build-up on a case neck can become lopsided, can have much the same effect as uneven thickness of the brass itself, and primer pockets loaded with crud obviously are not going to ensure proper primer seating. The idea, then is to be careful, to repeat everything, work on the basis of constant duplication and identical materials. Just don't be a damned fool about it.

The business of believing in what you see out there in that mystery land of wind and mirage between you and the target is, I feel, of vast importance if you enter the accuracy game with any idea of winning. Let no man tell you different—the chap who is consistently shooting good groups in a set of conditions that has other shooters, at least his peers and maybe his betters, mumbling to themselves has for whatever reason

Feature of every range because it is the scene of both triumph and bitter disappointment is the Wailing Wall, where targets are posted after measuring and recording. This one happens to be in Pennsylvania but the scene is universal. So today is the presence of lady shooters both at and in the competition. The dark-haired damsel at right, Jim Stekl's wife Donalee, is not only mother of two but also the bane of most male shooters' existence, since she wins aggregates and breaks records as easy as making breakfast toast, and almost as often.

on that day not only found the combination but really *believes* he has found it. He can *think* that fifth shot plunk into the hole.

Bear in mind that your view of the conditions and that of the guy one or two benches along the line is not the same. Repeatedly neighbor shooters have this experience: A reads the pickup of wind and mirage as being worth, say, a half-inch. Lacking time to wait things out, he holds accordingly and his bullet goes just about where he wants it to. B, one or two benches over, at the same time reads the conditions in much the same way, holds over half an inch, but sees his bullet hole prove that he obviously should have aimed over a whole inch and a half! Yet both shot at virtually the same instant. Or, A sees things as above, holds his half-inch, and hits in the group. B reads the conditions differently, feels he should hold over an inch, and still plops it in, firing at the same time as A and from only a bench or two away. What *you* think is going on, and what its effect will be, is nine times out of ten more nearly correct than what some other gink thinks; and just because Joe Hotshot has, or says he has, discovered that watching the extreme right-hand flag at the 100-yard line is the secret of his dinky little groups at 200 is not necessarily reason to believe you should pin your faith in that particular bit of wavering ribbon. Pay no attention to what the other geniuses say. Work out your own pattern, bearing in mind, of course, that whatever combination of flags and mirage gives you solid indications at one end of the range may not work for sour apples at the other. That's why rotation of benches separates the men from the boys.

Finally, let me again repeat that the successful accuracy shooter is usually a man of smooth and even temper. He does not let himself become disturbed readily. He does not, for example, swear and kick the bench post because an unseen Wapwallopen zephyr has just moved his fifth shot an inch over into nice clean paper. He does not gnash his teeth when he discovers that one of the milder Midland hurricanes has him holding four inches upwind of the whole blooming target paper in order to get his group somewhere inside the borders. And of course he does not smash his loading stool and scream that he'll never come near the place again when one of those sneaky little Fassett flippers flips his second shot over $\frac{3}{4}$ inch when every flag in the place was hanging straight down. No, the accuracy bug is a marvel of even temperament. It says here!

21

The Improvement
of the Breed

One of the more famous firearms writers of our time, a man widely respected in the trade and by the shooting public, has several times expressed the idea that those accuracy fans who manifest themselves as bench rest shooters are a bunch of nuts. They deal, he contends, with rifles of such weird characteristics that they're impractical anywhere but on a bench, and are working toward a level of perfection which is so impossible of attainment as to verge on the absurd. In total, he indicates, they're messing about with the ridiculous and contributing nothing at all to the practical.

The man has never, so far as I know, attended a bench rest match. It is certain that he has never shot in one. Hence his opinions are decidedly suspect. They smack of the attitude of the countryman who, when he viewed his first street car, stoutly averred, "It won't run," and when the tram did indeed move off down the street shouted, "It'll never stop."

The plain fact is that the accuracy search, whether it be conducted by the lone reloader and rifle-tinkerer who tests his tries over a log or off a handy bench rest, or by the more sophisticated shooter who dives into the mysteries of bench rest competition, has indeed contributed to modern riflery. Not always in the amount or direction hoped for, to be sure, but a major contribution nonetheless.

When the concept of a national association for the bench rest clan was new, its announced purposes were (a) to develop extreme accuracy in rifles, ammunition, equipment, and shooting methods; (b) to standardize on a national basis a bench rest shooting program so that targets, ranges, scoring methods, and match procedures were uniform; (c) to assist individuals or organizations in the promotion of bench rest shooting; and (d) to gather and make generally available pertinent statistical and technical data. These purposes were a good mixture of the noble and the functional, and while what was then NBRSA may now have a split-off sister group known as IBS, the intent of the *entire* accuracy crowd has not changed in the slightest.

Early on, one very practical justification announced for bench shooting was the development of combinations of rifle and cartridge that could be supreme in 300-meter international competition. International Shooting Union rules demand a rifle of weight and barrel dimension not dissimilar to our present heavy-varmint category, albeit necessarily stocked in a different form because the 300-meter competition calls for a three-position iron-sight race, prone, kneeling, and standing, 40 rounds each, in a centerfire caliber. Twenty years ago and even earlier the loading preferred by U.S. shooters was a combination in the .30-06 of somewhere between 33.5 and 37.6 grains of HiVel No. 2 powder, to give the 173-grain boattailed military bullet a speed of about 2200 f.p.s. The records show the smallest ten-round test group *ever* attained with this was 1.4 inches at 300 meters. Since the innermost ring of the 300-meter ISU target is actually about $2\frac{5}{8}$ inches across, what is needed would be a rifle-cartridge combination *regularly capable* of shooting ten-shot groups at the $\frac{7}{8}$ minute of angle level, to give a perfect-score potential. That is, the rifle and ammunition must have this capability under optimum circumstances—what the shooter does under match conditions is of course dependent on him. Actually, since some shooter error and misjudgment of wind or mirage must be expected, the idea was to get not $\frac{7}{8}$ but $\frac{5}{8}$ minute capability.

At first that seemed beyond attainment, but it really did not take very long. More than ten years ago, Mike Walker stopped off at my place with a batch of four .308 rifles that had just

An early dream of bench rest competitors was the development of cartridges and rifles to make the United States Olympic teams tops in the world, and while we may never have quite swept the boards there can be no doubt of the contribution made by civilian experimenters in the calibers, bullets, and rifle designs equipping our shooters, like this 300-meter rifleman practicing at Ft. Benning.

been through tests in the tube range in Bridgeport. They were essentially free rifles, but equipped with scopes and stripped of the paraphernalia of three-position shooting. On the Camp Fire Club range, which no one has ever been able to read successfully in respect to its fluky mirage and wind conditions, the result of its odd topography, we shot all four rifles all one day. Half the time the ten-shot strings were at $\frac{5}{8}$ or better; all the time they were under $\frac{7}{8}$. Since that was a day of weird conditions indeed, it struck me that the 300-meter capability was demonstrated. Since that time the .308 has been the basic cartridge in a great many rifles capable of staying well under the $\frac{1}{2}$-minute mark. The $10\frac{1}{2}$-pound sporter aggregate level for five-shot strings at 100 yards now stands at .2904 m.o.a., but in five-shot terms some .308s and some shooters of them regularly beat .3 m.o.a. in single matches and clobber the smaller calibers. On breezy days the .30s are time and again champs. The 300-meter demands have been complied with and then some. That U.S. riflemen have won the 300-meter event in the Olympics of '72, '68, and '64 would itself seem to be an indication of that accomplishment.

In point of fact, if you strip aside the equipment needed for the satisfaction of the ISU procedures, and look at the barrel, action, and basic stock-bedding procedures of the modern 300-meter rifle used by U.S. competitors, you'll find it is a thinly disguised heavy-varmint rifle, bench rest style, in .308. One Australian shooter at the 1970 World Championships, in Phoenix, Arizona, showed up with a musket featuring the barrel-block system of attaching the barrel to the stock. U.S. bench

Colonel Tom Sharpe, now retired and with Remington Arms, was the original presiding genius over the Fort Benning training grounds for Olympic and ISU riflemen. Tom is shown here with the 1968 Olympic group.

shooters have just about abandoned that in favor of better schemes, but for some years now have had postal matches and information exchange with the Aussies, so more such adaptation is likely.

One interesting point has developed from bench rest experience to help our ISU shooters. Where the 300-meter loadings of earlier days developed only some 2200 f.p.s., were indeed so mild that there must have been ignition variances in the .30-06 case, today's .308 shooters stuff the load in the smaller case up to maximum. They push the 168-grain Sierra, for example, to 2750 or so with a virtually full case of H-380, or 48 grains of 748 BR and similarly extreme dosages of faster powders. Once in a blue moon, of course, some recoil-conscious shooter backs off to the 2200-f.p.s. level and scares people for a match or two, but in general the full loads give the better groups.

All of which may suggest something to the hunting rifleman, too, who uses the .308. It does its best not with dangerous loads but with the loadings over toward the right-hand side of the handbook page.

The impact of bench rest activity on certain cartridges has been considerable. First off, any loading-company salesman will admit that the vast commercial success of the .222 has in part been due to its remarkable performance in accuracy competition. A matter of reputation. And that cartridge was conceived and created by a handful of accuracy bugs.

This has also worked the other way. The demand for ordinary commercial varmint-hunting rifles and ammunition that would in some degree approach what could be done with custom equipment and handloads has forced the manufacturers to comply. You can today go to a sporting-goods store and buy off the shelf a rifle, scope, and boxed ammunition in .222 and usually in .22-250 which is capable, with minimal titivating and bedding check, of beating a minute of angle. Back in the days of the varminting greats of the 1920s and 1930s, the time of men like Gebby, Donaldson, Wotkyns, Morse, J. B. Smith, and the rest, any rifle-cartridge combination, custom-made and loaded, that would regularly beat the minute mark was some pumpkins. Today, it is not at all uncommon for factory-made rifles of varminting weight, firing reloads, to be fairly consistent at $\frac{1}{2}$ minute, with virtually any one of the cartridges now used in the varminting field. Somebody has learned something somewhere and put it to work. To work for the shooter, that is.

The immensely popular .243 is another case in point. The cartridge derives from a casual conversation between me and the late Al Marciante, a true accuracy nut and superb gunsmith of the early '50s. I had mysteriously acquired a sample case of a similarly mysterious short .30-caliber then being worked on by Ordnance people. It later, much later, as you know, became the 7.62 Nato or the .308 Winchester. Al and I agreed that the mysterious experimental case was about the right size (we had spent years messing about with such wildcats as the .240 Cobra, the .243 Ackley Express, .243 Rockchucker, and a cartload of others) to make a good .24-caliber. I took it home, ran it through various dies until I had a fair length of neck and what seemed a 30-degree shoulder, and sent it out to Hal Mallett of H&M Tool and asked him for a set of reamers "like that." No calculation, no dimensional hairsplitting.

With the reamers, Bill Cotter of upstate New York chambered up not a sporter but a bench rest rifle as they were in those days, about 18 pounds, because we thought of the original .240 Page as an accuracy cartridge. And it was surprisingly good, although it never really got competitive with smaller and less violent cartridges, so since we got some very fancy velocity data out of it I then proposed to Winchester that they run the idea through commercial development as a combination hunting and varminting round.

After a certain amount of shy backing and filling, that they did, their compromise being to retain the short neck and easy 17-degree shoulder of the original 7.62 Nato (which made production easier but didn't help the cartridge any), and ultimately we had the .243 Winchester. You know the rest. What you may well not know is that the .240 Page as Winchester went for it was originally called by them the 6 mm. Winchester. One of the original experimental M70 Varmint-weight rifles, so marked, still stands on my racks.

But when the .243 hit the streets its primary reputation was made less on the game-killing or varmint-busting performance factors, although these were considerable, than on the amazing accuracy level displayed by the original M70 featherweights in the caliber. The reason was probably less in the rifles than in the cartridge as factory-made. It was held to far tighter accuracy specifications than most hunting rounds.

The story can be repeated both ways. Consider the hotrock pistol varmint-shooting cartridges which popped onto the market at one stage. Tried in rifles, some were basically accurate, some were klunkers. Only the accurate ones lived very long in either rifle or handgun. Why? Because the accuracy expectations for varminting rounds or rifles had been shoved skyward by the accuracy bugs, the bench resters.

At least half the designers and production engineers of firearms companies whom I have known over the past twenty-odd years have at one time or another said: "You guys, you scribblers and the bench rest crowd, have made life miserable for us." What they meant, in simple words, was that the combination of the rise of reloading and the use of benches in either testing or competing with rifles had forced the factories, not only in ammunition but in production rifles, to improve their products. They *had* to make better-shooting guns, or be pounced on by irate outspoken customers.

Where once stood the ancient British *Textbook of Small Arms* concept of 3 minutes of angle, 3 inches at 100 yards, as adequate accuracy—and that is still all right for certain classes of deer rifle, or for elephant busters meant for use only at spitting distance—today a bolt-action sporter of such limited capability gets the big razzoo from all the gun experts, is a source of customer annoyance, and usually achieves a sorry sale indeed—it only takes about seven minutes for word of inaccuracy in a new rifle model to sweep the entire country! The better-advised riflemen today expect 2 inches from untouched factory rifles and ammunition, and a half-inch better than that with reloads, just as a standard, not as an exception. And plenty of today's equipment can beat that. This is not an accident; it is not altruism on the part of manufacturers; it is the result of pressures from the accuracy bugs.

22

A One-Hole Future

It is customary in virtually every book related to shooting to do the crystal-ball bit, to peer into the future. I suspect I am the world's lousiest prognosticator, never having been able even to pick a horse race except by the stick-a-pin-anywhere method, but here goes.

I venture to say that before this book goes out of print the *competitive* individual bench rest group records will have been chipped at here and there but not lowered by any vast amounts, since this is a slow process, involves considerable luck, and the present record lists have few soft spots in the events and courses of fire regularly shot. I feel sure, on the other hand, that the aggregate listings will continue to shrink, at a more rapid rate for 200-yard than for 100-yard averages, so that very shortly $\frac{1}{4}$-minute levels will be attained for a whole course of one-rifle fire, and the three-rifle aggregate will touch .35 now and again.

I am willing to risk the guess that the way most rifles have of being brand-new entities one season to the next, demanding different loads, etc., will be reduced by the use of the no-bedding or glued-up scheme which certain experimenters are now applying in order to eliminate the troublesome fit of inert steel to ever-moving wood.

I should devoutly hope that any differences between NBRSA and IBS will be reconciled by changing times, changing personnel and conditions, so that within the near future bench competition will be under one roof in this country, the extant situation being a sorry one for the sport save in the one instance that it has, at least seemingly, increased total bench-associated memberships. In this connection I should hope that it will prove feasible to establish in the eastern sector of the country at least one and preferably two fifty-bench ranges, since only with such firing lines is it practical to run off a really large entry, over a hundred in a class, within the number of off-work days practicable for the working man. I should further venture the hope that the development of more fifteen- and twenty-five-bench clubs be accelerated, perhaps even subsidized, to offer more weekend opportunities to shoot in competition without expensive and time-consuming long-distance travel. There are today federal funds available of possible application to such projects.

As far as hunting rifles are concerned, I see nothing but accelerated progress, so long as the anti-hunting, anti-gun forces in this country are held in their proper place. The devout rifleman tends to have tunnel vision, as it were, on this subject, in that he believes that the gun-control rumpus has spawned the hate-hunting movement, when the opposite is the true case and the existence of even the most completely devoted synthetic shooter, who aims at nothing but paper or clay, is threatened by the blither of the "big brown eyes" group, rapidly growing as this nation is urbanized.

But assuming we do not lose this conflict, it is my conviction that more and more the major firearms concerns will become involved in the pursuit of accuracy. Just as Savage vaunts their Anschutz imports, and Remington the 40X series and related projects, so I think will Winchester enter the lists with .22 rimfire fodder of truly competitive quality, more rifles which like the International M52 are designed more to win matches than to make immediate profits, and so on. I believe that reloading will continue its growth not as a money-saver but as a means of achieving better performance from any given rifle and the far greater satisfaction of hunting with personalized loads.

The aim of the whole exercise is to develop ammunition, rifles, and scopes that will hit the target as surely as a ray-gun, and be deadly if the piece is intended not for paper targets but for varmints or game. If my spouse hits the chuck she and a companion are looking at in the middle of that pasture, the rifle, a Ruger single-shot .222, is a triumph. If they manage a miss, which is hard to do with ultra-modern gear, it's a bust. I refuse to say whether or not she made the shot!

The sporting rifle must inevitably improve, if only for political or sociological reasons. With increasing population, decreasing wild-land availability, but sharply increased accessibility to a growing urban mass, the basic competition of the hunting sport, man versus nature in the forms of man versus the animal and man versus climate or terrain, will become three-legged in that a man-versus-man competition for hunting opportunity may be added. Undesirable this undoubtedly is, but it's probably inevitable.

In such a situation, the quality of the hunter's equipment becomes steadily more vital. He won't sensibly hunt elk with a rusty old thutty-thutty because he may well have no chance within its effective limits, but should equip himself with a rifle of loading, sights, and accuracy level dead sure of taking an elk at the top end of the park or on the next ridge. I call to mind the not uncommon situation of a respected arms-business friend who laid out considerable shekels for an elk hunt in what I knew to be good country. But what with one thing and another, his only chance at a bull came in a broad basin where shooting opportunity had to be, by virtue of that terrain, anywhere from 200 to 600 yards. He was, alas, equipped with a short-barreled rifle in a light cartridge. It might have done well enough on a 100-yard shot but simply did not have the stuff in terms of either accuracy or potency at range, for what he encountered, and all he encountered, which was time to get off five rounds at a bull traveling across the basin at from 350 to 450 yards. Two or three days later, in the same basin, with a rifle fully adapted to the problem, I busted my elk at what had to be over 400 with little or no trouble. The difference was very much more in the equipment than in the man, and under the clearly competitive stresses that are going to face hunters of the future that equipment will become more and more critical—and I suspect better and better to match.

For a cluster of related reasons I expect the accuracy impetus to increase, and the number of shooters devoting themselves by either competition or experiment to making rifles shoot better to grow. The slow loss of hunting space, the ultimate effect of the handgun excise tax and of other excises on the public range facilities in this country, to which half that money can be devoted when met with matching state dollars, the "civilization" of men, if indeed it can be so called, under which it is fine to shoot at chunks of clay or pieces of paper but not fine to crop game that is eating itself out of house and home, all tend to add impetus to synthetic sport.

With rifles, that sport can take few directions, and the chief of these is the pursuit of accuracy, by individuals and by competing groups. That pursuit has motivated men since the rifle's earliest beginnings; it will continue to do so as long as rifles endure.

Handy Addresses

AMMUNITION

C-I-L Ammunition Inc., P. O. Box 831, Plattsburgh, N. Y. 12901
Federal Cartridge Co., 2700 Foshay Tower, Minneapolis, Minn. 55402
Frontier Cartridge Co., Inc., Box 906, Grand Island, Neb. 68801
NORMA-Precision, South Lansing, N. Y. 14882
Omark-CCI, Inc., Box 856, Lewiston, Idaho 83501
Remington Arms Co., Bridgeport, Conn. 06602
Smith & Wesson-Fiocchi, Inc., 3640 Seminary Rd., Alton, Ill. 62002
Speer-DWM, Box 896, Lewiston, Idaho 83501
Stoeger Arms Corp., 55 Ruta Ct., So. Hackensack, N. J. 07606 (RWS)
Super-Vel Cartridge Co., Box 40, Shelbyville, Ind. 46176
Winchester-Western, East Alton, Ill. 62024

BULLET AND CASE LUBRICANTS

Alpha-Molykote, Dow Corning Corp., 45 Commerce Dr., Trumbull, Conn. 06601
Birchwood-Casey Co., Inc., 7900 Fuller Rd., Eden Prairie, Minn. 55343 (Anderol)
Jet-Aer Corp., 100 Sixth Ave., Paterson, N. J. 07524
Lenz Products Co., Box 1226, Sta. C, Canton, Ohio 44708 (Clenzoil)
Lyman Gun Sight Products, Middlefield, Conn. 06455 (Size-Ezy)
Micro Shooter's Supply, Box 213, Las Cruces, N. M. 88001 (Micro-Lube)
Nutec, Box 1187, Wilmington, Del. 19899 (Dry-Lube)
RCBS, Inc., Box 1919, Oroville, Calif. 95965 (case lubes)
SAECO Rel. Inc., 726 Hopmeadow St., Simsbury, Conn. 06070

CHRONOGRAPHS AND PRESSURE TOOLS

Avtron, 1049 Meech Ave., Cleveland, Ohio 44105
B-Square Co., Box 11281, Fort Worth, Texas 76110
Chronograph Specialists, P. O. Box 5005, Santa Ana, Calif. 92704
Herter's, Waseca, Minn. 56093
Micro-Sight Co., 242 Harbor Blvd., Belmont, Calif. 94002 (Techsonic)
Oehler Research, P. O. Box 9135, Austin, Texas 78756
Sundtek Co., P. O. Box 744, Springfield, Ore. 97477

CLEANING AND REFINISHING SUPPLIES

Birchwood-Casey Chem. Co., 7900 Fuller Rd., Eden Prairie, Minn.
   55343 (Anderol, etc.)
Bisonite Co., Inc., Box 84, Buffalo, N. Y. 14217
Jim Brobst, 299 Poplar St., Hamburg, Pa. 19526 (J-B Compound)
Geo. Brothers, Great Barrington, Mass. 01230 (G-B Linspeed Oil)
J. Dewey Gun Co., Clinton Corners, N. Y. 12514 (rods)
Dri-Slide, Inc., Industrial Park, Fremont, Mich. 49412
Robert Hart, Nescopeck, Pa. (throat-saver)
Frank C. Hoppe Div., P. O. Box 97, Parkesburg, Pa. 19365
Jet-Aer Corp., 100 Sixth Ave., Paterson, N. J. 07524 (blues and oils)
K. W. Kleinendorst, Taylortown Rd., Montville, N. J. 07045 (rifle clg.
   rods)
LEM Gun Spec., Box 31, College Park, Ga. 30337 (Lewis Lead Remover)
Liquid Wrench, Box 10628, Charlotte, N. C. 28201 (pen. oil)
Marble Arms Co., 1120 Superior, Gladstone, Mich. 49837
Micro Sight Co., 242 Harbor Blvd., Belmont, Calif. 94002 (bedding)
Mill Run Products, 1360 W. 9th, Cleveland, Ohio 44113 (Brite-Bore
   Kits)
Nutec, Box 1187, Wilmington, Del. 19899 (Dry-Lube)
Rig Products Co., Box 279, Oregon, Ill. 61061 (Rig Grease)
Service Armament, 689 Bergen Blvd., Ridgefield, N. J. 07657 (Parker-
   Hale rods)
Shooter's Service and Dewey (SS&D), Clinton Corners, N. Y. 12514
   (rods)
Southeastern Coatings, Inc. (SECOA), Bldg. 132, P.B.I. Airport, W.
   Palm Beach, Fla. 33406 (Teflon Coatings)
Taylor & Robbins, Box 164, Rixford, Pa. 16745 (Throat Saver)
WD-40 Co., 5390 Napa St., San Diego, Calif. 92110 (anti-rust oil)

COMPONENTS—BULLETS, POWDER, PRIMERS

Bahler Die Shop, Box 386, Florence, Ore. 97439 (17 cal.)
Bitterroot Bullet Co., Box 412, Lewiston, Idaho 83501
Centrix, 2116 N. 10th Ave., Tucson, Ariz. 85705
Kenneth E. Clark, 18738 Highway 99, Madera, Calif. 93637 (bullets)
Colorado Custom Bullets, Rt. l, Box 507-B, Montrose, Colo. 81401
Clarence Detsch, 133 Larch Rd., St. Marys, Pa. 15857
DuPont, Explosives Dept., Wilmington, Del. 19898
Frank A. Hemsted, Box 281, Sunland, Calif. 91040
Hercules Powder Co., 910 Market St., Wilmington, Del. 19899
Hi-Precision Co., 109 Third Ave., N. E., Orange City, Iowa 51041
B. E. Hodgdon, Inc., 7710 W. 50th Hwy., Shawnee Mission, Kans. 66202
Crawford Hollidge, Cotuit Road, Marston's Mills, Mass. 02648

Hornady Mfg. Co., Box 1848, Grand Island, Neb. 68801
David Ingram, Box 4263, Long Beach, Calif. 90804 (17/20 cal. bullets)
Jurras Munition Corp., Box 140, Shelbyville, Ind. 46176
Lyman Gun Sight Products, Middlefield, Conn. 06455
Norma-Precision, So. Lansing, N. Y. 14882
Nosler Bullets, P. O. Box 688, Beaverton, Ore. 97005
Red Diamond Distributing Co., 1304 Snowdon Dr., Knoxville, Tenn.
    37912 (black powder)
Remington-Peters, Bridgeport, Conn. 06602
Sierra Bullets Inc., 10532 So. Painter Ave., Santa Fe Springs, Calif.
    90670
Sisk Bullet Co., Box 398, Iowa Park, Texas 76367
Speer Products Inc., Box 896, Lewiston, Idaho 83501
Winchester-Western, New Haven, Conn. 06504

CUSTOM GUNSMITHS

T. H. Boughton, 410 Stone Rd., Rochester, N. Y. 14616
Leonard M. Brownell, Box 6147, Sheridan, Wyo. 82801
Tom Burgess, Rte. 3, Kalispell, Mont. 59901 (metalsmithing only)
Carpenter's Gun Works, Gunshop Rd., Box C, Plattekill, N. Y. 12568
Kenneth E. Clark, 18738 Highway 99, Madera, Calif. 93637
J. Dewey Gun Co., Clinton Corners, N. Y. 12514
Freeland's Scope Stands, 3737—14th Ave., Rock Island, Ill. 61201
Tom Gillman, Hot Springs, Ark. 71901
Griffen & Howe, 589—8th Ave., New York, N. Y. 10017
Dale M. Guise, Rt. 2, Box 239, Gardners, Pa. 17324 (Rem. left-hand
    conversions)
Robert W. Hart & Son, 401 Montgomery St., Nescopeck, Pa. 18635
    (actions, stocks)
William Hobaugh, Box 657, Philipsburg, Mont. 59858
Hyper-Single Precision SS Rifles, 520 E. Beaver, Jenks, Okla. 74037
Paul Jaeger, 211 Leedom, Jenkintown, Pa. 19046
Kennedy Gun Shop, Rte. 6, Clarksville, Tenn. 37040
Monte Kennedy, R. D. 2-B, Kalispell, Mont. 59901
R. J. Maberry, 511 So. K, Midland, Texas 79701
Harold E. MacFarland, Star Route, Box 84, Cottonwood, Ariz. 86326
Pat B. McMillan, 1828 E. Campo Bello Dr., Phoenix, Ariz. 85022
Clayton N. Nelson, 1725 Thompson Ave., Enid, Okla. 73701
George Schielke, Washington Crossing, Titusville, N. J. 08560
Shilen Rifles, Inc., 930 N. Belt Line, Suite 134B, Irving, Texas 75060
Shooters Service & Dewey Inc., Clinton Corners, N.Y. 12514
Keith Stegall, Box 696, Gunnison, Colo. 81230
Taylor & Robbins, Box 164, Rixford, Pa. 16745
Weber Rifle Actions, Box 515, Woodbridge, Calif. 95258
C. A. Williams, 1213 Patricia Lane, Garland, Texas 75042 (actions,
    triggers)
Lester Womack, Box 17210, Tucson, Ariz. 85710

EAR PROTECTORS

American Optical Corp., Mechanic St., Southbridge, Mass. 01550 (ear
    valve)
Bausch & Lomb, 635 St. Paul St., Rochester, N. Y. 14602
David Clark Co., 360 Franklin St., Worcester, Mass. 01604

Curtis Safety Prod. Co., Box 61, Webster Sq. Sta., Worcester, Mass. 01603 (ear valve)

Hodgdon, 7710 W. 50 Hiway, Shawnee Mission, Kans. 66202

Human Acoustics, Inc., 888 E. Williams St., Carson City, Nev. 89701 (molded plugs)

Sigma Engineering Co., 11320 Burbank Blvd., No. Hollywood, Calif. 91601 (Lee-Sonic ear valve)

Willson Products Div., P. O. Box 622, Reading, Pa. 19603 (Ray-O-Vac)

ENGRAVERS

Sid Bell, Box 188, Tully, N. Y. 13159

Joseph Fugger, c/o Griffin & Howe, 589 8th Ave., New York, N.Y. 10017

Donald Glaser, 1520 West St., Emporia, Kans. 66801

Paul Jaeger, 211 Leedom, Jenkintown, Pa. 19046

Pachmayr Gun Works, Inc., 1220 S. Grand Ave., Los Angeles, Calif. 90015

E. C. Prudhomme, 302 Ward Bldg., Shreveport, La. 71101

John E. Warren, P. O. Box 72, Eastham, Mass. 02642

A. A. White Engr., Inc., P. O. Box 68, Manchester, Conn. 06040

GUNS

Champlin Firearms, Inc. Box 3191, Enid, Okla. 73701

Colt's, 150 Huyshope Ave., Hartford, Conn. 06102

Firearms Development, Inc., 218 Austin St., Denton, Texas 76201

Harrington & Richardson, Park Ave., Worcester, Mass. 01610

High Standard Mfg. Co., 1817 Dixwell Ave., Hamden, Conn. 06514

Ithaca Gun Co., Ithaca, N. Y. 14850

Iver Johnson Arms & Cycle Works, Fitchburg, Mass. 01420

Marlin Firearms Co., 100 Kenna Dr., New Haven, Conn. 06473

O. F. Mossberg & Sons., Inc., 7 Grasso St., No. Haven, Conn. 06473

Plainfield Machine Co., Inc., Box 447, Dunellen, N. J. 08812

Ranger Arms Co., Box 704, Gainesville, Texas 76240 (Texan Mag)

Remington Arms Co., Bridgeport, Conn. 06602

Savage Arms Corp., Westfield, Mass. 01085

Sturm, Ruger & Co., Southport, Conn. 06490

Winchester Repeating Arms Co., New Haven, Conn. 06504

Winslow Arms Co., P.O. Box 578, Osprey, Fla. 33595

GUNSMITH SUPPLIES

Alamo Heat Treating Co., Box 55345, Houston, Texas 77055

Alley Supply Co., Box 458, Sonora, Calif. 95370

Bonanza Sports Mfg. Co., 412 Western Ave., Faribault, Minn. 55021

Bob Brownell's, Main & Third, Montezuma, Iowa 50171

M. H. Canjar, 500 E. 45th, Denver, Colo. 80216 (triggers, etc.)

Clymer Mfg. Co., 14241 W. 11 Mile Rd., Oak Park, Mich. 48237 (reamers)

Dayton-Traister Co., P. O. Box 93, Oak Harbor, Wash. 98277 (triggers)

Dem-Bart Hand Tool Co., 7749 15th Ave., NW., Seattle, Wash. 98107 (checkering tools)

Dremel Mfg. Co., P. O. Box 518, Racine, Wis. 53401 (grinders)

F. K. Elliott, Box 785, Ramona, Calif. 92065 (reamers)

E-Z Tool Co., P. O. Box 3186, East 14th Street Sta., Des Moines, Iowa 50313 (taper lathe attachment)

Forster Appelt Mfg. Co., Inc., 82 E. Lanark Ave., Lanark, Ill. 61046

Gopher Shooter's Supply, Box 246, Faribault, Minn. 55021 (screwdrivers, etc.)

H. & M., 24062 Orchard Lake Rd., Farmington, Mich. 48024 (reamers)

Paul Jaeger Inc., 211 Leedom St., Jenkintown, Pa. 19046

Marker Machine Co., Box 426, Charleston, Ill. 61920

Viggo Miller, P. O. Box 4181, Omaha, Neb. 68104 (trigger attachment)

N & J Sales, Lime Kiln Rd., Northford, Conn. 06472 (screwdrivers)

Palmgren, 8383 South Chicago Ave., Chicago, Ill. 60167 (vises, etc.)

Ponderay Lab., 210 W. Prasch, Yakima, Wash. 98902 (epoxy glass bedding)

Riley's Supply Co., 121 No. Main St., Avilla, Ind. 46710 (Neidner buttplates, caps)

A. G. Russell, 1705 Hiway 71N, Springdale, Ark. 72764 (Arkansas oilstones)

Timney Mfg. Co., 5624 Imperial Hwy, So. Gate, Calif. 90280 (triggers)

Charles A. Williams, 1213 Patricia Lane, Garland, Texas 75042 (triggers, actions)

Wilton Tool Corp., 9525 W. Irving Pk. Rd., Schiller Park, Ill. 60176 (vises)

LOAD TESTING

Carter Gun Works, 2211 Jefferson Pk. Ave., Charlottesville, Va. 22903

Hutton Rifle Ranch, Box 898, Topanga, Calif. 90290

Jurras Co., Box 163, Shelbyville, Ind. 46176

Shooters Service & Dewey, Inc., Clinton Corners, N. Y. 12514 (daily fee range also)

H. P. White Lab., Box 331, Bel Air, Md. 21014

MISCELLANEOUS

Barrel-bedding device, W. H. Womack, 2124 Meriwether Rd., Shreveport, La. 71108

Bench rest accessory case, Walden Leisure Prods., 1040 Matley Lane, Bldg. 4, Reno, Nev. 89502

Bench rest pedestal, Jim Brobst, 299 Poplar, Hamburg, Pa. 19526

Bench rest sandbags, Basil Tuller, 29 Germania, Galeton, Pa. 16922

Bench rest stands, Suter's, 332 Tejon, Colorado Springs, Colo. 80902

Bench rest tripod, E. L. Beecher, 2155 Demington Drive, Cleveland Heights, Ohio 44-06

Bore collimator, Alley Supply Co., Box 458, Sonora, Calif. 95370

Borescope, Eder Inst. Co., 5115 N. Ravenswood Ave., Chicago, Ill. 60640

Cartridge boxes, Llanerch Gun Shop, 2800 Township Line, Upper Darby, Pa. 19083

Cartridge boxes, Shooters Supplies, 1589 Payne Ave., St., Paul, Minn. 55101

Custom bluing, J. A. Wingert, 124 W. 2nd St., Waynesboro, Pa. 17268

Ear-Valv, Sigma Eng. Co., 11320 Burbank Blvd., N. Hollywood, Calif. 91601 (Lee-Sonic)

Gun-bedding kit, Resin Div., Fenwal, Inc., 400 Main St., Ashland, Mass. 01721

Portable bench, Walden Leisure Prods., 1040 Matley Lane, Bldg. 4, Reno, Nev. 89502

Portable gun rest, Central Specialties Co., 630 Northwest Hwy., Chicago, Ill. 60631 (Gun-Rak)

Porto-Bench, Universal Std. Prods., 926 N. Memorial, Racine, Wis. 53404

Pressure-testing machine, M. York, 19381 Keymar Way, Gaithersburg, Md. 20760

Shooting/testing glasses, Clear View Sports Shields, P. O. Box 255, Wethersfield, Conn. 06107

Shooting glasses, Bausch & Lomb, Inc., 635 St. Paul St., Rochester, N.Y. 14602

Shooting glasses, Bushnell Optical Corp., 2828 E. Foothill Blvd., Pasadena, Calif. 91107

Shooting glasses, M. B. Dinsmore, Box 21, Wyomissing, Pa. 19610

Swivels, Michaels, P. O. Box 13010, Portland, Ore. 97213

Trap buttplates, Albright Prod. Co., P. O. Box 695, Bishop, Calif. 93514

Triggers, Canjar Rifle Acc., 500 E. 45th St., Denver, Colo. 80216

Trigger-pull gauge, Ohaus, 29 Hanover Rd., Florham Park, N. J. 07932

Trigger shoe, Flaig's, Babcock Blvd., Millvale, Pa. 15209

REBORING

A & M Rifle Co., Box 1713, Prescott, Ariz. 86301

P. O. Ackley Inc., 5448 Riley Lane, Salt Lake City, Utah 84107

Ward Koozer, Box 18, Walterville, Ore. 97489

Morgan's Custom Reboring, 707 Union Ave., Grants Pass, Ore. 97526

Sharon Rifle Barrel Co., P. O. Box 106, Kalispell, Mont. 59901

R. Southgate, Rt. 2, Franklin, Tenn. 37064 (Muzzleloaders)

RELOADING ACCESSORIES

Bahler Die Shop, Box 386, Florence, Ore. 97439

Bair Machine Co., Box 4407, Lincoln, Neb. 68504

Belding & Mull, P. O. Box 428, Phillipsburg, Pa. 16866

Bonanza Sports, Inc., 412 Western Ave., Faribault, Minn. 55021

A. V. Bryant, 72 Whiting Rd., East Hartford, Conn. 06424 (Nutmeg Universal Press)

Carbide Die & Mfg. Co., Box 226, Covina, Calif. 91706

Clymer Mfg. Co., 14241 W. 11 Mile Rd., Oak Park, Minn. 48237 ($\frac{1}{2}$-jack, swaging dies)

Cole's Acku-Rite Prod., P. O. Box 25, Kennedy, N. Y. 14747 (die racks)

J. Dewey Gun Co., Clinton Corners, N. Y. 12514 (bullet spinner)

W. H. English, 4411 S. W. 100th, Seattle, Wash. 98146 (Paktool)

Fitz, Box 49797, Los Angeles, Calif. 90049 (Fitz Flipper)

Forster-Appelt Mfg. Co., Inc., 82 E. Lanark Ave., Lanark, Ill. 61046

Gopher Shooter's Supply, Box 246, Faribault, Minn. 55021

Hart Products, 401 Montgomery St., Nescopeck, Pa. 18635

B. E. Hodgdon, Inc., 7710 W. 50 Hiway, Shawnee Mission, Kans. 66202

Lee Engineering, 21 E. Wisconsin St., Hartford, Wis. 53027

Lyman Gun Sight Products, Middlefield, Conn. 06455

McKillen & Heyer, Box 627, Willoughby, Ohio 44094 (case gauge)

Pat B. McMillan 1828 E. Campo Bello Dr., Phoenix, Ariz. 85022

Normington Co., Box 156, Rathdrum, Idaho 83858 (powder baffles)

John Nuler, 12869 Dixie, Detroit, Mich. 48239 (primer seating tool)

Ohaus Scale Corp., 29 Hanover Rd., Florham Park, N. J. 07932
Omark-CCI, Inc., Box 856, Lewiston, Idaho 83501
Pacific Tool Co., Box 4495, Lincoln, Neb. 68504
Ferris Pindell, R. R. 3, Box 205, Connersville, Ind. 47331 (bullet spinner)
Marian Powley, 19 Sugarplum Rd., Levittown, Pa. 10956
RCBS, Inc., Box 1919, Oroville, Calif. 95965
Redding-Hunter, Inc., 114 Starr Rd., Cortland, N. Y. 13045
Remco, 1404 Whitesboro St., Utica, N. Y. 13502 (shot caps)
Rochester Lead Works, Rochester, N. Y. 14608 (lead-wire)
Sil's Gun Products, 490 Sylvan Dr., Washington, Pa. 15301 (K-spinner)
L. E. Wilson, Box 324, Cashmere, Wash. 98815 (dies, gauges)
A. Zimmerman, 127 Highland Trail, Denville, N. J. 07834 (case trimmer)

RIFLE BARREL MAKERS

A & M Rifle Co., Box 1713, Prescott, Ariz. 86301
Apex Rifle Co., 7628 San Fernando, Sun Valley, Calif. 91352
Christy Gun Works, 875 57th St., Sacramento, Calif. 95819
J. Dewey Gun Co., Clinton Corners, N. Y. 12514
Douglas Barrels, Inc., 5504 Big Tyler Rd., Charleston, W. Va. 25312
Federal Firearms Co., Inc., Box 145, Oakdale, Pa. 15071 (Star bbls., actions)
Hart Rifle Barrels, Inc., RD 2, Lafayette, N. Y. 13084
Wm. H. Hobaugh, Box 657, Philipsburg, Mont. 59858
SS&D, Inc., Clinton Corners, N. Y. 12514 (cold-formed bbls.)
Sharon Rifle Barrel Co., P. O. Box 106, Kalispell, Mont. 59901
Ed Shilen Rifles, 4510 Harrington Rd., Irving, Texas 75060
Titus Barrel & Gun Co., Box 151, Heber City, Utah, 84032

RIFLE RESTS

E. L. Beecher, 2155 Demington Dr., Cleveland Heights, Ohio 44106
Cole's Acku-Rite Prod., Box 25, Kennedy, N. Y. 14747
Rob. W. Hart & Son, 401 Montgomery St., Nescopeck, Pa. 18635
Basil Tuller, 29 Germania, Galeton, Pa. 16922 (Protecktor sandbags)

SCOPES, MOUNTS, OPTICAL EQUIPMENT

Alley Supply Co., P. O. Box 458, Sonora, Calif. 95370 (Scope collimator)
Bausch & Lomb, 635 St. Paul St., Rochester, N. Y. 14602
Browning Arms, Rt. 4, Box 624-B, Arnold, Mo. 63010
Maynard P. Buehler, Inc., 17 Orinda Highway, Orinda, Calif. 94563
D. P. Bushnell & Co., 2828 E. Foothill Blvd., Pasadena, Calif. 91107
Freeland's Scope Stands, Inc., 3734 14th, Rock Island, Ill. 61201
E. C. Herkner Co., Box 5007, Boise, Idaho 83702
Paul Jaeger, 211 Leedom St., Jenkintown, Pa. 19046 (Nickel)
Kuharsky Bros., 2425 W. 12th St., Erie, Pa. 16500
T. K. Lee, Box 2123, Birmingham, Ala. 35201 (reticles)
E. Leitz, Inc., Rockleigh, N. J. 07647
Leupold & Stevens Inc., P. O. Box 688, Beaverton, Ore. 97005
Lyman Gun Sight Products, Middlefield, Conn. 06455
Premier Reticles, Ocala, Fla. 32670
Redfield Gun Sight Co., 5800 E. Jewell Ave., Denver, Colo. 80222

Remington Arms Co., Ilion, N.Y. 13357
Stoeger Arms Co., 55 Ruta Ct., S. Hackensack, N.J. 07606
Swift Instruments, Inc., 952 Dorchester Ave., Boston, Mass. 02125
Tasco, 1075 N.W. 71st, Miami, Fla. 33138
John Unertl Optical Co., 3551-5 East St., Pittsburgh, Pa. 15214
Vissing Co., Box 437, Idaho Falls, Idaho 83401 (lens cap)
H. P. Wasson, Box 181, Netcong, N. J. 07857 (eyeglass aperture)
W. R. Weaver Co., 7125 Industrial Ave., El Paso, Texas 79915
Carl Zeiss Inc., 444 Fifth Ave., New York, N. Y. 10018 (Hensoldt)

STOCKS (COMMERCIAL AND CUSTOM)

Al Biesen, West 2039 Sinto Ave., Spokane, Wash. 99201
E. C. Bishop & Son Inc., Box 7, Warsaw, Mo. 65355
Lenard M. Brownell, Box 6147, Sheridan, Wyo. 82801
Mike Conner, Box 208, Tijeras, N.M. 87059
Crane Creek Gun Stock Co., Box 268, Waseca, Minn. 56093
Reinhart Fajen, Box 338, Warsaw, Mo. 65355
Clyde E. Fischer, Rt. 1, Box 170-M, Victoria, Texas 77901
Flaig's Lodge, Millvale, Pa. 15209
Dale Goens, Box 224, Cedar Crest, N. M. 87008
Harris Gun Stocks, Inc., 12 Lake St., Richfield Springs, N. Y. 13439
Monte Kennedy, R.D. 2B, Kalispell, Mont. 59901
Leonard Mews, R. 2, Box 242, Hortonville, Wis. 54944
Robert U. Milhoan & Son, Rt. 3, Elizabeth, W. Va. 26143
Oakley and Merkley, Box 2446, Sacramento, Calif. 95801 (blanks)
Carl Roth, Jr., P. O. Box 2593, Cheyenne, Wyo. 82001
Keith Stegall, Box 696, Gunnison, Colo. 81230
Stinehour Rifles, Box 84, Cragsmoor, N. Y. 12420
Roy Vail, Rt. 1, Box 8, Warwick N. Y. 10990

Joining an Organization

The originally established group of accuracy fans is known as the National Bench Rest Shooters Association. Its headquarters are operated by the Secretary, Mrs. Bernice McMullen, at 607 West Line Street, Minerva, Ohio 44657. Membership, which includes a subscription to *The Rifle* magazine (official organ of the NBRSA), the right to vote, to buy official brassards at $1.50 each, and to compete in NBRSA-registered matches, plus a membership card, is $8 per year. Application may be made directly, without any special form, to Mrs. McMullen. Associate membership is available to spouses and children of regular members at $3.50, and includes all privileges except the magazine.

More recently established but of similar size is International Benchrest Shooters, often referred to as IBS, whose Recording Secretary is Mr. Emory Tooly of 8 Cline Street, Dolgeville, New York 13329, telephone 315 429-9227. The IBS annual membership fee is also $8 (life membership $125), which gives the member a subscription to *Precision Shooting*, official organ for the IBS, and the right to compete in IBS-registered matches, to buy either charter-member or regular patches at $2 each, to receive official rule books and IBS bylaws at $.50 per copy, and to buy official bench rest targets and hunter-class targets at a discount. Affiliated club memberships are free. Memberships are open to Canadian and Australian citizens with whom postal and direct matches are conducted.

Every individual seriously interested in accuracy, even if he does not plan to compete in bench rest matches, should belong to one or the other of these associations. If possible, they should join both. Their aims are virtually identical, there is a considerable overlap in personnel—many shooters are like me, members of both and competitors in the matches of both—and from both official publications much can be gained in accuracy knowledge, sighting procedures others have employed, etc. It is not, of course possible to compete in the matches of either without membership certification, and membership applications can be processed at any registered shoot to permit compliance therewith.

The secretaries of either organization will upon request furnish you with a listing of all affiliated clubs so that a prospective member can locate one near him and establish contacts. The magazines also frequently publish such club lists; and as the schedules develop they will announce the dates and gun types, etc., of all matches planned, plus their local contacts or shoot directors.

At matches contestants are expected to pay entry or daily registration fees usually ranging from $5 to $10 per gun, which go to defray shoot expenses, awards, etc. At virtually all matches provision is made, in some instances excellent provision, for meals at the range and for the parking and plugging in of trailer or camper equipment. The shoot officials named in the magazine announcements will gladly answer all questions about local housing, match procedures, etc.

The Accuracy

Records

1953 WORLD RECORD GROUPS

100 yard—5 shots—.1057″	Paul Dinant—.250/3000
100 yard—10 shots—.3268″	Olive Walker—.222 Rem.
200 yard—5 shots—.3896″	Bill Guse—.22/250
200 yard—10 shots—.6378″	Frank Cooper—.22/250
300 meter—5 shots—.6735″	Sam Clark, Jr.—.250 Don Ace
300 meter—10 shots—1.740″	Clair Taylor—.219 Don

IBS WORLD RECORDS as of January 1, 1973

Single Groups	Heavy Bench Rest Rifles	Heavy Varmint	Light Varmint	Sporter
5-100	.063" Zeiser 8/30/58	.090" Oakley 5/25/68	.095" Beard 7/17/65	.096" D. Hall 7/5/69
5-200	.161" D. Pickens 7/15/67	.192" Gillman 6/24/64	.236" F. James 8/7/69	.259" L. Hunt 7/5/69
5-300	.605" Gottschall 5/9/65	.787" Bassett 10/6/68	.887" D. Hall 5/30/69	.817" D. Kiel 5/30/69
10-100	.138" F. Pindell 8/27/69	—	—	—
10-200	.298" Miller 7/20/68	—	—	—
10-300	.918" Rinehart 8/30/57	—	—	—

Aggregates—MOA

	Heavy Bench Rest Rifles	Heavy Varmint	Light Varmint	Sporter
5-5-100	.1852 Berger 9/24/66	.2189 Hunt 7/12/64	.2425 Cornelison 8/19/67	.2928 A. Blensinger 7/27/72
5-5-200	.2290 Engelbrecht 11/4/67	.2505 D. McIlwain 10/10/71	.2772 Suchan 5/13/67	.3193 F. James 6/8/69
5-5-300	.3547 Demoise 5/14/66	.4640 Mick 5/7/67	.5527 T. Seitz 6/22/68	.4898 W. Dunn 5/30/69
5-10-100	.2278 Cornelison 10/22/66	—	—	—
5-10-200	.2496 E. Walker 8/11/62	—	—	—
5-10-300	.5105 A. Angerman 6/1/69	—	—	—

Grand Aggregates—MOA

5-5 (100 plus 200)	.2275 Carden 11/4/67	.2491 Suchan 6/26/65	.2810 Suchan 5/13/67	.3740 J. Deming 7/24/70
5-5 (200 plus 300)	.3639 P. Gottschall 5/9/65	.4703 Kiel 10/6/68	.5000 T. Seitz 6/22/68	.5469 W. Dunn 5/30/69
5-10 (100 plus 200)	.2563 Roberts 8/11/62	—	—	—
5-10 (200 plus 300)	.4627 A. Angerman 6/1/69	—	—	—

Note 1: Ten shot groups or aggregates are no longer contested in any of the Varmint or Sporter classes.

Note 2: Heavy bench rest rifle records were split into restricted (bag) rests and unrestricted (mechanical) rests effective January 1, 1963. Effective January 1, 1970 this rule was rescinded by action of the Directors of NBRSA. Accordingly the heavy bench rest rifle world records shown in the above table are the **smallest** regardless of class as of January 1, 1970.

Note 3: The numbers 100, 200, and 300 in the table refer to 100 yards, 200 yards and 300 meters (328.08 yards) respectively.

Table Compiled By IBS Measurement Committee.

NBRSA WORLD RECORDS as of January 1, 1973

Single Groups	Bench Rest Rifle	Heavy Varmint	Light Varmint	Sporter
5-100	.063″ Hap Zeiser 8/30/58	.070″ A. J. Freund 12/6/70	.095″ Larry Beard 7/17/65	.090″ Donalee Stekl 9/4/72
5-200	.161″ David Pickens 7/15/67	.192″ Tom Gillman 6/24/64	.236″ Frank James 8/7/69	.259″ Lynn Hunt 7/5/69
5-300	.605″ Paul Gottschall 5/9/65	.553″ Stan Buchtel 7/8/71	.757″ Edward Owen 7/17/71	.817″ Dave Kiel 5/30/69
10-100	.138″ Ferris Pindell 8/27/69	—	—	—
10-200	.298″ Melvin Miller 7/20/68	—	—	—
10-300	.918″ Omar Rinehart 8/30/57			

Aggregates—MOA

	Bench Rest Rifle	Heavy Varmint	Light Varmint	Sporter
5-5-100	.1852 Walt Berger 9/24/66	.2189 Lynn Hunt 7/12/64	.2393 Art Blensinger 9/4/72	.2807 Art Blensinger 9/4/72
5-5-200	.2290 L. Engelbrecht 11/4/67	.2474 A. J. Freund 7/18/70	.2725 C. E. Seitz 6/25/72	.3193 Frank James 6/8/69
5-5-300	.3547 Thomas Demoise 5/14/66	.4492 Jesse Corder 5/31/70	.5527 C. E. Seitz 6/22/68	.4798 P. Rechnitzer 5/21/72
5-10-100	.2270 Leo Harrison 8/26/72	—	—	—
5-10-200	.2496 Ed Walker 8/11/62	—	—	—
5-10-300	.4248 Herb Stark 5/31/70	—	—	—

Grand Aggregates—MOA

5-5 (100 + 200)	.2275 Bud Carden 11/4/67	.2491 Ed Suchan 6/26/65	.2810 Ed Suchan 5/13/67	.3540 Jim Stekl 6/6-7/72
5-5 (200 + 300)	.3639 Paul Gottschall 5/9/65	.4261 Al Angerman 5/21/72	.5000 C. E. Seitz 6/22/68	.5068 George Kelbly 5/21/72
5-10 (100 + 200)	.2563 Al Roberts 8/11/62	—	—	—
5-10 (200 + 300)	.4419 Herb Stark 5/31/70	—	—	.4990 Jim Gilmore 10/14/72

Note 1: Single groups of 5-100 indicates five shots at 100 yards, etc.; Aggregates MOA of 5-5-100 indicates five five-shot groups at 100 yards, etc.; Grand Aggregates MOA of 5-5(100 + 200) indicates the MOA average of five five-shot groups at 100 yards and five five-shot groups at 200 yards, etc.

Note 2: The numbers 100, 200 and 300 in the table refer to 100 yards, 200 yards and 300 meters (328.08 yards) respectively.

Note 3: Ten-shot groups or aggregates are no longer contested in any of the Varmint or Sporter classes.

Index